The Origins of the Bible

Theological Inquiries

Studies in Contemporary
Biblical and Theological Problems

General Editor
Lawrence Boadt, C. S. P.

PAULIST PRESS

The Origins of the Bible

Rethinking Canon History

John W. Miller

Paulist Press
New York • Mahwah, NJ

ACKNOWLEDGMENTS

The Publisher gratefully acknowledges use of the following materials: excerpts from *The New Jerusalem Bible*. Copyright © 1985 by Doubleday, a division of Bantam Doubleday Dell Publishing Group, Inc. and Darton, Longman & Todd, Ltd. Used by permission of Doubleday, a division of Bantam Doubleday Dell Publishing Group, Inc; excerpts reprinted from *The Formation of the Christian Bible* by Hans von Campenhausen, copyright © 1972 Fortress Press. Used by permission of Augsburg Fortress.

Library of Congress Cataloging-in-Publication Data

Miller, John W., 1926-
    The origins of the Bible: rethinking canon history / by John W. Miller.
      p. cm.
    ISBN 0-8091-3522-1 (pbk.)
    1. Bible—Canon. 2. Bible—History of Biblical events. 3. Bible—History of contemporary events. I. Title.
BS465.M55   1994
220.1′2—dc20
                                         94-33902
                                          CIP

Published by Paulist Press
997 Macarthur Boulevard
Mahwah, NJ 07430

Printed and bound in the
United States of America

CONTENTS

Preface 1

1. How the Hebrew Scriptures Became
Part of the Christian Bible 5

2. A First Look at When and Why They Were Compiled............17

3. The Wider Background: Israel's Rival Priestly Houses............31

4. Differing Theologies Among the Priestly Houses.....................49

5. Heightened Tensions Due to the "Battle of the Prophets" 67

6. The Ezra–Nehemiah Reforms as a Response 89

7. The Birth of a Scripture Based Community:
The Law and the Prophets 104

8. Custodians and Teachers of the Second Temple Library 127

9. Editing and Adding "The Other Books"...................................139

10. The Christian Bible in Its Final Form:
Concluding Reflections 161

Appendix...169
The Hebrew Scriptures...170
Jewish, Catholic and Protestant Bibles Compared..........171

Why Jewish, Catholic and Protestant Bibles Differ
(A Synopsis) 172

A Note to Bible Publishers..173

Notes 176

Annotated Bibliography of Recent Canonical Studies............220

Index 245

Dedicated to Conrad Grebel College
and its constituent Mennonite churches

"Do not imagine that I have come
to abolish the Law or the Prophets." *

PREFACE

For a great variety of reasons the normative place of the Bible in our churches and culture has suffered erosion and can no longer be taken for granted. Intuitive awareness of this among theologians, biblical scholars and pastors has given birth to a flood of research and publishing focused on the Bible as canon.[1] Many are now asking: What in truth *is* the Bible? How did it originate? What role was it meant to play in the communities that first formed it? What role should it play in today's world? In the following chapters I seek to make a contribution to this important field of study by showing how the Christian Bible was fashioned in the midst of two epochs of crisis and reform: the first, in the fifth to second centuries BCE when the Hebrew scriptures of the Jews were assembled; the second, during the first and second centuries CE when these same scriptures were defended, supplemented and reborn as the Bible of the church. Thus, at center stage in the following study are the Hebrew scriptures of the Christian Bible: when, why and how they were assembled, what their message was initially, and why they later became such an integral part of the Christian scriptures.

The need for a greater knowledge of the Bible's origins is widely recognized. Despite the growing body of literature on the subject, rank and file Christians know little or nothing about this subject. Biblical scholars too are in some confusion just now over how in particular the Hebrew scriptures were compiled and became authoritative. This is partly due to the collapse of an older theory which presumed that a first century CE Rabbinic council had played the decisive role in this development. Many now realize this was not the case, but are unaware that viable alternative proposals are beginning to take shape. My hope is that the following study will call attention to these possibilities and demonstrate that more can be known about this subject than is general-

1

ly recognized, and that such knowledge can contribute significantly to the search now underway in the churches for a renewed sense of the Bible's overarching message and relevance.

The study will begin in Chapter 1 with an analysis of how the Hebrew scriptures became part of the Christian Bible. For this aspect of the inquiry I have relied heavily on the research of others, but break new ground in the following chapters, where the focus shifts to the question of how and why this older body of Hebrew writings was assembled in the first place. What comes to light is that the form and content of the Hebrew scriptures were significantly shaped by long-standing institutional and theological conflicts between Israel's rival priesthoods, conflicts which persisted on into the period of the Second Temple (515 BCE) and were not fully resolved until the climactic Ezra-Nehemiah reforms (c. 458–430 BCE). Only then, in the midst of an unprecedented crisis, were the writings of these competing groups finally assembled and combined in such a manner that they could begin to serve as the legal, confessional and pedagogical foundation of a *united* Israel. It is thus no accident, I hope to show, that the books (or scrolls) so assembled were originally arranged so that the account of these reforms constitutes the collection's chronological apex and ending. Nor is it without significance that in the Christian Bible this is no longer the case. Instead, a story has been added that imbues the older Hebrew scriptures with a dramatically new chronological apex and meaning. Our study draws to a close in Chapter 10 with a discussion of the significance of this momentous development, seen against the backdrop of the message of the Hebrew scriptures.

The picture thus drawn of how the Hebrew scriptures were created and supplemented to become the Bible of the Christian church is admittedly different in some respects from the one now prevalent in scholarly literature. That it does not stand isolated or alone in contemporary studies will become evident from the footnotes and bibliographical references in the appendix. While issues of a more or less academic nature are repeatedly addressed in this study, and the book as a whole is directed in the first instance to students, pastors, teachers and scholars, my hope would be that it is written simply and clearly enough to be of value and interest to anyone wanting to gain a deepened understanding of how the Christian Bible originated and functioned as normative literature for those who created it and how it might still do the same for us today.

*   *   *

The gracious gift of a careful reading of this entire manuscript by my wife, Louise, and my son, Christopher, was invaluable in identifying innumerable organizational and stylistic infelicities. The opportunity to test its major theses in courses with graduate students has also contributed greatly to its development. Several colleagues, Elmer Martens, David Reimer and Mark Smith, generously took time to read parts or all of the manuscript at various stages of its development and have made many helpful comments and suggestions. As before, Lawrence Boadt's encouragement and advice were decisive in moving this project forward toward publication. Needless to say I am deeply grateful to each one—and to "him in whom we live and move and have our being."

Since 1969 I have had the privilege of being on the faculty of a Mennonite College affiliated with a vibrant Canadian university, the University of Waterloo. The time, energy and resources for writing a book of this kind would not have been possible apart from a supportive setting of this nature. The dedication of this book to Conrad Grebel College and its constituent Mennonite churches is meant as a small gesture of appreciation for affording me this opportunity.

John W. Miller
Emeritus Professor, Conrad Grebel College,
University of Waterloo

Chapter One

HOW THE HEBREW SCRIPTURES BECAME PART OF THE CHRISTIAN BIBLE

Not only were the Hebrew scriptures the first Christian Bible, they were deliberately retained and defended as such in the face of a powerful challenge to put them aside.

Does the Christian Bible itself offer any clues to its origins? Looked at as a whole, one of its most obvious features is its division into two unequal macrostructures: the first and larger known traditionally as the Old Testament, the second customarily referred to as the New Testament. Furthermore, on almost every page of the New Testament are references to the Old Testament, implying that this older body of writings was already in existence and regarded as authoritative by the authors of the New Testament. The Christian Bible must therefore have originated in two stages: first, there were older writings, most of which are in Hebrew; these were then supplemented with other writings, which are almost entirely in Greek, and the two parts functioned as one Bible. The canon-historical approach to the Bible that I hope to pursue will investigate these two canon-forming epochs.

Which should be investigated first? Only as we become familiar with the final stages of this process will it be at all clear as to why and how the Hebrew scriptures came to occupy the important place they did (and do) in the Christian Bible; so it is with this that we shall begin our study.

A. Final Stages in the Formation of the Christian Bible

The story of how the Hebrew scriptures came to be part of the Christian Bible is a long and complex one. Fortunately, excellent treatments of this subject are readily available.[1] Equally fortuitous is the consensus among those working in this field regarding essentially what happened. In summary, the picture they present is that the Christian Bible emerged in the first two centuries of the Christian era in three stages: Christianity began with an already existent Bible in its bosom, the sacred scriptures of Judaism (stage 1); however, as the movement spread into the wider world a challenge arose to abandon these scriptures in favor of a canon of exclusively Christian writings (stage 2); this precipitated an equally forceful response resulting in the retention of the Hebrew scriptures with appended Christian writings, creating the first uniquely Christian Bible (stage 3). I will now elaborate briefly on each of these three stages and conclude with some comments regarding how knowledge of these developments serves to highlight some of the essential qualities of this Bible.

1. Stage One: The First Christian Bible

The first Christians fell heir to an already existent canon of sacred writings, the Hebrew scriptures of Judaism. These scriptures were not at some point adopted or taken from the Jews, but were from the beginning part and parcel of Christian existence by virtue of the fact that, in the first instance, the church was Jewish and the first Christians were themselves Jews. This too is why these writings were not referred to as as "the Old Testament"[2] but as "scripture" (John 20:9; Gal. 3:22; 1 Pet. 2:6; 2 Pet. 1:20), or "scriptures" or "holy scriptures" (Rom. 1:2; 2 Tim. 3:15), or "the Law and the Prophets" (Matt. 5:17; 7:12; 22:40; John 1:45), or "the Law of Moses and the Prophets and the Psalms" (Luke 24:44), for this was how the Jews of that period knew them.[3]

But what books were being referred to in this manner? The New Testament writings themselves do not specify, for there was no need to do so. Their names were well known among those being addressed. That this was the case is confirmed by what a first century Jewish historian, Josephus, wrote regarding this library. In a treatise entitled, *Against Apion,* addressed to Gentiles, he states that Jews do not have an indeterminate number of books in their sacred library, but a more limited, "justly accredited" list. So revered were these scriptures, he adds, that despite the passage of "long ages of time, no one has ventured either to add, or remove, or to alter a syllable"; indeed, "it is an instinct with every Jew, from the day of his birth, to regard them as the decrees of God, to abide by them, and if need be, cheerfully to die for them."[4] Josephus goes on to specify that the number of these "justly accredited" books is twenty-two and then, historian that he was, names them according to the chronology of the times to which they refer. The more traditional numbering and arrangement of these writings in rabbinical sources and Bible manuscripts is set forth in a section of the Babylonian Talmud, Baba Bathra 14b, which can be dated to the second century CE.[5] Here the volumes identified as belonging to the Jewish scriptures are twenty-four and the books are listed in the traditional three-part arrangement alluded to in the New Testament. After the books of the Law (Genesis, Exodus, Leviticus, Numbers, Deuteronomy), which are not actually cited since they were well known by all, the books of "the Prophets" are listed in the following arrangement: Joshua, Judges, Samuel, Kings, Jeremiah, Ezekiel, Isaiah and the Twelve Minor Prophets; then "the Writings" or *Hagiographa* are itemized as follows: Ruth, Psalms, Proverbs, Ecclesiastes, Song of Songs, Lamentations, Daniel, Esther, Ezra[–Nehemiah] and Chronicles.[6] It may be assumed that these are the scriptures which many early Christians had studied from childhood (2 Tim. 3:15), which all regarded as inspired (2 Tim. 3:16), and which Jesus himself reportedly used when instructing his disciples (Luke 24:44).[7]

2. Stage Two: The First Christian Bible Challenged

How then did it happen that this first Christian Bible was enlarged and supplemented with specifically Christian writings? For an answer we must turn to sources outside the Bible itself, namely the writings of the early Church Fathers, certain early Christian Gnostic texts, and the work of the church historian, Eusebius (c. 263–340). Contemporary historians who have examined these sources are in substantial agreement that following stage one there was a gradual appearance of writings reflective of the new identity and message of the emergent Christian churches (Gospels, letters of the apostles, the book of Acts), and then, around the middle of the second century CE, the forceful challenge of a church leader named Marcion, who advocated that the Hebrew scriptures should be abandoned and replaced by a canon of writings made up exclusively of an edited selection of these newer Christian writings.[8]

What led to this radical proposal, Campenhausen has written, was not Marcion's analysis of "the uncertain state of Church tradition …" Rather, it was "theologically conditioned," the consequence of his uncompromising, passionately thought through and espoused conception of Christianity as a Gospel of the pure goodness and mercy of God which he interpreted not only as freedom from the Mosaic law (as did Paul), but as "hatred toward the creation, toward all the gods at work 'in Nature', and toward the cruelly-just Creator of this world himself." For Marcion, "this God of the world is the God of the old covenant and the Jewish 'scripture'. With him the Father of Jesus Christ has nothing in common and nothing to do."[9] Others prior to Marcion had also raised questions of a similar nature about the Jewish scriptures. Controversies over the proper interpretation of the Hebrew scriptures were a feature of the Judaism within which Christianity was born, as well as of the life and mission of Jesus himself as portrayed in the church's Gospels. But prior to Marcion "no one was in the least interested in rejecting the ancient Scripture altogether. It was only Marcion for whom such compromises had at one stroke become impossible."[10] His magnum opus was a book called *Antitheses* in which he systematically tabulated the contradictions ("antitheses") between the Hebrew scriptures and Christian teachings, "to prove," states Chadwick, "that the God of the Jews, the creator of this miserable world, was quite different from the God and Father of Jesus of whose existence the world had no inkling until the fifteenth year of Tiberius Caesar when Jesus suddenly appeared preaching the Gospel."[11] To Marcion "it was inconceivable," he adds, "that the divine redeemer could ever have been born of a woman …"; he consequently "rejected the story of the birth and childhood of Christ as a falsification imposed on the authentic story."[12] In Jesus, he believed, a new and totally unprecedented revelation of God had appeared.

What this systematic, frontal attack on the church's Bible meant for the second century church, writes Campenhausen, "is now hardly possible to appreciate. She had lost her 'scriptures'; at one and the same moment her proud claims to be the religion of the most ancient wisdom and the religion of historical fulfillment were both rendered invalid."[13] What then was left to hold on to? "That," writes Campenhausen, "was the question with which Marcion now saw himself unavoidably confronted."[14] Unlike some Gnostics he regarded himself neither as the founder of a religion nor as a prophet, and therefore did not appeal to 'secret' traditions or special revelations of his own. His belief was that the Gospel which the Jesus of history had proclaimed was radically different from that found in Hebrew scriptures, and also from that to be found in the church. In the church too this pure Gospel had been betrayed, Marcion believed.

> It was therefore necessary [he thought] to retrace one's steps, not in search of traditions, which even in the most favourable circumstances were still dubious and unconfirmed, but of definite written documents, which might possibly have preserved the original truth safe through all error and confusion, and which could therefore teach and safeguard it still. If the truth was again to be held in honour, and to be more permanently effective in the future, then there was only one way to achieve this: the ancient documents must once more be set upon the lampstand as the genuine and trustworthy witnesses to the message of Christ, and be exalted to the status of the normative rule, the 'Canon' of the Church. That is why Marcion's bible contains no new dogmatic, catechetical, or edifying texts of any sort, but exclusively ancient, traditional documents, which were merely edited in his own sense and purged of supposed distortions.[15]

The canon Marcion subsequently proposed as a substitute for the traditional scriptures was one that had two parts: an opening single Gospel account of the life and teaching of Jesus purged of its secondary accretions, and ten edited letters of Paul, for he was convinced that "in Paul he had found the meaning and true content of the 'Gospel'."[16] In Marcionite thought Paul was preeminent among the apostles, "*the* apostle and *the* evangelist of Christ," because "Paul alone knew the truth; for to him the mystery of Christ was made known by revelation."[17] It was on the basis of Paul that Marcion and his followers not only rejected and combated all other apostles and the whole of church tradition, but also fashioned their account of the life and teaching of Jesus in the solitary Gospel they perpetrated as alone the true one. This Marcionite Gospel no longer exists, but it was apparently a dogmatically revised version of Luke in which elements offensive to Marcionite theology were expurgated. Campenhausen pinpoints the reason for the enormous power of Marcion's challenge in the following words:

> The implacable logic with which Marcion thought through his basic ideas to their conclusion, and the practical consequences which he deduced from them, explains a great deal of the power and enthusiasm of the movement founded by him. It is only in the light of this that its consequences for the history of the Canon are to be understood.[18]

Marcion's forceful rejection of the first Christian Bible, the Jewish Hebrew scriptures, and his attempt at constructing a substitute Bible made up exclusively of words of Jesus and letters of Paul were the decisive events in the middle phase of the formation of the Christian Bible, a phase that set the stage for the final period in Christian canon formation.[19]

3. Stage Three: The First Christian Bible Defended and Enlarged

How would the wider church meet the challenge posed by Marcion? Here too we must rely for an answer on extra-biblical sources primarily, but are fortunate, once again, that a rather remarkable agreement exists among leading historians of the period as to what in general these are and how they should be read and interpreted. When it comes to tracing the history of the final formation of the canon in the early church, writes Rowan Greer, "all roads lead not to Rome but to Irenaeus and the last quarter of the second century," for it was he who at that time brought forth "a Christian Bible and Rule of faith thought to be derived from Scripture and supplying the proper key to the meaning of Scripture."[20] The beginnings of this development were of course earlier than this. However, before Irenaeus, writes

Greer, "we find no fully articulated definition of a New Testament canon and no clear framework for interpreting a Christian Bible."[21] It is in the late second century writings of Irenaeus and his enormously influential work, *Against Heresies,* that we encounter the ideas that successfully defended the Hebrew scriptures against the challenge posed by Marcion and gave birth to the bipartite Christian Bible.

This defense was complex and multifaceted and I can do no more here than try to summarize a few of its more salient points, three in particular.

a. Circumventing Marcion's Newly Contrived Christology

In seeking to rebut Marcion's Christology (which had drawn such a sharp distinction between the God revealed through Jesus and the God of Hebrew scripture), Irenaeus sought, first of all, to circumvent Marcion's newly contrived Gospel account of what Jesus taught and did by resorting to four older, more reliable Gospel portraits of Jesus in use in the churches of his time: Matthew, Mark, Luke and John (which he characterized as "writings" which "by the will of God had been handed down to us ... to be the foundation and pillar of our faith").[22] His main contention in doing this was that Marcion had not only

> abolished the Prophets and the Law [the Hebrew scriptures], and all the works of that God who made the world, whom he calls the World Ruler, [but] in addition to this he mutilated the Gospel According to Luke, removing everything about the birth of the Lord and much of the teaching of the words of the Lord, in which the Lord is recorded as clearly confessing the creator of this universe as his Father.[23]

Throughout his discussion of this issue Irenaeus repeats the point made here that in the earliest Gospel traditions (in contrast to the Gospel Marcion was putting forward) the God whom Jesus called Father was none other than the God whom Hebrew scriptures refer to as the maker of heaven and earth, and also that this is what all the apostles taught in all the churches worldwide. By linking this early apostolic confession of faith with the testimony of these earliest

Gospels Irenaeus was able to forge an unbreakable bond between the church's four oldest Gospels, the core beliefs of the early apostolic church and the God of Hebrew scriptures, and in this way defend the continuing use in the church of its first sacred writings, the Hebrew scriptures of the Jews. At the same time, he set in motion forces that would consolidate the emergence of a new or second version of this Bible, one which would include not just these older Hebrew scriptures but additional uniquely Christian writings as well: namely, the four apostolic Gospels (in place of Marcion's single edited version of Luke's Gospel).

b. Circumventing Marcion's One-Sided Concentration on Paul

What then was to be done about Marcion's other proposal: his ardent espousal of the theology and letters of Paul? Irenaeus' response to this issue may be thought of as his second major contribution to canon formation. Paul's letters had already begun to circulate freely in the churches and were by now (the middle of the second century) widely and highly regarded (see 2 Peter 3:15–18). Marcion's passionate advocacy of Paul's theology gave them an even higher visibility, but unlike the Gospel Marcion had created, their ascendant authority could not be put in question by resort to older *pre*-Pauline traditions. However, Paul was not the only apostle. What Irenaeus called for, therefore, was a recognition of the canonical status of Paul's letters, just as Marcion had done, but within the context of an expanded corpus of other apostolic writings which would supplement and balance Paul's one-sided emphasis. These included the book of Acts, plus certain pastoral letters intended for all the churches and the Apocalypse of John. It is Campenhausen's opinion that 1 and 2 Timothy, Titus, Philemon, Hebrews and James might have been composed at about this time (mid–second century) and with this need in mind, for like the writings of Polycarp they attack "godless philosophical discussions and the contradictions [literally, 'antitheses'] of the 'knowledge' which is not knowledge at all" (1 Tim 6:20), a text some think is directed quite specifically against Marcion. Here too we find the most explicit declaration of scriptural authority in the New Testament, namely, the text in 2 Tim. 3:15–16 that speaks of "all" Hebrew scripture being inspired and therefore profitable for instructing the people of God, a text that Campenhausen believes may be a "concealed piece of polemic against the narrow Marcionite canon."[24]

Therefore, in addition to defending the church's Christology against Marcion's attempt to loosen it from its monotheistic moorings in the Hebrew scriptures by replacing Marcion's truncated Gospel with four older Gospels, Irenaeus also sought to retain the Pauline letters by preserving them unedited within an enlarged apostolic canon that would provide a counterweight against Paul's too sharp contrast between grace and law. The subsequent discussions in the churches over precisely which additional books should be included in this list are unimportant compared to this step, writes William Farmer, for "with Irenaeus, the church had all the essential parts of what came to be its New Testament canon."[25]

c. Fashioning a New Perspective from Which To Read This Newly Enlarged Christian Bible

In conjunction with this discussion Irenaeus made yet another important contribution which can only be touched on in passing. Having defended the church's continuing use of its Hebrew scriptures on the basis of a scriptural canon that now included both these older sacred writings plus a sizeable number of newer explicitly Christian writings, Irenaeus also began to explore how this enlarged canon might be viewed and read as a single set of scriptures with an inherent organic unity. In explaining what this entailed, it is important to recall that not even at this juncture were either he or his church in the habit of referring to the newer writings of this canon as a "New Testament" sharply differentiated from an "Old Testament." Indeed, Campenhausen writes,

> This designation [New Testament]…was as yet unknown to Irenaeus. He has no name by which to distinguish the New Testament books from the ancient Scripture…. As occasion requires he speaks simply of the fourfold Gospel, of the Acts of the Apostles, or the letters of the Apostle. Sometimes he groups these books together with the Old Testament, and refers to the whole without differentiation by the long-hallowed names of 'scriptures of the Lord', 'the scriptures', or 'the scripture'.[26]

For Irenaeus, in what, then, lay the unity and coherence of this now expanded body of sacred writings? He sees it as a story of the human race in which progressive revelation of God has occurred, a revelation that begins with creation and moves forward to the final redemption in Christ and the new age. The chief figure in this redemptive plan is the God whom Jesus called Father. As Greer puts it, the revelation of God manifested in Christ according to Irenaeus,

> far from introducing the revelation of God for the first time, brings to focus God's self-disclosure in creation and in the Hebrew Scriptures.... Christ's revelation of the Father in Hebrew Scriptures takes place by stages. There are four covenants, under Adam, under Noah, under Moses, and the fourth "which renovates man, and sums up all things in itself by means of the Gospel, raising and bearing men upon its wings into the heavenly country" (*Against Heresies* 3.11.8).[27]

Greer goes on to suggest that Irenaeus' understanding of these four "covenants"

> is best explained by his use of the metaphor of education. The Word's revelation of the Father is really a teaching and a moral training that is designed to assist humanity's growth and persuade human beings of the perfection that is their destiny in God's purpose.[28]

Greer also states that

> regarding human history as an education correlates with another metaphor central to Irenaeus' thought. He understands the history of humanity on the analogy of the development of an individual human being as a growth from innocence of childhood to adult maturity. God did not create Adam perfect, because created things inevitably fall short of perfection and must grow from infancy to maturity. The creation of humanity is followed by growth, strengthening, abounding, recovering, and finally the glori-

fication of the perfect vision of God that renders humanity incorruptible (*Against Heresies* 4.38).[29]

Perhaps this will suffice to give the flavor of Irenaeus' theological perspectives. We might summarize by saying that he viewed the newly expanded "scriptures" of the church as conveying a continuous, providentially guided, redemptive story that unfolded by stages from creation to the consummation of creation in Christ.

B. The Final Form of the Christian Bible: Initial Thoughts and Questions

What light has this foray into the formation of the Bible shed on its nature and form? What questions does it pose? For one thing, it heightens our awareness of how integral were the twenty-four scrolls of the Hebrew scriptures in their original three-part arrangement to this Bible's initial development and design. These scriptures were not only the first Christian Bible, but were retained and defended as such in the face of a powerful challenge to set them aside. Since the heart of this challenge was Marcion's belief that the God whom Jesus called Father was not the same deity as the God of Hebrew scriptures, crucial to this defense was the recognition of their oneness. It is Lloyd Gaston's belief that the classic doctrine of the Trinity should have for this reason "logical priority over Christological doctrines," for the point being made is "that the 'Father' to whom the 'Son' relates is none other than the God of Abraham, Isaac and Jacob, the God of Sarah and Rebekah and Rachel and Leah, the God of Moses and Jeremiah and Ezra and Esther."[30] Polarizing or bifurcating law and grace, love and justice, the God of the New Testament and the God of the Old Testament is a betrayal of the Bible's canonical intentionality.[31]

The question arises as to whether the way the Hebrew scriptures of this Bible were subsequently renamed, rearranged and supplemented in the churches of the west has not contributed to a continuing tendency within Christianity to perpetuate just such a polarization. The practice of dividing the Christian Bible into two distinct parts and labeling them "Old Testament" and "New Testament" is a case in point. This custom which became entrenched when these scriptures were translated into Latin during the fourth century, has almost always resulted in "a hermeneutic of antithesis."[32] Similar consequences tend to follow from the changes in the list and order of "Old Testament" books that became commonplace as the churches of the west were increasingly reliant on translations and lost contact with the older list and arrangement of the Hebrew scriptures of the Jews and early Christians. Thus, in the large Greek (Septuagint) and Latin codexes which replaced the older scroll-libraries as the preferred mode of compiling these scriptures from the third and fourth centuries onward, certain books (the so-called Apocryphal or Deuterocanonical writings), which were originally not included in the Jewish scriptural collection, were added, and the whole corpus was rearranged in ways that seemed preferable to the Christian churches who created these volumes.[33] One innovation introduced during this period was an especially consequential one: the exchange of places between Ezra-Nehemiah and Chronicles, on the one hand, and the four books of the prophets, on the other. More specifically, it became customary for these latter books (Jeremiah, Ezekiel, Isaiah, and the Twelve Minor Prophets) to be moved from their older position following Kings to a position near or at the end of the Old Testament, while Ezra-Nehemiah and Chronicles, which had been at the end, were moved from there to the place after Kings where the prophetic books had been.[34] As a result the importance of the prophetic books within the thematic structure of "the Law and the Prophets" was lost sight of, as well as their significance for an understanding of "the Writings" that follow (in the older arrangement). Now, instead of the prophets serving as a framework for a proper interpretation of the events recounted in Ezra-Nehemiah, there was a tendency to see their futuristic visions as only relevant to the developments referred to in the New Testament scriptures.[35] Thus, the danger arose once again that Christians, rather than seeing their history and identity in continuity with Israel (and as an organic unfolding of the Hebrew scriptural story), would instead think of themselves as belonging to an alternative religion. The rebirth of canon-studies in our time marks this as an auspicious moment for reconsidering these important issues.[36]

Chapter Two

A FIRST LOOK AT WHEN AND WHY THEY WERE COMPILED

The chief impetus to the formation of the Hebrew scriptures in the listing and format they had at the threshhold of the Christian era was the reform movement spearheaded by Ezra and Nehemiah.

Having learned in Chapter 1 how the Christian Bible as a whole was formed, and having discovered how important were the Hebrew scriptures in that development, I want to turn now to the Hebrew scriptures themselves and begin the search for when and why they were compiled. Approximately when did this occur? Who initiated this process? For what reasons? These are the questions I will be addressing in this chapter.

A. Locating the General Time Period When the Hebrew Scriptures Were Compiled

The evidence has already been noted for believing the Hebrew scriptures were existent in the first century CE in much the same format they have since had in Jewish Bibles. The issue now facing us, therefore, is this: how long prior to this time was this collection created? Among the sources that may be relevant for answering this question, none is more important than the Translator's Foreword to Sirach, a text written by Sira's grandson in 132 BCE to explain why he had translated his grandfather's book (Sirach) into Greek.[1] Three times in his brief discourse the grandson refers to writings which the Jewish community of his time held in highest esteem and which were being assiduously studied by Jewish scholars like his grandfather. In naming these writings the grandson uses titles that are virtually identical with those later found in Jewish and Christian sources for the Jewish scriptures. He first calls them, "the Law, the Prophets, and the others"; then, "the Law, the Prophets and the other books of the Fathers"; and finally, "the Law, the Prophets and the other books." While the name of the third section of this collection fluctuates from citation to citation, the titles used all have the definite article ("*the* others"; "*the* other books of the Fathers"; "*the* other books")—this plus the fact that this section can be referred to as "the other books *of the Fathers*" suggests that it too must have included a quite specific and venerable block of books. Notable too is the fact that in the grandson's introductory comments a clear distinction is drawn between this older collection and books produced by scholars like his grandfather. "The Law, the prophets and the others," as he introduces them, are an already established body of respected writings which "have passed on to us great lessons, in consequence of which Israel must be commended for learning and wisdom." On the other hand, the literary productions of scholars like his grandfather are described as having arisen from their study of these older writings and as being aimed at helping people acquire the disciplines necessary for living in accordance with their teachings. The specific and respectful manner in which the Hebrew scriptures are here identified and discussed presupposes their existence as a major force in Jewish affairs at least two centuries before the Christian era.

How sure can we be, however, that the actual list and organization of books in this library were the same or similar to that which existed later on? Perhaps the best indication of this is the review of this library which Sira himself undertakes in chs. 44–49 of his book. There key figures in biblical history are identified and highlighted, beginning with those mentioned in Genesis (Enoch, Noah, Abraham, Isaac and Jacob), and then proceeding sequentially, book by book, right through Exodus, Leviticus, Numbers, and Deuteronomy (Moses, Aaron, Phinehas), the books of Joshua, Judges, Samuel and Kings (Joshua, Caleb, the Judges, Samuel, Nathan, David, Solomon, Rehoboam, Jereboam, Elijah, Elisha, Hezekiah, Isaiah, Josiah), the prophetic books (Jeremiah, Ezekiel, omitting Isaiah, since he was previously mentioned), right down to the final volume of "the Law and the Prophets," "the twelve [minor] prophets" (49:11). In other words,

Sira's library of "the Law and the Prophets" included the very same books in the same order as those in Jewish Bibles today. Furthermore, at the very end of Sira's historical survey, Zerubbabel, Jeshua and Nehemiah are also mentioned (Sirach 49:13–15), implying that the books of Ezra and Nehemiah were also in this collection as part of the "other books" section (again precisely as in the arrangement in Jewish Bibles since then). While it is unlikely that all the books that were later included in this third section were among the volumes that Sira was familiar with, it appears that many were, for elsewhere in Sirach there are allusions to Psalms and Proverbs (Sirach 44:4–5; cp. 39:3; 47:8, 14–17), Chronicles (Sirach 47:9–10) and possibly Job (Sirach 49:9). Hence, it can be said with some confidence that a body of authoritative scriptures similar in content and organization to the one found in Jewish Bibles today was already firmly in place at the beginning of the second century BCE.[2]

How old then *was* this collection? How many years, decades or centuries prior to *this point* in time had it been compiled and edited? There are at least two ways of arriving at an *approximate* answer to this question. One is by noting what bearing certain notable features of the Hebrew scriptures themselves might have on this issue; the other is by paying close attention to a quite explicit (although frequently neglected) reference in 2 Maccabees to the beginnings of this collection. Among the characteristics of the Hebrew scriptures themselves that might be of relevance to their origins is their frequently noted preoccupation with chronology. The main point to be considered, in brief, is the way these scriptures convey a story with a distinctive beginning, middle and end. At their opening is an account of the origins of the world and its peoples (Gen. 1–10); then, against this backdrop the story of Israel's origins and rise to national greatness is related (Exodus to Samuel), followed by the account of a precipitous decline and fall (Kings). After this, in the four scrolls of the Prophets we are introduced to the theme of restoration and future blessing for both Israel and the world. Finally, in the books of Ezra and Nehemiah we read of the dawning fulfillment of these hopes in the events of Israel's restoration and of the reforms spearheaded by Ezra and Nehemiah during which certain scriptures were introduced, taught and solemnly embraced (Neh. 8–10). It is the report of these latter events which brings this long history begun in Genesis to its climax and close. In other words, looked at as a whole, the Hebrew scriptures may be characterized as a literature which recounts the history of the world from the creation of the universe to Israel's restoration and the formation of a scripture-based community during the reforms of Ezra and Nehemiah.[3]

What bearing does this have on the question of when and why the tripartite Hebrew scriptures were first compiled? These scriptures could not have been created in their present form prior to the final events they record. Therefore, whenever this happened, it must have been during or following the reforms described at the end of Ezra-Nehemiah. What time-period was this? According to modern conventions for reckoning time, the destruction of Jerusalem by Babylon transpired in 586 BCE; the return from captivity was in 537; the temple was rebuilt in 515. If the Artaxerxes mentioned as monarch during the era of Ezra and Nehemiah was Artaxerxes I, then Ezra's return and the beginning of his reforms took place in 458 (Ezra 7:7). Nehemiah's mission began some twelve years later (Neh. 2:1). Hence, the reforms alluded to in Ezra-Nehemiah's final chapters were initiated and carried out during the middle and latter half of the fifth century BCE. Two and a half centuries later (as just noted), a prominent teacher in Israel was described by his grandson as having been a life-long student of "the Law, the Prophets, and other books of the Fathers." Therefore, it must have been from about 450 to 200 BCE that the Hebrew scriptures were assembled in the approximate form they then came to have. Since our sources refer to no other event in this time-period that would remotely match that of the Ezra-Nehemiah reforms as an explanation for this development, it may be concluded these reforms were the precipitating event.[4]

Added support for this conclusion can be derived from a set of comments in a letter that is now part of 2 Maccabees, one which was purportedly sent from the Jews of Jerusalem to the Jews of Egypt in 164 BCE (see 2 Macc. 1:10–2:18).[5] In this letter passing reference is made to an otherwise unknown source, the *Memoirs of Nehemiah,* in which was recorded (it is said) "how Nehemiah founded a library and made a collection of the books dealing with the Kings and the Prophets, the writings of David and the letters of the kings on the subject of offerings" (2 Macc. 2:13). The point of this citation was to inform the Jews of Egypt that just as Nehemiah had earlier done, so "similarly, Judas [Maccabeus] made a complete collection of the books dispersed in the late war, and these we still have" (2:14). The "late war" referred to was the Maccabaean uprising that was successful in liberating the Jews of Palestine from the religious persecutions of Antiochus Epiphanes. What the report implies is that the library of scriptures begun by Nehemiah had been dispersed for safekeeping during this war, but was now fully reassembled, and the "complete collection" was again available to those who might want one or another of its books. "If you have need of any of them," the letter concludes, "send someone to fetch them" (2 Macc. 2:15). The only "collection" of books of this kind in this period that we know of is that of "the Law, the Prophets and the other books of the Fathers" which Sira's grandson reports his grandfather had been studying all his life. Thus, 2 Macc. 2:13–15 makes explicit what the story recounted in the Hebrew scriptures themselves implies: namely, that the collection of books later regarded as authoritative scriptures by the Jews was *begun* in the aftermath of the reforming work of the figures described in its closing chapters.[6]

B. A PROVISIONAL LOOK AT THE CRISIS THAT MAY HAVE PROMPTED THIS DEVELOPMENT

With this possibility in mind (that these scriptures began to be compiled at this point in time), I want to turn now to the era of the Ezra-Nehemiah reforms and begin inquiring into what may have prompted these reforms and this development. Naturally, writings that purport to tell us what was happening at this juncture, such as the books of Ezra and Nehemiah themselves, are of very special interest for our study at this point, but other volumes too can be related to the events of this period. Several prophets, for example (notably Isaiah 56–66, Haggai, Zechariah 1–8 and Malachi), can be dated to a time-period just prior to the reforms in question. Furthermore, if this is in truth the epoch when the Hebrew scriptures were compiled, it is only to be expected that many aspects of this corpus might bear the imprint of this development. Our resources for understanding the developments of this era may, therefore, be far richer than is often realized.[7]

As important as the sources themselves, however, is the angle from which they are approached and studied. A crucial first question might be why at this late date in biblical history reforms of the kind alluded to in Ezra-Nehemiah were at all necessary. Was Israel at this stage of its existence not an ancient, well-established people? Did it not have a plenitude of venerable legal, moral and liturgical traditions to draw upon for guidance and support? Did it not have tested institutions and leadership groups for governing itself? If so, what had gone wrong? I have come to believe that students of this period have seriously underestimated the depth of the divisions this community was facing. For example, Paul Hanson, after surveying the strife among contending parties that characterized this era, concludes that nevertheless they all shared a "common legacy" that "far outweighed" the "differences in emphasis" among "the contending groups."[8] It is this quite commonly accepted perspective that I have come to question and have also concluded that closer attention must be paid as well not just to what the difficulties were at a point in time *just prior* to the reforms in question (that is, their *near*-historical background), but to a cluster of very old, unresolved institutional, theological and cultic tensions and disagreements which had plagued this community for centuries (the *far* historical background).

My goal in the remainder of this chapter will be to highlight a few of the more *immediate* problems facing this community as these come to light through a more or less naive, surface reading of the more pertinent sources. To understand the true nature of the crisis this community was facing, it will be essential that we then undertake a more detailed analysis of the "far historical background" of these issues, before returning (in Ch. 6) to a closer analysis of what the Ezra-Nehemiah reforms themselves sought to accomplish.

1. Critical Issues Facing This Community Just Prior to the Ezra-Nehemiah Reforms

As a first step in identifying some of the problems this community was facing, the identity of the community itself needs to be clearly established. In the edict of Cyrus quoted in the opening lines of Ezra, the people whose fate is being described is characterized as one whose God is Yahweh ("the God in Jerusalem"); they are also referred to as "survivors" of the Babylonian captivity who were authorized by the Persian monarch Cyrus to return to their Judean homeland. This information is followed in Ezra 1:5 by a more specific characterization of

them as "the heads of families of Judah and of Benjamin, the priests
and the Levites, in fact all whose spirit had been roused by God," and
who were "prepared to go and rebuild the Temple of Yahweh in
Jerusalem...." In Ezra 2–6 we are then informed of events that transpired in their midst from this point in time (537 BCE) until the
rebuilding of the Second Temple twenty-two years later (515). Only at
Chapter 7 of Ezra do we arrive at the period of the Ezra-Nehemiah
reforms. There we are first informed of Ezra's initial mission which
began during the seventh year of the Persian monarch Artaxerxes (Ezra
7:7). Assuming this to be Artaxerxes I, Ezra's arrival at Jerusalem
would have occurred, as noted, in 458 BCE, or well over a half century
after the rebuilding of the temple in 515.[9] It was *this* fifty-seven year
period (515 to 458 BCE) in the life of *this* community (Judean and
Benjaminite families who had been "roused by God" to return from
Babylon to their homeland to rebuild the temple of Yahweh) that constitutes the *near* background to the Ezra-Nehemiah reforms.

What was happening in this community during this half century?
What were the difficulties that prompted the intervention and missions
of Ezra and Nehemiah as these are described in the subsequent chapters of their books? Our most vivid glimpses of these problems are to
be found in the following three sources: the conditions of the period as
these surface in the sharp critiques of the prophet Malachi, usually
dated to the period just prior to the reforms of Ezra;[10] the personal
diaries of Ezra (Ezra 8:15–9:15) which mention problems encountered
during the first stages of his mission to this community in 458; the can-
did journalistic reports of Nehemiah of the difficulties he faced during
his two terms as Judean governor (Neh. 1–2; 3:33–7:5; 12:27–13:31),
the first occurring some twelve or thirteen years after Ezra's mission
(Neh. 1:1), the second "some time" later, after the completion of his
initial mission during the thirty-second year of Artaxerxes, or 433 BCE
(Neh. 13:6).

Collating the glimpses afforded by these several sources, the following first provisional picture of the rather dismal state of affairs in
this community during this half century begins to emerge.

a. Demoralized Rival Priesthoods

The chief impression derived from reading the acerbic messages
of Malachi is that despite the fact that this community had been suc-

cessful in rebuilding the Yahweh temple and was now worshiping there, the performance of its priesthood was extraordinarily slipshod, and that there were enormous differences of opinion over what a priest's role and task at that temple should be. The words of Malachi (which are the culminating prophecies of the final scroll of the Prophets) may be characterized as an unrelentingly fierce attack on the priests then in charge of the Temple regarding not only their behavior, but their fundamental ideals. Thus he warns them that if they do not repent of the irreverent manner in which they are carrying out their duties, a curse will be laid upon them and their sacrifices (Mal. 2:1–3), and he further challenges them to adopt as an ideal the lofty example of Levi, whom he characterizes as a priest who "walked in peace and justice," "converted many from sinning," safeguarded "knowledge" and interpreted "law" as specified by Yahweh's "covenant with Levi" (Mal. 2:4–9).

Strangely, a covenant by this name is not elsewhere mentioned or described in the biblical sources, even though Malachi's words imply that this covenant was authoritative for the priesthood in question. The tradition he appears to be referring to is that of Moses' final words as recorded in Deut. 33:8–11, where Levi and his descendants are singled out as priests and teachers of Yahweh's law because they have kept Yahweh's word and "hold firmly" to his "covenant" (33:10).[11] As Malachi views it, this covenant required that a true priest be a person of character and a *teacher* (2:6), and not just that he preside at sacrifices. More specifically, he should hold Yahweh in respect, honor his name (2:5) and be his "messenger" (2:7).[12] The critique concludes with a stinging charge that the priests in charge of the temple have instead destroyed the "covenant with Levi," and not only that, but have themselves "turned aside" from this way and are causing others "to lapse" as well (2:8). Thus, in Malachi's eyes this priesthood was both itself unfit and chiefly responsible for the social, moral and spiritual disintegration of the community at large.

It comes as no surprise that those addressed do not concur—in fact, do not seem even to understand what Malachi is talking about. To his opening charge that their conduct in office was disrespectful of Yahweh's name, they reply: "How have we despised your name?" (1:6b); "How have we polluted you?" (1:7). Yet from Malachi's point of view, their behavior was so deplorable that were they to persist in what they were doing, it would be better if the temple were shut down altogether (1:10)—and should their behavior *not* change and should present conditions prevail, the most horrible consequences would ensue, he declares: not only will Yahweh curse their blessings, but break their arms, throw offal in their faces and sweep them away "with it" into oblivion (Mal. 2:3). One is hard pressed to imagine a more vitriolic critique. "Nowhere else does the priesthood receive such extended or scathing beratings," writes Julia O'Brien of this confrontation.[13]

Furthermore, it appears that this conflict between Malachi and this priesthood was of no recent origins, but involved issues of a longstanding nature. This is intimated by the prediction in Mal. 3:1–5 of an approaching event during which "suddenly" an "angel" or "messenger" of the covenant will appear who will "purify the sons of Levi and refine them like gold and silver, so that ... the offering of Judah and Jerusalem will then be acceptable to Yahweh as in former days, as in the years of old" (Mal. 3:4). The reference here to "former days" (or "years of old") points to a time long ago when the ideals of which the prophet spoke *were* accepted and adhered to.[14] Such is not the case now, his words imply, nor can a restoration of that former state of affairs be anticipated except through the agency of an extraordinary emissary; nothing short of the advent of a divinely commissioned "messenger of the covenant" will be able to sweep aside the resistance to the needed reforms, he prophesies (3:2). The words of other prophets of this era reflect similar disputes over priestly ideals and temple affairs (a subject to which I will return in Chapter 5).

Potent evidence of these conflicts may also be derived from a careful analysis of the detailed lists cited in Ezra 2:36–40 of those who first returned to this community. A peculiar feature of these is the manner in which "priests" and "Levites" are carefully distinguished, with the numbers of priests being registered in one column (2:36–39), and the numbers of the Levites in another (2:40). Having just observed Malachi's strident rebuke of the priesthood for having failed to embrace the ideals embodied in Yahweh's "covenant with Levi," we are prompted to ask why this was so. Were Levites not regarded as priests by those who compiled these lists? Were priests not regarded as Levites? Was Malachi not implying the identity of the two groups in his challenge that priests, if truly faithful to their calling, should adhere to Yahweh's "covenant with Levi"? Why then, in these texts, are "priests" listed separately from "Levites" as though the two are different groups altogether?

The mystery deepens as we pay closer attention to the actual *numbers* of personnel cited in each category. Those returnees listed as "priests" are said to have numbered 4,289, while those listed as "Levites" numbered only 74 (Ezra 2:36–40; cp. Neh. 7:39–42), a ratio of almost sixty to one. A century later when Nehemiah had succeeded in resettling Jerusalem, this imbalance between priests and Levites was seemingly rectified somewhat, for then the priests are said to have numbered 1,192 and the Levites 284, a ratio of four to one (see Neh. 11:10–18). However, other texts imply that even this modest increase of Levites in this community came about only as a result of actions taken in the face of considerable opposition from the priests. Thus, Ezra 8:15 informs us that, when assembling his entourage for the return journey to Jerusalem that would initiate his reforms, Ezra suddenly realized that not a single Levite was present, although numerous laymen and priests had joined his company. Only after extraordinary steps were taken was he finally able to bring with him thirty-eight heads of Levitical households (Ezra 8:18–19). We learn that not even then, however, was the fate of this guild a secure one during the following years in Judea. Illustrative of the problems they faced is an arresting addendum to Nehemiah's journal in which he reports of events occurring during his second visit to this community. At that time he discovered that every one of the Levites whom he had earlier settled in Jerusalem during his first visit had returned to their ancestral fields, because "they had not been receiving their allocations ..." (Neh. 13:10). We are then informed that Nehemiah reprimanded the officials for this neglect of duty in attending to the needs of this group and took immediate action to rectify matters by reassembling, resettling and reappointing them once again to their temple duties. To this end, we are told, a committee was formed of both priests *and* Levites to insure that from now on both groups would receive their due share of the "tithe of corn, wine and oil" which had been assembled for their support (Neh. 13:10–14). However, even this measure was insufficient, apparently, for Nehemiah's journal closes with the surprising notification that it was at this juncture that "regulations for the priests and the Levites, defining each man's duty," were finally drafted and adopted (Neh. 13:30).[15]

In summary, our sources are transparent regarding the existence of intense rivalries between priests and Levites during the period leading up to and during the Ezra-Nehemiah reforms, with one of these sources, Malachi, containing messages that threaten the priests with expulsion if they did not adhere to Levite ideals—and yet other sources (notably Ezra and Nehemiah) implying that right at this juncture Levites were in truth a minority group and not even regarded as priests by a dominant priesthood who resented their very presence at the temple. Clearly, something was seriously amiss and unresolved in this regard. The core leadership of this community was divided and at odds to an exceptional degree.

b. Widespread Religious Malaise and Confusion

The problems and needs of this community were not confined to the priestly elites only. Religious malaise and confusion were widespread among the populace generally, it seems. To what extent this was a result of the conflicts between leadership groups remains to be seen, but it is again in the messages of Malachi that this problem surfaces most vividly. To Malachi's declaration (in the opening message of his book) that Yahweh still loves them, the people addressed respond by asking, "How have you [Yahweh] shown your love [to us]?" (1:2). The depth of their doubts is captured in several quotes of a similar nature: "Any evil-doer is good as far as Yahweh is concerned; indeed he is delighted with them" (Mal. 2:17), the people say; and again, "Where is the God of fair justice now?" They are even reported to have said, "It is useless to serve God; what is the good of keeping his commands or walking mournfully before Yahweh Sabaoth?" (Mal. 3:14–15). They have reached the point, they say, where they are prepared to call "the proud the happy ones; the evil-doers are the ones who prosper; they put God to the test, yet come to no harm!" (3:15).

As in Malachi's critique of the priesthood, the impression we get from these statements is of an unbridgeable gulf between him and those he is addressing—so much so, that in the *final* instance he does not even try to respond to the cynicism expressed. Rather, we are told: "*then* those who feared Yahweh talked to one another about this, and Yahweh took note and listened; and a book of remembrance was written in his presence recording those who feared him and kept his name in mind" (Mal. 3:16). This suggests that in the midst of a sea of despair and cynicism a group characterized as "fearing" Yahweh had gathered and was talking. It may be conjectured that it was to this community that Malachi himself belonged.[16]

c. Non-Support for the Central Institutions

Another focus of Malachi's critique was the community's failure to bring to the central storehouses of the restored Temple the necessary tithes and offerings specified in Yahwistic law (see Mal. 3:6–12). A half century earlier Haggai had touched on a similar failure when he charged the people of his time with being too busy building their own houses to care about rebuilding the House of Yahweh (Hag. 1:9b). This lack of support for the community's most vital religious institution is regarded by both prophets as symptomatic of a loss of faith that needed urgent attention. For Malachi such behavior was tantamount to "cheating" God, a gross dereliction of religious duty. It is with this in mind that he characterized the renewal of support for the temple and its personnel through tithes and offerings as being tantamount to a "return" to Yahweh (3:7), an event that would "open the floodgates of heaven" (3:10). From Nehemiah we learn that Jerusalem itself was being grossly neglected even after Ezra's efforts at reform, for it was news of this that overwhelmed him with emotion and prompted him to take action on the community's behalf (Neh. 1:3–4). This community was so directionless and discouraged during this time, it appears, that it had ceased caring about its most vital institutions: neither the needs of the Jerusalem temple, nor of Jerusalem itself, were being properly attended to.

d. Socio–Economic Disorders

Another foreboding sign of communal disarray among the populace during this period was the socioeconomic situation we read of in Nehemiah 5. From the opening verses of this chapter it is apparent that a wide gulf had opened up between a wealthy elite and others who had fallen into abject poverty or debt slavery. The description of this state of affairs in Neh. 5:1–4 is such an unusually vivid one that it deserves being quoted in full:

> There was a great outcry from the people, and from their wives, against their brother Jews. Some said, "We are having to pledge our sons and daughters to get enough grain to eat and keep us alive." Others said, "We are having to

mortgage our fields, our vineyards and our houses to get
grain because of the shortage." Still others said, "We have
had to borrow money on our fields and our vineyards to
pay the royal tax; and though we belong to the same race
as our brothers, and our children are as good as theirs, we
shall have to sell our sons and our daughters into slavery;
some of our daughters have been sold into slavery already.
We can do nothing about it, since our fields and our vineyards now belong to others.

The immediate causes of the poverty referred to were shortages
of produce due to drought (Neh. 5:3) and excessive royal taxes (5:4),
not oppressive measures as such. However, a wealthy class made up of
nobles and officials (5:7) benefited from these bleak circumstances
through default on the loans they had made. Wealth obtained in this
manner and with these consequences, Nehemiah pointed out, was hard-
hearted and callous no matter how legitimate from a legal point of
view, especially when it involved fellow Jews who had only recently
been liberated (Neh. 5:6–13). Socio-economic divisions and tensions
between a powerful elite and others in this society are again the motifs
reflected in this incident.[17]

e. Intermarriage with Foreign Women

Perhaps the most striking indicators of the crisis of identity
which this community was experiencing are the references in both
Malachi and Ezra-Nehemiah to intermarriage with foreign women.
Malachi termed it a "profanation" of the ancestral covenant and threatened those involved with the prospect of excommunication (see Mal.
2:10–12). His additional teachings against divorce (2:13–16) suggest
that to marry such women, Israelite men were abandoning the wives of
their youth, an action he regarded as a breach of solemn pledges made
in the presence of Yahweh (2:14). The extent to which such religiously
syncretistic marriages were occurring at this time is underscored by the
report in Ezra 9 and 10 of what occurred soon after Ezra took up resi-
dence in this community. Not just lay people were involved in this
practice, we learn there, but priests and Levites as well (Ezra
10:18–22). Ethnic purity per se was not the issue (as sometimes suggested), but the potential loss of values and identity resulting from too

close contact with the "disgusting practices" of the foreigners resident in this region (Ezra 9:1).[18]

So, in summary, not only were there seemingly unbridgeable divisions among the priestly elite of this community, not only were the people at large demoralized and increasingly disinterested in its central religious institutions, but many were adrift in a form of syncretism that could only spell extinction were these trends not halted. This is the bleak picture that emerges from a first, provisional look at a few of our more important biblical sources for understanding what was happening in this community during the half century prior to the Ezra-Nehemiah reforms.

2. Why These Conditions?

It surprises us to discover how fragile this community was at this late stage of its existence, and especially right at this juncture when it had successfully resettled its land and had managed to rebuild its temple. Why after centuries of existence would priests and people be as divided and demoralized as they seem to have been—and to the point of compromising their ancestral faith? What could have produced a spiritual crisis of this magnitude? The bitter controversies among priestly leaders of this community are especially perplexing. What accounts for Malachi's devastating diatribe against those in charge of the temple? What group does *he* belong to that he can speak as he does of the critical importance of the "covenant with Levi" as guide and norm for priestly conduct? Why are the priests he addresses so impervious to the challenge he brings them? These are questions which can only be answered by looking farther back into the history of this people. Our brief review of the priest-lists in Ezra and Nehemiah reinforces this suggestion. The puzzling distinction made there between "priests" and "Levites" raises questions about the prehistory of these groups. What groups are these? At what point in Israelite history were they distinguished in this manner? Why do Ezra and Nehemiah experience such great difficulties in bringing them together? The thought arises that there might have been more than one claimant to priestly leadership in this community and that the intense rivalry between them was not the least of the factors contributing to the crisis we read of in our sources for this period.

Chapter Three

THE WIDER BACKGROUND: ISRAEL'S RIVAL PRIESTLY HOUSES

Following Solomon's dismissal of the Levite priests from Jerusalem, worship at Israel's national shrines was administrated by priesthoods who either disagreed with or were unacquainted with Levite tradition.

The possibility posed at the conclusion of the last chapter, that rival priesthoods were contending for power in postexilic Israel, is one I now wish to examine more closely. Is it possible that contentions among priestly guilds were a major factor in the crisis Israel was facing at this time, and in the reforms enacted and the scriptures compiled in the service of these reforms? I will try to answer this question by advancing two theses: first, that the Hebrew scriptures themselves are forthcoming about the fact that for centuries prior to the Ezra-Nehemiah reforms (and right up to that point) Israelite religious tradition had been channeled through diverse priestly houses or traditions that were often at odds with one another; secondly, that these tensions between priestly groups were severely exacerbated by a succession of prophets who appeared in this community during the three centuries when the two Israelite kingdoms were destroyed, followed by a period in exile and then a new beginning in the Israelite homeland. The first of these theses will be the subject of this and the following chapter, the second the focus of Chapter 5.

A. Preliminary Considerations

The enormous importance of priesthoods in Israelite culture (and ancient cultures generally) is sometimes overlooked or underestimated

in contemporary studies of the Hebrew scriptures. This is partly due to
the demise in modern secular cultures of religious institutions or hier-
archies of equivalent status or power. As a consequence we fail to realize that as custodians of sacred teachings and traditions (Jer. 18:18)
and as guardians of national shrines (see Amos 7:13; Jer. 26:7–11),
these ancient priests were among the most powerful figures of their
time. Thus, among David's first acts when founding Jerusalem as the
base of operations for his kingdom was his decision to establish a tent
shrine there (Psalm 132; 2 Sam. 6–7) under the administration of venerable priestly guilds (2 Sam. 8:16). Also, Jeroboam when founding
the northern Israelite kingdom, took pains to establish at once his own
national shrines lest the integrity of his kingdom and the loyalty of his
people be diminished (1 Kings 12:26–27). The range and nature of the
competencies and learning required for priestly duty at such centers
are reflected in the writings of the Jerusalem priest-prophet Ezekiel,
where an astonishing wealth of knowledge is to be found regarding the
varied historical, legal, cultic and confessional traditions not only of
his own temple and people, but of surrounding cultures as well.

The possibility, therefore, that rival priesthoods may have been
active in Israel over long periods of time, and even as late as the period
just prior to the Ezra-Nehemiah reforms, properly arouses our curiosi-
ty. Was this really the case? If so, why would this have been so, and
how might these priesthoods have compared or been different from
one another? For answers, we must turn to documents within the
Hebrew scriptures themselves that purport to tell us about the history
of this community in olden times. If priestly rivalries did exist in
Israel, one presumes that something will be said about this in the historical accounts that are such a prominent feature of these writings.
There are two such histories, the first extending from Genesis through
the books of Kings, the second a much more compact and limited
work, the two books of Chronicles. Before looking at these books
more closely for what they might tell us about Israel's priestly houses,
it will be important to characterize them briefly as works of history.

A feature of 1 and 2 Chronicles is the way these volumes borrow
verbatim significant sections of the history recounted in Genesis-
through-Kings, especially passages from the books of Samuel and
Kings.[1] This would suggest that Chronicles was composed later than
these volumes and with other purposes in mind. Recent studies have

supported this suggestion and demonstrated that a primary aim of Chronicles (whose composition may be dated to the aftermath of the Ezra-Nehemiah reforms) was to serve primarily as a warrant for Second Temple priestly duties and perspectives, not as a revision or replacement for the older histories.[2] What then are we to make of Genesis-through-Kings—how might these books be characterized as historical writings? An important development in the modern study of these volumes is the recognition that two once independent and distinct collections of documents lie before us in this large scriptural corpus: the first extending from Genesis through Numbers (sometimes called the Tetrateuch), the second extending from Deuteronomy through Kings (sometimes called the Deuteronomistic History). Important too is the recognition that the *second* of these collections (the Deuteronomistic History) reached its present form *prior to* the final formation of the Tetrateuch. In other words, it is now widely believed that the great array of documents found in the Tetrateuch was assembled in the approximate form we now have them *after* the Deuteronomistic History was completed, and that only then was the Deuternonomistic History attached to it, and with minimal editorial adjustments.[3]

The significance of these observations for the topic at hand becomes evident when it is realized that the priesthood at the center of the story recounted in the Deuteronomistic History is almost exclusively that of the Levites,[4] while in the Tetrateuch the Levites are only rarely mentioned and then mostly to make clear that their role in the cult was to be subservient to that of the Sons of Aaron, as the priesthood there is called (cf. Num. 3:5–10; 4:27; chs. 16–18). In our review in Chapter 2 of the problems the Israelite people were experiencing in the period just prior to the fifth century reforms of Ezra and Nehemiah it was noted that the precise role these Levites were to play within the restored Temple was unclarified and open to debate and abuse.[5] Tetrateuchal Legislation which decisively resolves this issue in favor of the priestly primacy of the Sons of Aaron must, therefore, postdate this period and reflect accommodations worked out in the wake of these reforms. The Deuteronomistic History, on the other hand, seems to offer us an older Levite perspective on cultic developments in Israel, one which predates this period.

It is, therefore, this older "Levite" account of Israel's history (as

I prefer to call the Deuteronomistic History) that would appear to offer us our best hope of finding answers to the kinds of questions we are now asking. However, is even this set of documents of a type that can be relied on for the historical information we are seeking? Recent investigations have shown that the interests and concerns of its compilers were in setting forth what actually did happen during Israel's first settlement in Canaan, and in doing this from the perspective of a specific cultic point of view.[6] In other words, "antiquarian" as well as cultic matters were among its author's chief interests. Hence, this source is an obviously important one for discovering what there is to know about Israel's preexilic priesthoods, and will be examined first of all. Only when we have understood what the Levite historians have to say on this subject will we turn to other texts that might shed additional light on the matter.

B. ISRAEL'S RIVAL PRIESTLY HOUSES FROM THE POINT OF VIEW OF THE LEVITE HISTORIANS

The impression conveyed by the great majority of speeches and teachings in the book of Deuteronomy is that one group (and one group only) had been appointed by Moses for priesthood in Israel, and that was the tribe of Levi. It was this tribe, we are told, that was set apart to carry the ark of Yahweh's covenant and to stand in Yahweh's presence "to serve him and to bless in his name, as they still do today" (Deut. 10:8–9). It is further specified that it was for this reason that "Levi has no share or heritage with his brothers," for "Yahweh is his heritage, as Yahweh your God then told him" (10:9).[7] As noted, this representation stands in stark contrast to the way Israel's priesthood is portrayed in the prior books of the Tetrateuch. There, those appointed to priestly office are called "sons of Aaron" (cf. Exod. 28:1; Num. 18:1), and Levites, with one exception (Exod. 32), are represented as being subservient to the Aaronites (Num. 16:8–11; 18:1–7). By contrast, in Deuteronomy those appointed to the priesthood are with one exception (Deut. 10:6) called Levites (18:6–8) or "levitical priests" (10:8–9; 17:9, 18; 18:1–6; 33:8–11), and Aaron is the one who is denigrated (Deut. 9:20).[8] How did it happen that Levites, if once the only priesthood in Israel appointed by Moses, were demoted in this manner?

Do the Levite historians themselves offer any explanation for this puzzling cultic development? They do, although the story they tell is one modern readers often overlook or undervalue, unattuned as they are to the importance of this aspect of the history being related. In summary, the picture presented in Levite sources of cultic developments in the pre-exilic era (from the last days of Moses to the destruction of the two Israelite kingdoms) may be roughly outlined as follows:

–During Israel's first period of settlement in Canaan Israelite tribes were united under a common law (Joshua 24–25), at a common shrine, Shiloh (Joshua 18:1), where the venerable "ark of the covenant" was housed (1 Sam. 3:3) that Moses had fashioned and assigned to the Levites for their care (Deut. 10).[9]

–However, in the days of the judges problems arose at that shrine that would forever alter the fate of its priesthood. Because of the failure of a levitical priest, Eli, in disciplining his sons who "cared nothing for Yahweh" (1 Sam. 2:1–17, 22–26), a "man of God" appeared at this shrine with the message that despite Yahweh's promise that "your family and your father's family would walk in my presence for ever, now, however, this is what Yahweh declares—nothing of the sort!" (1 Sam. 2:30). Instead, Eli's sons were going to be destroyed (2:33), his ancestral priesthood was going to be terminated (2:27–30) and an "enduring House" would replace it that would serve in the presence of Yahweh's "anointed for ever" (2:35).[10]

–Soon thereafter the Philistines raided this region, captured the "ark of God" (which had been taken into battle) and destroyed the Shiloh temple (1 Sam. 4). The remaining Levite priests retreated to Nob (1 Sam. 22) where with the exception of a single priest named Abiathar, they were all massacred by soldiers of Saul because of their hospitality to David (1 Sam. 22:1–23).

–At this point the sources assembled in 1 Sam. 23–2 Sam. 8 relate how both Abiathar and the "ark of God" eventually ended up with David at Jerusalem. The impression conveyed is that it was nothing short of a miracle that the ark escaped from the hands of the Philistines and was returned to Israelite territory (1 Sam. 5–6), where it was rescued by David and brought to Jerusalem (2 Sam. 6). Equally fortuitous were the events that resulted in Abiathar's survival and appointment by David to the priesthood at Jerusalem (note how carefully the connections are traced between his ancestors who survived the debacle at Shiloh and his installation under David at Jerusalem: 1 Sam. 14:3; 22:9; 22:20–23; 2 Sam. 8:17; 20:25).

–However, yet another ominous turn of events is hinted at in 2 Sam. 8:16–17, when David's priestly appointees at Jerusalem are said to be not just the Levite Abiathar, but also Zadok son of Ahitub.[11] In this unobtrusive manner we are informed that when David established the Jerusalem shrine not just Levites were installed there as priests, but another priestly group as well: the Zadokites.

–It is this brief notice that sets the stage for the climactic sequence of events that the opening chapters of 1 Kings relate happened right after David's death. There we learn of Abiathar's swift dismissal from Jerusalem to his ancestral village, Anathoth, because of his opposition to Solomon as David's successor (1 Kings 2:26–27). With this shocking turn of events the Levite heirs of the Shiloh priesthood were suddenly deprived of the role that both Moses and David are reported to have given them as priest-custodians of the ark of Yahweh. "Solomon," we are told, "deprived Abiathar of the priesthood of Yahweh, thus fulfilling the prophecy which Yahweh had uttered against the House of Eli at Shiloh" (1 Kings 2:27). Subsequently, "in place of Abiathar," the king appointed "the priest Zadok" (1 Kings 2:35). With these solemn words the Levite historians concluded this segment of their historical narrative.

–Since never again do they refer to the Levites as having been restored to service as priests at the Jerusalem temple, the assumption conveyed is that they never were and that from this moment onward until Jerusalem's fall, some three centuries later, the priesthoods of this community were divided in the following manner: the Levites of Shiloh whose responsibility it had been to care for the ark of God and its associated traditions were now deprived of their responsibilities at the Jerusalem temple; presiding there instead (and exclusively so) was the priesthood of the sons of Zadok.[12] Many questions are thereby posed for the readers of this history. What will happen at this shrine now that the Levites are no longer allowed to preside there as priests? How will this temple fare under Zadokite leadership alone? Will Levite traditions still be transmitted and taught there? What will happen to the Levites themselves? Will they simply forfeit their priestly calling? Will they forget about Jerusalem and the ark of God there, or will they regard the priestly mandate given them by Moses (and reinforced by David) as still valid and the Jerusalem shrine as still theirs in some sense?

–What we are informed happened is that from the time of Abiathar's dismissal from Jerusalem by Solomon until the reign of Hezekiah some 200 years later, not a single king in Jerusalem was wholly loyal to Yahweh exclusively and alone. Rather, king after king (including Solomon) permitted other gods to be worshiped alongside of Yahweh—and with apparent Zadokite complicity and approval, as in the notorious case of the collaboration of Uriah and King Ahaz in bringing the altar of an Assyrian deity to the Jerusalem temple (2 Kings 16:11).[13]

–To make matters worse, upon Solomon's death the Israelite tribes of the north broke free and established an autonomous kingdom with national shrines at Bethel and Dan. There calf-icons were erected and yet another priesthood installed (1 Kings 12:28–23)—and, again, prior to Hezekiah's reign, not a single king or member of the national priesthoods opposed these developments (2 Kings 18:1–8). On the contrary, not only was this deviant northern worship and priesthood uncontested by the officials of both kingdoms, but the worship of Canaanite gods was at times supported and promoted on a massive scale, as during the days of King Ahab (see 1 Kings 16–18).[14]

–In short, according to the Levite historians from the time the Levites were banished from temple service at Jerusalem during the early days of Solomon's reign until the Assyrian invasions that brought about the destruction of the northern Israelite kingdom, during the reign of Hezekiah (2 Kings 18:9–12), the leading priesthoods at the two national shrines paid little or no attention to "the commandments which Yahweh had laid down for Moses" (2 Kings 18:6). Indeed, it was not until Hezekiah's reign that the "high places" were destroyed, "the pillars" and "sacred poles" of the Canaanite deities broken down and pulverized in strict accordance with what Moses had taught (Deut. 12:1–3). "No king of Judah after him could be compared with him—nor any of those before him" (2 Kings 18:5).

–However, even that noble effort was only temporarily successful, it is reported, for in the half century following Hezekiah's reign, during the reign of his son, Manasseh, the doors of the Jerusalem temple were once again thrown open to the altars, images and practices of the religions of the surrounding peoples (2 Kings 21), setting the stage for what the Levites must have regarded as the apex of their story: the reforms of Josiah.

–It was then that an awe–inspiring book was found in the temple by the Zadokite high priest Hilkiah, who gave it to his secretary for reading, who in turn had it read to the king (2 Kings 22:8–10). Deeply moved by its message, the king sought a revelation from Yahweh regarding the validity of its contents and received such from a prophetess named Huldah (2 Kings 22:12–20). Sweeping reforms were then enacted that purged the nation of alien priesthoods and cultic practices and united Israelites north and south in the worship of Yahweh alone at the Jerusalem temple. Not since "the judges ruled Israel" had anything like this been accomplished, we are told (2 Kings 23:2–2).

–The book upon which these reforms was based seems to have been some version of Deuteronomy, for only it, of the books of the Pentateuch, contains laws calling for the kind of sweeping changes enacted at this time: the centralization of the worship of Yahweh at one place (2 Kings 23:4–20; Deut. 12:3–17), with even the Passover celebrated at that place as the crowning act of this reform (2 Kings 23:21–23; Deut. 16:1–8; cp. Exod. 12:43–51).[15] The uncertainty which the Levites report ensued among those who found this book over what to think about it, and Josiah's decision to consult Yahweh regarding this very matter (2 Kings 22:8–20), convey the clear impression that its teachings were either unknown or unrecognized in these circles in the period prior to Josiah. It was largely through his initiatives, their history implies, that the way was opened for the reacceptance of Levite teachings at Jerusalem and their reentry into the mainstream of Israelite cultic affairs. "No king before him turned to Yahweh as he did ... in perfect loyalty to the Law of Moses, nor did any king like him arise again" (2 Kings 23:25).

–However, not even Josiah's bold reforms could stay the judgment that was building due to the flagrant apostasy of prior kings and priests, Manasseh in particular (2 Kings 23:26–27)—such are the closing thoughts of those who drafted the Levite history. Responsibility for the demise and destruction of the two Israelite kingdoms lay at the feet of those kings and priests who had rejected the legacy of Moses.

What priests were they who had failed in this manner? Strangely, the Levite historians (after telling us quite a bit about the history and fate of their own group) have almost nothing to say about the priesthood that replaced them in Jerusalem when they were banished, nor about the priests of the northern calf-shrines, except to emphasize how apostate they were on the matter of worshiping other gods besides Yahweh. Who then were these "other" priests? Are there any other sources to turn to for information about them?

C. ALTERNATIVE PRIESTLY PERSPECTIVES

If the Zadokites of Jerusalem or the priests at Bethel or Dan had parallel or complementary things to say about themselves to that which the Levites relate in their history, it is no longer known to us. However, there are here and there texts or fragments of texts which do bear upon the existence of these priesthoods and, when properly assembled and interpreted, they do enable us to say at least something about them. I will try now to indicate what these are and will begin with an attempt at summarizing what might be said about the "sons of Zadok" (or Zadokites), first of all, since they were the priests in charge of Israel's preeminent shrine in the period under review (see Ezek. 44:15).

1. The Zadokites

It is to the Levite historians that we are indebted for the information that two priestly families (not just one) were initially appointed by David at Jerusalem when he centralized his rule there: the one headed by Abiathar, the other by Zadok (2 Sam. 8:17). However, as noted, after telling us a good bit about Abiathar's ancestry and fate, almost nothing is said about the ancestry of Zadok, even though his was the priesthood left in charge at the Jerusalem temple when Abiathar was banished to Anathoth under Solomon (1 Kings 2:26–27). If there is anything further to be known about Zadok, we must turn elsewhere. But where? Surprisingly (given its importance), solid information pertinent to an understanding of the origins and history of this priesthood is scant elsewhere as well. Indeed, even the few relevant genealogies in late sources (1 Chron. 5:27–41; 6:36–38; 9:11; Ezra 7:1–5; Neh. 11:10) are so fraught with textual difficulties that some have concluded they were contrived.[16] With this possibility in mind others have hypothesized that Zadok's lineage might not even be Israelite, but that he was a descendant of the Canaanite priest-king Melchizedek (Gen. 14), who presided at the pre-Israelite shrine of Jerusalem (cf. Psalm 110)—and in that case, it is conjectured, we must imagine that when capturing Jerusalem, David adopted a Canaanite priesthood already functioning there.[17] But why, it has been countered, would "a primitive Yahwist of well-documented piety" like David "invite a pagan priest as one of the high priests of the national cultus"?[18]

A more believable scenario is gradually replacing this one in contemporary studies of this baffling issue. It is based in part on a passing reference in Chronicles to troops of armed men who rallied to

David at Hebron early in his fight to succeed Saul as king over all Israel (1 Chron. 12:24–41). Among these recruits "Aaronites" are singled out (vss. 27–29), and among them, "a young and valiant champion" named Zadok, "and twenty-two commanders of his family" (12:28). It is suggested this might be the Zadok whom David later installed as priest in Jerusalem, for not only is he mentioned as having supported David at this critical juncture of his career, but the Zadok mentioned here is also identified as belonging to the "Aaronites."[19] This is significant, since other sources refer to the priestly ancestors of the Jerusalem Zadokites as "sons of Aaron" (Num. 18:1–7) and a close connection reportedly existed between these Aaronites and Hebron where David was first crowned king by the men of Judah (2 Sam. 2:1–4) and later by "all" Israel (2 Sam. 5:1–3).

The conclusion to which this leads is that Hebron, a city to the *south* of Jerusalem, might have been sacred to the Aaronite-Zadokites in much the same way that Shiloh, a village to the *north* of Jerusalem, was to the Levite family of Abiathar. This being the case, David's subsequent transfer of his base of operations to Jerusalem, a site geographically in the middle between Hebron and Shiloh, makes a great deal of sense and takes on added significance. Since Shiloh had by then been destroyed and its sacred ark was available to David for transfer to Jerusalem, he was now able to unify his kingdom, north and south, by installing there both the ark and a Levite priesthood from the north and Zadok of the Aaronite priests of Hebron in the south.[20]

If this is what happened, we are still left wondering who these Hebron Aaronites might have been. Where did they come from? If they were priests, who appointed them to that role *in the period prior to* David? Do our biblical sources provide us with any clues or answers? They do, but the information is elusive, fragmentary and scattered throughout our sources, and therefore not easily assembled into a coherent picture. The following are among the more relevant of the texts bearing on this subject and what they seem to be saying:

> –Even if flawed, the already mentioned Aaronite geneologies which trace the line of Zadok back to Aaron (1 Chron. 6:3, 50–52; Ezra 7:1–5) might still be correct in linking Zadokite ancestry to the Aaronites.[21] However, this would still leave us

wondering who the Aaronites were and who appointed them as priests.

–Several pentateuchal texts state that Aaron was Moses' *elder* "brother" (Exod. 4:14; 6:20; 7:7; Deut. 32:50), but if that were so, Aaron's absence from the older accounts of Moses' Levite family in Egypt is puzzling. In these the impression is given that *Moses* was both the first-born and only son in this family (Exod. 2:1f.). Furthermore, in subsequent narratives Aaron appears, as it were, out of nowhere at "the mountain of God" (Exod. 4:14, 27), where Moses was tending his father-in-law's sheep (Exod. 3:1). This suggests that Aaron might have come from *this* region; perhaps he was Moses' brother-in-law[22]— other texts linking him to Moses' father-in-law reinforce this conjecture, as will be noted later. In any case, it seems a bit contrived when he is first introduced as "the Levite" (Exod. 4:14), an aspect of his portraiture that may have been added in the Pentateuch's final redaction when Levites and Aaronites were finally reconciled and both groups recognized Aaron as the name to be written "on the branch of Levi" signifying its "head" (Num. 17:3; cp. Ezek. 44:15).[23]

–A few texts in the Tetrateuch state that it was Moses who appointed the sons of Aaron to the priesthood (Exod. 28:1) and even defended him against his Levite critics and opponents (Num. 16:8–11; 17:1–10); it is also specified there that Aaron himself went on to legislate what the respective roles and duties of his priesthood should be vis-à-vis these contentious Levites (Num. 18:1–7). However, older Levite sources (as noted above) say nothing of this and paint a quite different picture of how Levites came to be demoted and how the Aaronite-Zadokites became their superiors (1 Sam. 2:30–33; 1 Kings 2:26–27).

–Another late *Zadokite* source also poses questions regarding this development. This is a chapter in the writings of the Jerusalem priest-prophet Ezekiel which contains legislation he (or his school) produced after the destruction of the first temple. In it the issue of the respective roles Zadokites and Levites are to have in the soon-to-be-built second temple are specified (Ezek. 44:10–31). This legislation is both similar and different from that in the Tetrateuch, giving it the appearance of a "first draft" of what would later become official policy. By implication the tetrateuchal legislation on these matters must post-date that of Ezekiel, for were it already in place earlier, Ezekiel's provisional sketch would not have been needed.[24]

–This opens the door for a second look at other tetrateuchal sources in which Aaron is portrayed, not as an appointee of Moses, but as an autonomous priestly figure who acts apart from, or even in opposition to Moses. The first such text is the account in Exod. 18:1–12 of how Moses' Midianite-Kenite father-in-law, after hearing of all that Yahweh had done in delivering Israel from Egypt, presided as priest over "sacrifices to God" in which honor was given to "Yahweh as greater than all other gods" (Exod. 18:9–11). Attendant at this rite, we are told, was "Aaron and all the elders of Israel" (18:12), but not Moses. In other words, Aaron alone without Moses is associated with this event.

–The narrative concludes by stating that after this and a subsequent episode in which Moses' father-in-law advised Moses on the handling of judicial matters, his father-in-law departed and "travelled back to his country" (Exod. 18:20). The implication is that while Moses' father-in-law learned of the traditions regarding Israel's escape from Egypt and embraced them as significant for his understanding of Yahweh, he was in no way a participant or heir to what occurred later on under Moses' leadership at Sinai. Yet, it is to the father-in-law's faith-tradition that Aaron is linked by this text.[25]

–That there were tensions between Aaronite tradition and the Moses-Sinai traditions is reinforced by yet another text which portrays Aaron as acting not just apart from, but in opposition to Moses during this period. This is the account in Exod. 32 where Aaron is shown at the base of Sinai, while Moses was absent, fashioning a calf-icon, building an altar and proclaiming a festival in Yahweh's honor (Exod. 32:5). Here Aaron is represented as functioning as a priest in his own right, and his actions were reportedly abhorrent to Moses when he found out about them (Exod. 32:19–29). With this narrative before us, the question becomes a very real one as to whether Aaronite and Moses traditions did not both originate in the vicinity of Sinai, but independent of each other.

–Were that the case, how might we imagine their *subsequent* histories—if at first independent, how were these disparate traditions preserved and passed on to subsequent generations? Although somewhat speculative, surprisingly, several bits and pieces of information related to the way the Israelite tribes reportedly entered Canaan seem to offer us a possible set of answers. Two strikingly different accounts of how this happened are woven into the fabric of the Levite history of this period: the one in Joshua 14 and 15, the other in Judges 1. Both sets of tradition seem to agree that the *southern* region of Canaan was occupied by Judean clans—however, Joshua 14 and 15 attribute the *initial* conquest of this region to the leadership of Joshua invading from the east, while Judges 1 states it was settled by the Judeans themselves invading from the south. More specifically, the Joshua-led invaders are reported to have started out from "Yahweh's mountain" (Num. 10:33), then, after moving north to a position east of the Jordan, to have penetrated westward into the central Canaanite highlands (Joshua 2:1), eventually setting up their base at Shiloh from which the land was distributed (Joshua 18:1). By contrast, the Judean settlers are said to have started from "the City of Palm Trees" (Judges 1:16), then invaded northward, but only as far as the vicinity of Hebron (Joshua 15:13–14; Judges 1:11–15).[26] From this the conclusion can be drawn that central and northern Canaan was introduced to Yahwism through the invasions led by Moses' successor Joshua (see Joshua 24:14–15), while the southern part of this region became Yahwist through the influx of the Judeans, with the Judean Calebites playing the leading role in the settlement in and around Hebron (Kiriath-Sepher; Judges 1:13; 3:7–11).[27]

–Supplementing this picture are those traditions which report that while the Kenite descendants of Moses' father-in-law *rejected* Moses' request that they accompany him and his people on their journey to Canaan (Num. 10:29–32), they *did* join the Judeans on their trek northward (1:16). This is consistent with the picture drawn of Aaron (in Exod. 18:1–12) as someone religiously closer to Moses' father-in-law than was Moses.[28] It may also explain Aaron's actions in fashioning a calf-icon for the festival of Yahweh he presided over at Sinai (Exod. 32:4). Abhorrent as such an icon was to the Moses tradition, it might have been viewed quite differently among the Kenite-Midianites whom Moses' father-in-law served as priest (see further to this point below).

–Dovetailing with this emergent picture of southern Aaronite Yahwism are several tetrateuchal texts tracing the origins of the shrine at Hebron to a period before the settlement of this region by the Judean Yahwists. So far as we know, Shiloh (center for the Levite Moses traditions) had no prior history as a shrine before being taken over by the Joshua-led invaders. This was not the case with Hebron, however. Long before the Judean-Aaronite invaders captured it, we learn in Genesis, the patriarch Abraham had built an altar there (Gen. 13:18); hence, the earliest traditions of this shrine were from a pre-Yahwist era, and one imagines these were appropriated and fused with their own by the Aaronite-Judeans who later occupied this region and laid claim to this shrine.[29]

–It is worth noting in this connection that several Genesis sources characterize Abraham as originally a worshiper, not of Yahweh, but of the Canaanite father-deity El (Gen. 14:17–20; Exod. 6:2f.) and that in both biblical and extra-biblical texts this deity is not infrequently characterized as a "Bull" (cf. the "Bull" of Jacob, Gen. 49:24).[30] Cross believes the name Yahweh itself was originally used as an epithet of El among the tribes of this southern region.[31] Thus, there appears to have been a quite special affinity between the faith of the Aaronite and

> Kenite Yahwists who invaded this region and the pre-Yahwist
> El worshipers at Hebron referred to in our Genesis sources.

From all this the conclusion can be drawn that the Zadokite priesthood installed by David in Jerusalem had a quite different background and history than that of the Levite priesthood simultaneously installed there. Both priesthoods were devoted to Yahweh; both traced their origins to groups of Yahwists who had escaped from Egypt under providential circumstances; both situated their beginnings in the general time-period of Moses and in the region to the south of Canaan. But the Zadokites were heirs to a southern Aaronite tradition of Yahweh worship that was more akin to the beliefs of the pre-Moses patriarchs and other settlers of this region (like the Kenites) than to the traditions of those whose cult center was at Shiloh, who traced their origins to the teachings of Moses.

2. The Priests of the Northern Kingdom Calf-Shrines

Support for this hypothesis may be found not only in what is said in our sources about the Aaronite-Zadokites, but in what is related there about another group of priests in Israel: those in charge of the shrines at Bethel and Dan which Jeroboam founded when establishing the Israelite kingdom of the north. It should not be forgotten that according to the Levite historians there were not just two, but *three* priesthoods in Israel during the period of the two Israelite kingdoms. In addition to the Levites and Zadokites, whom David installed as priests at his national shrine at Jerusalem, yet another priestly group was put in charge of the northern kingdom shrines at Bethel and Dan when that kingdom was founded. The decision to do this was deliberately arrived at, we are told in 1 Kings 12:28. Only after Jeroboam "thought this over," we learn there, did he make "two golden calves" and then say to his people, "You have been going up to Jerusalem long enough. Here is your God, Israel, who brought you out of Egypt!"

The terminology used in this text to describe the theology of these shrines is identical to that found in Exod. 32:5 to describe the creed of those who worshiped at the shrine of the calf-icon Aaron created at Sinai. This seems to be deliberate; by this we are informed that a direct link exists between the form of worship inaugurated by

Jeroboam at Bethel and Dan and the cult tradition founded by Aaron at Sinai. Nevertheless, in the Levite history it is clearly specified that these priests were "from ordinary families who were not of levitical descent" (1 Kings 12:31), implying that they not only were not Levites, but not Aaronites either. I see no reason to doubt this characterization as does Cross,[32] although it is worth noting that in tetrateuchal sources Bethel's cultic origins, like those of Hebron, are traced back to a period prior to the settlement of this region by Yahwists, more particularly, to the patriarch Jacob, who, like Abraham, is said to have been a worshiper of the Canaanite father-deity El (Gen 28:19; 35:7, 9–15). More specifically, it is he who at the conclusion of the patriarchal narratives in Genesis reportedly blessed Joseph (largest tribe of the northern bloc) "by the power of the Mighty One [Bull] of Jacob, by the Name of the Stone of Israel ... El Shaddai who blesses you" (Gen. 49:24f.). It seems, therefore, that the priestly cohorts in charge of the calf-shrines at Bethel and Dan, if not "sons of Aaron," had close theological affinities with the Aaronites of Hebron (and later Jerusalem), and like them were receptive to the modes and forms of Canaanite El worship and saw no problem with imaging Yahweh as a "Mighty One" (or Bull) who had proven himself powerful in liberating Israel from Egypt.

D. LOOKING BACK, LOOKING AHEAD

The picture of Israel's rival priestly houses that has begun to emerge from our study so far is an ironical one. From the point of view of the Levites, it was Moses' original intention that their House alone would be custodians of authentic Yahweh worship and that they would exercise this role by being caretakers of the ark of God and its associated traditions. And yet the shrine at Shiloh that had once housed this sacred object was destroyed by the Philistines, and the Levites themselves were subsequently banished by Solomon as priests from the shrine at Jerusalem, where they had been brought by David along with their ark. Fiercely loyal as they were to David for having installed them as priests there (and to the shrine he and Solomon had built for their ark), nevertheless, from that point onward they were without official priestly duties at the national shrines of both Judah and then also of northern kingdom Israel, when the northern calf-shrines with their non-Levite priests were established there.[33]

The evidence mustered so far regarding the rival priestly traditions all suggests that worship at Israel's national shrines during the centuries following this Levite dismissal from Jerusalem by Solomon was supervised by cultic personnel who were either in disagreement with or ignorant of Levite tradition. It would appear, therefore, that the Levites were correct when they implied (in their history) that during this entire period, except for the reigns of Hezekiah and Josiah, their point of view was either unknown or unheeded in the conduct of the national and religious affairs of either kingdom. Students of the Hebrew scriptures have been slow to recognize the implications of this fact for an understanding of the scriptures that were brought together in the Second Temple period at a point when the tensions and conflicts between these rival priesthoods had become intolerable. In order to appreciate all that was at stake in the resolution of the crisis that did occur at that time, more must be said regarding the respective theologies of these competing priesthoods.

Chapter Four

DIFFERING THEOLOGIES AMONG THE PRIESTLY HOUSES

The theologies of Israel's priestly houses were not absolutely at odds, but there were fundamental differences between them: certitude and hope based on God-given promises were at the forefront of the one, an allegiance to uprightness was at the center of the other.

Having gotten some initial sense of the *history* of Israel's rival priestly houses in the period prior to the Ezra-Nehemiah reforms, we now want to go a little deeper into their respective theologies. This will serve as background for an understanding of the great prophets of the era, as well as of the subsequent Ezra-Nehemiah reforms and the scriptural library born at that time. In approaching a subject as vast and complex as this one, we must be selective. I will attempt a brief characterization of the key theological distinctives of the three Israelite priestly traditions: the Aaronite-Zadokites of Jerusalem, the priests of the calf-shrines at Bethel and Dan, and the Levites.

A. THE THEOLOGY OF THE AARONITE-ZADOKITES OF JERUSALEM

We will begin this overview with the Aaronite-Zadokites of Jerusalem because theirs was Israel's oldest, most prestigious *national* shrine during the centuries under review. The Aaronite-Zadokite tradition may be likened to a small stream that swelled into a great river. To become acquainted with its distinctive features as it came to fullness, I propose to look first at the pre-Jerusalem stage and then at developments occurring after Zadok's transfer to Jerusalem. Keep in mind that

Zadok, who is mentioned as one of the two priestly heads David appointed when first establishing the shrine at Jerusalem (2 Sam. 8:17), in all likelihood came from Hebron (1 Chron. 12:29), and that his Judean ancestors had entered this region from the south in close association with the Kenite descendants of Moses' father-in-law (Judges 1:16). The other appointee was a Levite whose ancestors entered the land from the east under the leadership of Joshua. Hence the two priests whom David appointed to serve at Jerusalem may have been heir to alternative Yahwist traditions.

1. Pre-Jerusalem Aaronite Traditions

The theology of the Aaronite priesthood at Hebron appears to have been fashioned out of two older traditions: one of them associated with the figure of Abraham who is said in our sources to have founded the shrine at Hebron long before the Judeans entered the land; the other stemming from the Judeans and Kenites who began invading this region from the south at approximately the same time as the groups led by Joshua were settling in regions to the north. The older of these two traditions (and the point of origins to which our biblical sources trace the history of the shrine at Hebron) is to be found, therefore, in stories associated with the patriarch Abraham's settlement at Hebron (Gen. 13:18). Two things are emphasized in these stories, one having to do with the identity and nature of Abraham's God, the other with the promises this God is said to have made to him. Links between Abraham's God and the Canaanite father-deity El (cf. Gen. 14) have already been drawn (in Ch. 3). What remains to be emphasized are a few of the theological distinctives associated with this deity. Canaanite literary sources make evident that in worshiping El the biblical patriarchs were affiliating themselves with the high primordial father-deity of the Canaanite pantheon, one who is known in both Canaanite and biblical sources as the creator of heaven and earth.[1] The other theme emphasized in these stories is that of an oath sworn by this God to Abraham promising him land and progeny (Gen. 15, 17, 18)—or, more specifically, that *this* land where he and his clan had settled in south Canaan, the land of "the Kenites, the Kenizzites, the Kadmonites," would one day be theirs (Gen. 15:19a). Implicit in this oath is a conviction regarding the ability of the one making it to fulfill this promise, but also his *right* to do so (the land belongs to him). Implied too is a religiously based land claim: that is, El, the deity who owns this land, has a right to dispose of it as he wills and has made an irrevocable oath to give it to Abraham's descendants.[2]

The next step in the history of this shrine, as nearly as we can trace it from our sources, occurred when this region was invaded by Judean and Kenite clans moving northward to Hebron from the Sinai peninsula (Judges 1:1–7). As previously noted, it is Cross' opinion, based on his studies of ancient south Canaanite and Sinai texts, that although these clans were Yahweh worshipers, the name Yahweh was for them a cultic name for El.[3] This would explain, he suggests, why "many of the traits and functions of 'El appear as traits and functions of Yahweh in the earliest traditions of Israel."[4] Not just the "traits and functions of Yahweh" can be better understood in this light, Cross adds, but many other worship practices as well, such as "the early cultic establishment of Yahweh and its appurtenances—the Tabernacle, its structure ... its curtains embroidered with cherubim and its cherubim throne, and its proportions according to the pattern ... of the cosmic shrine...."All these "reflect Canaanite models, and specifically the Tent of 'El and his cherubim throne."[5]

Awareness of how embedded these southern clans of Yahweh worshipers were in Canaanite religious culture may help us arrive at a better understanding of the religion of Moses' father-in-law as portrayed in Exodus 18. There he is said to have functioned as a priest who honored Yahweh as "greater than all other gods," because of the way Yahweh helped Israel escape from Egypt (Exod. 18:10f.). The form of Yahwism reflected in this text (a Yahwism which Exod.18:12b implies that Aaron but not Moses espoused) may not have differed much from the Canaanite worship of El, except for the way faith in Yahweh as "the highest of all gods" had been dramatically intensified through the experience of his help in the escape from Egypt (Exod. 18:9–11). It appears this was the tradition in which the Canaanite calf-icon was at home, which Aaron is said to have fashioned (Exod. 32:4–6) and Jeroboam later adopted for use at Bethel and Dan (1 Kings 12:28). In any case, what is emphasized in this instance is the way this icon functioned to remind Yahweh worshipers of their God's supremacy in delivering Israel from Egypt.[6]

Some of the contrasting emphases in the pentateuchal law codes may be explainable in this light as well. For example, as presently redacted, the Decalogue (Exod. 20:1–17; Deut. 5:1–22), Covenant Code (Exod. 20:22–23:19) and Deuteronomic Code (Deut. 12–26) are all linked exclusively to Moses and say nothing about the "Sons of Aaron"; by contrast, "Sons of Aaron" figure prominently in the instructions for building a wilderness "Dwelling" or "Tent of Meeting" (Exod. 25:1–31:17; 35–40) and in the laws pertaining to what was to be done there (Lev. 1–16); they are also prominent as well in the appended "Holiness Code" (Lev. 17–26). Perhaps, therefore, this rich complex of texts was Aaronite-Kenite in origin before being edited, supplemented and placed under the authority of Moses in the Pentateuch's final redaction.[7] This would suggest that a shrine modeled on a cosmic prototype (emphasizing the mystery of Yahweh's greatness and holiness as cosmic king of the universe) was vital to Aaronite-Kenite tradition, and it follows that foremost among the rules for the people who worshiped at this shrine was that they "be holy, for I, Yahweh your God, am holy" (Lev. 19:2; 22:2).

A striking contrast is afforded right at this point by a parallel "Tent of Meeting" tradition in passages where only Moses is present (Exod. 33:7–11). The "Tent of Meeting" of this tradition was not a dwelling for God, but a place where Yahweh spoke with Moses "face to face, as a man talks to his friend" (33:11). Hence, in the one tradition (the Moses sources) the will of God revealed through Moses was central; in the other (the Aaronite-Kenite sources) the worship of God as cosmic king according to the pattern revealed on the sacred mountain (Exod. 25:1–9). The oracle-tent of Moses was so small that Moses could pitch it by himself (Exod. 33:7) and only Joshua resided there when Moses was absent (33:11). The Aaronite "Tent of Meeting" was so elaborate that it required a skilled Judean craftsman to design it (Exod. 35:30–32) and many assistants for its construction (Exod. 35:34–36:1); when completed, a large group of priests was needed to implement the numerous sacrificial offerings (Lev. 1–10). Our records suggest that the simpler oracle-tent of Moses, with the ark of the covenant, was set up at Shiloh when the Joshua-led invaders entered Canaan from the east (Josh. 18:1), and was later rescued and brought to Jerusalem when Shiloh was destroyed (1 Sam. 4–7; 2 Sam. 6). The more elaborate Tent of Meeting of Aaronite tradition may have been located at Hebron, before being taken to "the high place at Gibeon" (1

Chron. 16:37–42) and then placed in the Solomonic temple (1 Kings 8:4; 2 Chron. 1:3; 5:5).[8]

From this admittedly sketchy account of the shrine at Hebron at which the Aaronite-Zadokites served as priests in the period before David at least four key features of its theology begin to emerge: (1) In olden days, worship at this shrine was directed to the Canaanite father deity El, known and honored as "creator of heaven and earth" (Gen. 14:19, 22). (2) Among the most important legends recited at this shrine were stories of an oath made by El to Abraham promising him progeny who would inherit the surrounding lands (Gen. 15:4–21; 17:4–8). (3) When clans of Judeans and Kenites, whose favorite name for El was Yahweh and whose faith in Yahweh as greatest of all gods had been heightened by the way he had liberated their ancestors from Egypt, invaded this region, they joined their faith to that of those who believed in the oath made by El to Abraham that this land would be theirs one day—it was through them that Yahweh's promises were being fulfilled. (4) As a consequence, a most powerful sense of the holiness and sovereignty of Yahweh-El over all other gods and all other peoples (and an elaborate ritual of sacrifices) came to be celebrated at this Hebron shrine in the setting of a Tabernacle richly adorned with cosmic imagery.

2. Jerusalem Developments

A number of texts which can be assigned to Aaronite tradition *after* the transfer of Zadok from Hebron to Jerusalem indicate that with the rise to kingship of David over all Israel, first at Hebron and then at Jerusalem (and especially after the construction of the Zion temple), an imposing theological superstructure began to be built on an older foundation of beliefs. What this "superstructure" was can best be sensed in those Psalms of the Jerusalem-Psalter that may with some likelihood be assigned to the pre-exilic era.[9] One such is Psalm 132 which recalls and celebrates Yahweh's choice of Zion as a "home for evermore" (132:13f.; cp. Psalm 48). In this particular Psalm this conviction is related to David's action in bringing the ark of God to Jerusalem (132:1–10), but the remembrance of that event also becomes the occasion for a prayer that Yahweh would honor his pledge that a son of his would always be on the throne (132:11, 17; see also Psalm 89). In other words, it would appear that within the Zadokite tradition of Jerusalem the ark came to be viewed as a symbol, not of Yahweh's covenant law (as in Deut. 10:1–5), but of Yahweh's irrevocable promise of his presence at the Zion temple, and of his equally unbreakable promise to "raise up a line of descendants for David" (132:17).[10] One has the impression that with the passage of time these newer promises threatened to eclipse the older patriarchal promises of progeny and land, although Psalm 47 indicates that the sense of being "the people of the God of Abraham" remained strong (47:9), as did the patriarchal tradition of worshiping Yahweh as the "Most High" king of the universe (47:2).[11] Indeed, the pre-Israelite celebration of El's cosmic greatness (Gen. 14:17–20) seems to have taken on new life in Jerusalem when the magnificent Solomonic temple was completed with its rich array of cosmic symbolism (1 Kings 7:13–51). Now the venerable ark of God, once housed so simply at Shiloh, could be given a much grander home in this temple's "holy of holies" (2 Chron. 5:7).

It was at this juncture that the cultic artifacts of the two priestly traditions, the ark and the Tabernacle (the one the chief artifact of the Shiloh tradition, the other the chief artifact of the Hebron tradition), were united for the first time.[12] Worship of Yahweh as creator and king of the cosmos must have flourished now at this temple as never before (Psalms 47; 89; 91; 93–99).[13] Noteworthy is the way this emphasis on Yahweh's cosmic kingship is interwoven with that of Davidic kingship in several Psalms (Psalms 89, 72), with the one (Yahweh's rule of the universe) being seen as guaranteeing and providing a model for the stability and rule of the other (Davidic sovereignty). As in other religions and cultures of the period (and in Canaanite religion in particular), Yahweh's wise, just rule of the cosmos (Psalm 72:1–2; 104:24; 136:5) was regarded as foundation, model and mandate for the practice of wisdom and justice by the human ruler in his governance of the people. So in the Jerusalem of the Zadokites it was not the heritage of law stemming from Moses that guided the affairs of state, but a system of justice based on wisdom (1 Kings 3:4–12).[14]

The theological outlines of both the Jerusalem and pre-Jerusalem stages of this complex tradition are synopsized in several recitative poems which, even if post-exilic, seem to weave together the theological motifs just noted into a single confession of faith. Thus, in Psalm 135, for example, Yahweh is first lauded for his election of the patriarchs and his cosmic rule as greatest of all gods (135:1–7); following this, his help in Israel's escape from Egypt and entry into Canaan is remembered (135:8–12), all motifs already at home in the pre-Jerusalem Aaronite traditions of Hebron. Then the Psalm concludes with a summons to bless Yahweh who "dwells in Jerusalem" (135:21)—so here we see how older themes have been carried over and given a new home at the shrine at Jerusalem.[15] Psalm 136 has a similar outline, only in this instance the Psalm says nothing about the promise to the patriarchs, but begins with praise for Yahweh as creator (136:4–9), then moves directly to the story of how he helped Israel escape from Egypt and enter Canaan (136:10–22). A notable feature of both of these recitations is the absence of any reference to Moses or the covenant mediated by him at Sinai-Horeb; rather in each case the historical synopsis proceeds from creation and the promises to the ancestors, to the exodus from Egypt, then straight to the land-entry theme. Even the longer recitations of this type in Psalms 105 and 106, which are likely post-exilic, adhere to this basic pattern. True, Moses *is* mentioned in Psalm 105, but not in his role as covenant mediator, but as miracle-worker alongside of Aaron during Israel's exodus from Egypt (105:26–41). Thus, the only "covenant" referred to here is Yahweh's "everlasting covenant" or promise to Abraham, Isaac and Jacob (105:42–45). The same is true of Psalm 106, a post-exilic hymn which recites in detail the story of Israelite apostasy, mentioning in the process Moses' role as intercessor (106:23), but again saying nothing at all of his activity as lawgiver or mediator of a covenant. In fact, the Aaronite, Phinehas (106:30–31), not Moses (106:32–33), appears to be the hero of this Psalm.[16]

In summary, the heart of Aaronite-Zadokite theology was the belief in the greatness, goodness and wisdom of God made manifest through his creation of the universe, his promises to Abraham of progeny and land, his deliverance of Israel from Egypt, and the fulfillment of these promises in and through the Davidic kingdom and dynasty and the Jerusalem shrine where Yahweh chose to be at home forever. This theology was marked by an exuberant faith in Yahweh's gracious rule of the cosmos as highest of all gods, especially as this manifested itself in Israel's emergence as a great Abrahamic people (Gen. 17:4–8; Psalm 47). There was also a moral vision in this tradition based on wisdom (Psalm 104:24), but it should be noted that there does not appear to have been the same kind of strict prohibition against worshiping other gods that stood at the forefront of Levite law codes (Exod. 20:3). Emphasized instead was Yahweh's holiness (Lev. 19:2; 22:2) and his cosmic rule over the assembly of lesser gods (cf. Psalm 97:9).[17]

B. THE THEOLOGY OF THE CALF-SHRINES AT BETHEL AND DAN

It is sometimes forgotten that since the northern kingdom was the larger of the two Israelite kingdoms, more Israelites would have worshiped Yahweh at its calf-shrines at Bethel and Dan than anywhere else at the time of their existence, and there is no evidence that either the Zadokites of Jerusalem or the kings of either kingdom questioned their cultic legitimacy. In other words, before their destruction these shrines and their priesthoods, and especially Bethel (the larger and more centrally located of the two), were accepted as bona fide Israelite cultic insitutions. And yet, so discredited were they later on that a true picture of their theology is difficult to come by.[18] Nevertheless, their theological profile does emerge from two sources in particular: from what is said in Genesis and Kings regarding the patriarchal and national origins of the shrine at Bethel, and from the writings of their prophetic critics.

What do we learn about the priesthoods of Bethel and Dan from these sources? Traditions in the book of Genesis inform us that the shrine at Bethel, like the shrine at Hebron, dates back to the period of the patriarchs who first settled this land. In the case of Bethel, however, it was Abraham's grandson Jacob, rather than Abraham himself, who figures most strongly in the history of this shrine. Although it is mentioned in passing that Abraham too had built an altar there (Gen. 12:8), it is Jacob who is especially singled out as having located and named this site (Gen. 28:18f) and as having established it as a place where "El-Bethel" would be worshiped (Gen. 35:1–15). And to him too an oath was reportedly given by his God: "a nation, indeed an assembly of nations, will descend from you, and kings will issue from your loins" (Gen. 35:11; cp. 17:1). So Bethel was heir to many of the same theological traditions that are associated with Abraham at Hebron. In Kings we learn how this tradition was enhanced at the time of the founding of the northern kingdom by the addition of calf-icons which were meant to symbolize Yahweh's miracle-working power when delivering Israel from Egypt (1 Kings 12:28). Thus, here as in Jerusalem, older pre-kingdom patriarchal traditions were invigorated by the recollection of Israel's miraculous deliverance from Egypt, but note again the absence of any references to *Moses* or the covenant he mediated at Sinai. Hence, while the deity worshiped was Yahweh (cp. Exod. 32:5), it was apparently a Yahweh known and celebrated primarily for the way he had fulfilled ancient promises of progeny and land through liberating his people from slavery and bringing them to Canaan (Exod. 32:5; 1 Kings 12:28), not because of any definitive covenant law for which the people were held responsible.

Prophetic critics of this shrine, notably Amos, Hosea, Jeremiah and Ezekiel, confirm the impression that the priestly traditions transmitted at Bethel and Jerusalem were similar. An oracle of Amos outlines the rich pattern of ritual in vogue there: sacrifices each morning, tithes every third day, thank-offerings of leaven, and free-will offerings (Amos 4:4–5), yet according to both Amos and Hosea, a missing element was a certain "teaching of God" tradition (Hosea 4:6) that would have curbed the social and religious breakdown if it were taught (Hosea 4:1–3; Amos 2:6–8). Jeremiah compares the Israelite kingdoms to twin sisters, so alike in their adulterous behavior (openness to worshiping other deities alongside of Yahweh) that one can hardly tell them apart (Jer. 3:6–10; cp. Micah 6:16). The Zadokite priest-prophet Ezekiel, who picked up and elaborated this metaphor (in Ezek. 23), agreed that their besetting sin was their propensity to assimilate with other religions. While Yahweh was no doubt viewed as "greater than all gods," there does not appear to have been any strong sense of incongruity in either tradition (that of Jerusalem or Bethel) about worshiping "other gods," a charge explicitly made in 2 Kings 17:33 about the conduct of the Yahwists of the north in the period after that region fell to the Assyrians in 721 ("They worshiped Yahweh and served their own gods at the same time ... ").

It would appear that except for different cult symbols (calf-images in the north in place of the ark of God and the tabernacle in the south), and differing views of kingship (non-Davidic kings in the north, the Davidic dynasty in the south), the basic theology of this northern priesthood was similar to that of Jerusalem. Indeed, according to the Levites, it was precisely this that Jeroboam was aiming at when he created the northern shrines: that they would serve as a substitute for the one at Jerusalem, so that his people would stop going south to worship and confine their worship activities to the territory of his own newly established kingdom (1 Kings 12:26–28). Israelite worship at the national shrines of both Israelite kingdoms during the two hundred years of their dual existence was under the administration of priesthoods whose traditions were rooted in the pre-Moses patriarchal traditions of Canaan. These priesthoods were Yahwist, but Yahweh was regarded as the greatest of all gods, not the only God to be worshiped. In this respect he was much like the Canaanite father deity El, except that Israel's unique history of captivity in Egypt, exodus and land-entry was seen as a fulfillment of divine promises made to their forefathers specifically, and as a special proof of and support for their national destiny.

C. The Theology of the Levites

We are much better informed about Levite history and theology for the period under consideration than we are of the Zadokites of Jerusalem or of the priesthoods of the northern bull-shrines, for (as noted in Ch. 3) it was the Levite history that was given pride of place (when the Hebrew scriptures were assembled) as the definitive account of what happened in this community from a period just prior to Moses' death (Deuteronomy) until the destruction of the two Israelite kingdoms by the Assyrians and Babylonians (Joshua through Kings). This encompassing work is not only a history but a theology. In and through these writings the Levites presented *their* convictions regarding why Israel fared as it did and what led to the disasters that struck during these centuries.

Closer scrutiny of the volume which stands at the forefront of this encompassing history, the book of Deuteronomy, has led to the conclusion that despite its claim to being a "book" that Moses compiled (Deut. 31:9–13, 24–27), it was not drafted in the form it has now until near the end of the story related in the Levite history. This point is confirmed by the history itself through its own silence regarding the existence of such a "book" during the period extending from Joshua 24 until the reforms of Josiah (2 Kings 22:3–23:25).[19] Rather, the picture conveyed of this community during this long stretch of time is that of a people living by religious covenants and laws of a much simpler, more restricted scope and nature, such as those inscribed in the "Book of the Law" referred to in Joshua 24:25–28. This may have been a code much like the older "Deuteronomic" type laws in "the Book of the Covenant" in Exod. 20:22–24:33 (24:7), a legal compendium generally dated on internal evidence to the period of Israel's first settlement in Canaan.[20]

Already these older traditions have much to teach us regarding the fundamentals of Levite theology. Its ritual and cultic aspects were obviously much simpler than in Zadokite tradition: altars were to be made of undressed stone (20:25–26); all males of the community (not just a priestly elite) were to gather three times each year at the central shrine for a festival in Yahweh's honor (23:14–19); Israel seems to have viewed itself as a veritable "kingdom of priests" (Exod. 19:5). Furthermore, it is apparent that ritual sacrifice of animals played a much diminished role in the cult of this tradition—more important was loyalty to a code of conduct entailing avoidance of perverse sexual practices, of sacrifice to other gods, of ill treatment of aliens, widows and orphans, of lending money on interest, of taking a poor man's cloak on pledge, spreading false rumors, cheating the poor, taking bribes, and the like (Exod. 22:18–23:13).

Note, however, that not even this "Book of the Covenant" (Exod. 24:7) plays much of a role in the Levite history of the settlement period (as recounted in the book of Judges), nor even in their accounts of the history of Israel's first kings (in Samuel), even though documents relevant to the constitutional foundations of kingship *are* alluded to (for Saul, see 1 Sam. 10:17; for David, see 2 Sam. 5:3). Indeed, their stories about the priesthood of Eli at Shiloh (1 Sam. 2:12–17) suggest that a deterioration had occurred in the transmission and practice of Moses' teachings. It is implied that these trends were reversed with the rise of David and the transfer of the ark of God and the Levites to Jerusalem's newly founded shrine. Nevertheless, in the end David's handling of both his personal and family affairs was fraught with moral tragedy, and his son Solomon, even though advised to do otherwise (1 Kings 2:1–3), was also a great disappointment, especially after his dismissal of the Levites (1 Kings 2:26–27; 11:1–13). Indeed, it was Solomon, we are told, who "built a high place for Chemosh" and established a tradition of worshiping other gods alongside Yahweh at Jerusalem (1 Kings

11:6–8), practices that were never fully challenged until the reign of Hezekiah. Only then, the Levite historians inform us, did a national leader arise who was wholly "devoted to Yahweh, never turning from him, but keeping the commandments which Yahweh had laid down for Moses" (2 Kings 18:6).[21]

A growing body of research suggests that it was at this juncture, when the Assyrian invasions of this region had brought about the collapse of northern kingdom Israel (in 721 BCE), that the original nucleus of the book of Deuteronomy in the approximate form we now have it was composed.[22] Because of the prominent role Levites play in the book, it seems probable that its origins were in one or another of their communities, perhaps the descendants of the priesthood of Shiloh whom David put in charge of the Ark when he had it brought to Jerusalem, and whom Solomon subsequently banished to Anathoth (1 Kings 2:26–27). In any case, it is only of the fate of this community of Levites that we learn anything substantive at all in the Levite history.[23] Evidence of the ongoing existence of these Levite priests at Anathoth and of their devout adherence to Levite tradition may be found a generation later in the writings of their most famous son, Jeremiah (Jer. 1:1–3). As will be shown in the next chapter (Ch. 5), other prophets of this same general period can also be identified as having belonged to Levite communities where Levite traditions were being taught and lived, Hosea being chief among them. Levites such as these had seemingly come to believe that with the destruction of northern kingdom Israel now a virtual certainty, the hour had struck for their banished guild to re-enter the arena of public discourse and address a bold warning to "all Israel" (Deut. 5:1).[24] Their instruments for doing so were speeches and teachings of the one whose legacy they felt themselves commissioned and pledged to preserve and promulgate, Moses, a prophet without peer, "the man whom Yahweh knew face to face" (Deut. 34:10). It appears from contemporary literary parallels that these speeches and teachings were put forth in a format traditional at that time for national covenants.[25]

Their book is now generally regarded as the fullest flowering of Levite theology in the period of the two Israelite kingdoms. Some regard it as the most comprehensive statement of theology in the Hebrew scriptures. An exceptionally wide range of issues are addressed, including the errors (as they perceived them) of the theologies of the rival priesthoods then in charge of the national shrines. What its Levite authors appear to be aiming at is a sweeping reform and renewal of the Jerusalem shrine and Davidic commonwealth along lines deemed essential by adherents of the Moses traditions.[26] The following is a brief sampling of this book's more important emphases and themes.

1. Bearing in mind that Deut. 1:1–4:43 was probably added at the time the book was incorporated into the larger Deuteronomistic History as its opening volume, it follows that the original Reform Document began at Deut. 4:44.[27] Its very first words were those in 4:44–49 which carefully specify that what follows is the teaching (law or *torah*) of Moses which was presented to the Israelites at a certain time and place: "after" the Israelites had left Egypt and were in possession of "the whole Arabah east of the Jordan ... at the foot of the slopes of Pisgah" (4:49)—in other words, at the very end of Moses' life as the community stood poised to enter Canaan. What follows, therefore, is Moses' last and final Torah: teaching that updates and supersedes all previous teachings. The Levite reforms set forth in this book are put forward as an updated and final version of Moses' teaching.[28]

2. The first thing stated that Moses wanted "all Israel" to hear and to heed in this final teaching are the "laws and customs" of the Horeb "covenant" (5:3)—*this* is the covenant (and none other) that Israel should hear and heed. In making this point the text is deliberate in specifying that "Yahweh made this covenant not with our ancestors, but with us ... on the mountain, from the heart of the fire ... while I stood between you and Yahweh to let you know what Yahweh was saying ..." (5:2–5). The Levite authors of this text appear to be aware of an ancestral covenant with Abraham, Isaac and Jacob to which the Zadokites of Jerusalem ascribed such great importance (and which they interpret as being fulfilled in the Davidic dynasty and kingdom), but here and elsewhere in Deuteronomy one has the impression that the Levites were taking steps to subordinate *that* covenant to the Horeb covenant which Moses received, thereby depriving the Abraham covenant of its place "in the forefront of Israel's existence."[29] The covenant with Abraham was not ignored by the Levites. They too considered it the basis of Israel's inheritance of Canaan as a homeland (see Deut. 6:10; 7:12; 8:18; 9:5, 27; 11:9). However, "No longer ... does it

point forward to the rise of the Davidic empire, but to the covenant of Horeb and the subsequent conquest under Joshua."[30] In other words, only by observing the Horeb covenant will Israel's future be secure, not simply by trusting in an oath sworn to Abraham.

3. The task to which the Levites felt supremely called was caring for "the ark of Yahweh's covenant" (10:8). It is not, therefore, by accident that this Reform Document is so exceptionally precise about the fact that the two stone tablets deposited in this ark were inscribed with "the words that were on the first tablets" which were broken: that is, "the Ten Words" which Yahweh had spoken "on the mountain, from the heart of the fire, on the day of the Assembly" (10:2–4). The stress placed here on the two tablets in the ark being those inscribed with words that were on the first tablets which were broken seems designed to address a controversy regarding which of several texts should be accorded the status of a definitive (or canonical) summation of the Horeb covenant mediated by Moses. Since there are in fact *two* versions of a decalogue-like document to be found in the Exodus accounts, with the one, the list of cult laws in Exod. 34:17–27, introduced in such a manner that it could be regarded as a replacement for the other (the decalogue of Exod. 20: 1–17), it is difficult not to see the clarification made in Deut. 5:2–5 (see also 5:22 and 10:2–4) as an opening salvo in a theological war.[31] What these verses seem to insist on, in effect, is that the words which were addressed to the community at that time as foundational for their religious covenant were those specified in Deut. 5:6–21 and not any other. By transcribing these stipulations right at the beginning of their book and by defining their status as clearly as they have, the Levites forcefully staked out a claim for a renewed place in the life of this community for this quintessential set of teachings.

4. There was one especially important point on which the ideals of this decalogue were crystal-clear and where those of the priestly rivals at the Jerusalem temple were not (as the Levites viewed it). That had to do with the legitimacy of worshiping other gods (Deut. 5:6, 7). Within the wider religious culture of the time the various deities were seen as co-existing and bound together in a manner that mirrored the authority structures of human society. Seen in this way, relating to more than one deity was as natural as relating to more than one human authority. Peoples, kingdoms and individuals may differ as to which

deities are supreme, yet respect and relate to a plurality of other deities as well. Such was the basic attitude of the priesthoods in charge at Israel's national shrines during the period of the kings. Yahweh was Israel's "high god," not the only deity to be worshiped.[32] Looked at in this way, it was not seen to be wrong, for example, for an Israelite king who married foreign wives to permit them to worship their domestic gods in their customary way, or even to open the doors of the Yahweh temple itself to foreign altars and deities, so long as Yahweh continued to be honored there as the highest and greatest. It was apparently only the Levites who believed that the foremost commandment of authentic Israelite faith was that *no* other gods except Yahweh were to be worshiped and served (Deut. 5:7).[33] To put this revolutionary understanding of Yahweh's will into effect at Israel's national shrines was at the forefront of Levite concerns as they fashioned their Reform Document.

5. Some of the boldest proposals of the authors of Deuteronomy relate to the implementation of this imperative, especially their call for the elimination of certain foreign peoples (Deut. 20:15–18) and the centralization of all sacrificial worship at a single shrine chosen by Yahweh "to give his name a home" there (Deut. 12:2–13:1). It is clear from the words of the Levite prophet Jeremiah that the temple spoken of here as the place where Yahweh's "name" dwells (Deut. 12:5) was meant to refer to the Jerusalem temple. In his speech at this temple a century later he refers to it similarly as "this temple that bears my name" (Jer. 7:10). In this part of their document (Deut. 12) the Levites state what they believe will be necessary if their convictions about Yahweh are ever to triumph as the faith of a united Israelite commonwealth. The permissive Zadokite policy toward other religions will have to end and all foreign peoples and cults in the Israelite homeland will have to be eradicated (Deut. 12:2–3, 8–12, 29–13:1; 20:15–18);[34] and to prevent a return to the former permissiveness, all worship must be consolidated at one shrine (12:4–7) to which the Levites will again be given full access as bona fide priests (Deut. 18:6–8).[35] Furthermore, this central shrine must be thought of, not as the place chosen by Yahweh to be his "home forever" (as in Zadokite theology), but as the place chosen by him "to set his name [there] and give it a home" (12:5), for even the highest heavens cannot contain Yahweh, much less the Jerusalem temple (1 Kings 8:27).[36] Sweeping proposals such as these were apparently first heard and adopted by Hezekiah (2 Kings

18:3-4), then lost for a time during Manasseh's reign, then rediscovered and fully implemented by Josiah in the territories belonging to both kingdoms, just prior to this temple's destruction by the Babylonians in 586 (2 Kings 22–23). They came too late to save the nation, but they mark the beginning of a new era in the history of this faith.

6. While cultic reform was important to those who drafted the Deuteronomic Reform Document, it was by no means their only concern. Their aim was a reformed Israelite commonwealth, beginning at the bottom with the solitary individual in the family (6:1–9), and the local village courts (17:1–13), and then proceeding right to the top, with a reformed kingship (17:14–20). Unique to this document is the attention devoted to the family as a vital center of continuous religious instruction (6:6–9; 11:18–21).[37] Noteworthy too is the emphasis on king as well as commoner being subject to the *same* laws. The point made in Deut. 17:18–19 is that the king, above all, must have his very own copy of this Reform Document by his side so that he can read it every day of his life. This challenges the concept of kingship in Zadokite tradition where the monarch is idealized as an autonomous source of divine wisdom by virtue of his being God's "son" (Psalm 2, 72). While wisdom is not derogated, true wisdom, it stresses, can be found only in the laws and customs taught by Moses (see Deut. 4:5–8).

7. This teaching is put forward in such a way as to supersede and render conditional the covenants made with the ancestors. "Listen then, Israel," says Moses in its opening addresses (Deut. 6:3): "keep and observe what will make you prosperous and numerous, as Yahweh, God of your ancestors, has promised you, in giving you a country flowing with milk and honey." Here is the crux of what the Levites were seeking to say to the Zadokites: only by keeping and observing the teaching of Moses will the promises of land and prosperity be fulfilled. For the Zadokites this promise was unconditional, based as it was on an irrevocable oath of Yahweh to the forefathers; for the Levites, its full realization was conditional on keeping and observing the teachings of Moses. For this reason the Reform Document closes with Moses summoning all Israel to make a covenant in which this conditionality of the relationship between promise and fulfillment is radically expressed (26:16–28:68). Only "if" the commandments of Yahweh taught by Moses are kept will God raise Israel

"higher than every other nation in the world, and all these blessings will befall and overtake you, for having obeyed the voice of Yahweh your God" (Deut. 28:1–2); if, on the other hand, the commandments and laws are *not* observed, diseases, exploitation, and ruinous invasions will befall this people and they will be scattered across the face of the earth (28:15–68). This aspect of the Levite tradition is absent from the recitative Psalms of the Jerusalem Psalter, with one exception: Psalm 103; here the point that is made is that it was in truth to *Moses* that Yahweh revealed his ways (103:7). While this Psalm praises Yahweh for his tender father-like love and compassion, it does not hesitate declaring as well that it is only for "those who fear" Yahweh that his love will be steadfast "from eternity and for ever"; only as long as "his covenant" and its "precepts" are carefully kept and obeyed will "his saving justice" be manifested to "children's children" (103:17f.).[38]

It was this truth forcefully expressed in the final chapters of Deuteronomy that must have unsettled King Josiah as he heard this book read to him—so much so that he was not willing to let the Zadokite priest Hilkiah pass judgment on its validity, sending instead for a prophetess to verify its truth or falsity (2 Kings 22:11–13). Only when she had spoken and confirmed it as Yahweh's word did Josiah feel emboldened to take matters in hand and summon "all Israel" ("priests, prophets and the whole population, high and low") to a reading of "the entire contents of the Book of the Covenant …" (2 Kings 23:2). According to the Levites' history, such were the events that brought about the adoption of this Levite Reform Document by the authorities in Jerusalem. Their record testifies to the degree to which Levite tradition was an alien one to the Jerusalem Zadokites even this late in Israelite history.

Concluding Thoughts

Deuteronomy may be viewed as a theological response on the part of the Levites to the Zadokite hegemony in Jerusalem. The two theologies had fundamental differences. In that of the Zadokites, God was thought of as a wise, benevolent creator, and a set of unconditional covenants (with Abraham, Zion and David) promising progeny, land, rule and blessing were preeminent; in Levite theology (as expressed in Deuteronomy) creation theology and the promises to the forefathers play a lesser, background role—here these themes are viewed as but a prelude to the work of Moses, and a sharply defined set of covenant conditions are regarded as definitive for Israel's future.

Hence, Yahweh's activity as creator and his unconditional oaths to Abraham, David and Zion were at the heart of Zadokite theology, and the conditional covenant with Yahweh mediated by Moses was at the heart of Levite theology.[39] Both Zadokite and Levite sources agree that the period of the two Israelite kingdoms under the leadership of the Zadokites in the south and the priests of the calf-shrines in the north was marked by recurrent episodes of religious instability and assimilation to surrounding religions and culture. It was only the disenfranchised Levites whose tradition resisted these tendencies, but in the period of the two Israelite kingdoms it was difficult to make their voice heard.

Chapter Five

HEIGHTENED TENSIONS DUE TO THE "BATTLE OF THE PROPHETS"

From the time of the Assyrian invasions right up to the threshold of the Ezra-Nehemiah reforms prophetic voices were heard in this community whose interpretations of events and developments reflected the differing theologies of Israel's rival priesthoods and heightened the tensions between them.

In the study so far I have deliberately bracketed out an important aspect of the conflict between Israel's priestly houses, one on which I now want to focus. At about the time of the attempted reforms of Hezekiah and Josiah and the destruction and rebirth of the Israelite kingdoms, there appeared a number of prophets whose words have been assembled in the four scrolls of the prophets: Isaiah, Jeremiah, Ezekiel, and the Book of the Twelve. More precisely, from about 750 BCE, through the destruction of the two Israelite kingdoms in 721 and 586, right up to the threshold of the Ezra-Nehemiah reforms in the middle of the fifth century, a sequence of prophetic voices was heard in this community whose interpretations of the events of this era were reflective of the differing points of view of Israel's rival priesthoods and served to heighten the tensions between them. My goal in this chapter will be to indicate how the conflicts giving rise to the Ezra-Nehemiah reforms were intensified by the often contentious "words" of these prophets.

A. GENERAL INTRODUCTION

As mediators of divinely inspired "words" (see Jer. 18:18), prophets were looked to for guidance especially where the more traditional means of discernment had been exhausted. Just such a conundrum was posed by the invasion and destruction of the Israelite kingdoms by international superpowers in the eighth and sixth centuries BCE. Why was this happening? What about the future? Traditional wisdom had few or no answers. A "word" of God was therefore needed to clarify what all this meant and what Israel's future might be in the wake of these developments. However, even a casual perusal of the prophetic writings will reveal that the prophets who stepped into this gap to speak this essential "word" of clarification did so, more often than not, in ways that were unacceptable to those they addressed. This polemical, confrontational aspect of the prophetic messages has sometimes been understood as the expression of a lonely dissent on the part of some uniquely insightful, courageous individual. More recently, however, we have come to realize that these prophets were mostly members of marginalized communities whose dissenting theological perspectives and values found a voice in the messages they brought.[1] What I wish to suggest is that *many* (although not all) of the prophets whose words (or messages) were later assembled in the books of the prophets were from the *Levite* communities of their time and that it was they especially who spearheaded the renaissance of prophecy in Israel during the period under review by challenging the point of view of the dominant priesthoods at the national shrines.

What this implies is that even though excluded from a leadership role at the central shrines of the two Israelite kingdoms, Levite communities survived and even flourished during this era. Often overlooked in the discussion of these matters is the strategic presence during this period of Levite communities within the *Judean* kingdom of David, due to actions David himself apparently took when founding his kingdom. This is what is implied by the report in 1 Chron. 26:29–32 that Levites were assigned at this time to roles not only within the national shrine but as "officials and judges" (1 Chron. 26:29) in some of the more geographically and politically vulnerable territories of that kingdom. Knowing this helps to explain why many of the Levite villages mentioned in Joshua 21:1–42 can be identified as belonging to regions newly conquered by David.[2] This peculiar geographical distribution of Levite families, writes John Gray, "is hard to understand unless on the assumption that they [the Levites] had been deliberately settled as part of a regular policy in David's organization of his kingdom...."[3] Norman Gottwald believes that David's goal in this was for the Levites to help consolidate his "far–flung kingdom by wedding the old Yahwistic confederate ideology to the Davidic State."[4] In addition, according to Chronicles (2 Chron. 11:14), when the northern kingdom was founded, a second wave of Levites from the north fled south to Judah, due to their exclusion from the priesthood there and their ties with David's kingdom. Chronicles also informs us that this group of Levites worshiped at the Jerusalem shrine (2 Chron. 11:16) and were later involved in judicial reforms as well (2 Chron. 19:4–11).

In other words, it should not be overlooked that despite Solomon's dismissal of the Levites from active priestly duties at the Jerusalem shrine, both they and the Zadokites were loyal members of the Davidic commonwealth and their communities constituted a significant component of the social mix that made up Judean society in pre-exilic times. This cautions against assuming (as some have) that prophets loyal to Davidic or southern Judean tradition were all alike (or could not be Levite in background or orientation); rather, from the time of David onward Levites were as loyal to David's kingdom as were the Zadokites, in spite of their theological differences.[5]

B. Overview of the Prophets (750–450 BCE)

Against the background of this brief introduction I will now try to give an overview of the activities and messages of the more important of these prophets. From their books we learn that they appeared in three waves corresponding to the advent and impact on Israel of three international superpowers.

1.Prophets of the First Wave (c. 750–700)

Prophets of the first wave appeared in the latter half of the eighth century, prior to and during the Assyrian invasions that led to Assyrian domination of the fertile crescent for almost a century.

(a) Amos of Tekoa

The first to speak was Amos of Tekoa (1:1), a Judean fortress city directly south of Jerusalem (2 Chron. 5–12). The opening verse of his book refers to a Yahweh who "roars from Zion" (1:3); in the book's final oracle the hope is expressed that "the tottering hut of David" would one day be restored to its former greatness (9:11–13). This seems to identify him as someone who was loyal to Jerusalem and the Davidic kingdom, and this impression deepens when it is noticed that upon receiving a "word" of warning from Yahweh regarding an imminent invasion by Assyria (7:9), he took this grim message not to the Jerusalem temple, but to the competing bull-shrine at Bethel in the northern kingdom (7:10–17). However, when he calls upon his contemporaries to seek Yahweh, if they wish to survive, and specifies that in doing so they should avoid the shrines at Bethel, Beersheba, or Gilgal (5:4–6), he does not say they should go to Jerusalem as might be expected. Rather, to find Yahweh, he states, one must implement just decrees at the village "gate" or tribunal—that is where one should seek Yahweh and live, he says (5:14–15). What secures Yahweh's favor, according to Amos, is not sacrifice per se at Bethel or anywhere else (5:21–24). It is this emphasis on the implementation of fairness in accordance with well established judicial norms as essential for survival that seems to mark Amos as an adherent of covenantal traditions like those of the Levites (the crimes specified in Amos 2:6–8 and elsewhere echo the strictures of the old Levite Code in Exod. 20:22–23:19). His view of the cult appears to have been a widely shared Levite perspective based on ancient traditions (cp. Amos 5:25; Jer. 7:21–22; Micah 3:9–12).

What persuaded him to be a prophet after having twice prayed for the forgiveness of his people, he informs us, was a vision of Yahweh measuring Israel with a plumbline (7:8). Amos believed Yahweh had delivered Israel from Egypt and given it a homeland in Canaan (2:9–11), but says nothing about an oath to the forefathers being fulfilled through these events, nor about an unbreakable oath sworn to David or Zion that guarantees the existence of either Davidic kingdom or Jerusalem shrine (as in Zadokite-Jerusalem theology). What he emphasized instead is that a special bond was formed between Yahweh and Israel in the aftermath of the exodus, one which obligated Israel to do right (3:1–2) and practice justice (5:21–25); if not adhered to, there would be dire consequences (3:2). Although there is no direct reference in his messages to the Horeb-Sinai covenant (or to Moses), a covenant of that kind seems to be a background feature of his thinking.

The "word" (or divine message) which Amos received from Yahweh and felt compelled to bring to the bull-shrine at Bethel was simply that this bond (or covenant) between Yahweh and Israel was no longer intact (2:4), since Israel, in the way it was conducting its life and affairs, no longer measured up to the plumbline of Yahweh's law; Israel would therefore have to suffer the consequences of this deviation from Yahweh's will (7:8–9; 8:1–3). The clash that ensued at Bethel between Amos and the priesthood there (7:10–17) was between adherents of two theological worlds: the one governed by the covenantal codes of the Levite tradition, the other by the ritual codes and theology of the northern Yahwistic bull-shrines. That Amos did not go to Jerusalem with a similar warning may reflect the hopes the Levites still had that the shrine *there* might yet be reformed and the Davidic kingdom spared and restored (as it temporarily was by Hezekiah, with Levite help, a short time later). The Levites of Tekoa may have been descendants of those Levites who fled south into Judah when the northern kingdom was founded (2 Chron. 11:17), for it was right at that time that Tekoa was fortified "for the defense of Judah" (2 Chron. 11:5).

(b) Hosea of Israel

Not long after Amos of Tekoa appeared with his warning cry of danger ahead for northern kingdom Israel, Hosea, another prophet, appeared, this time in the north itself.[6] He challenged a certain priesthood of his time with having forgotten the "teaching" of their God (4:6) and of idol-worship at the shrine of a "calf" of their own invention (8:6–7). This immediately identifies Hosea as a Levite, for such was their point of view toward the national shrines of the northern kingdom (1 Kings 12:28–31). Furthermore, Hosea seems to know nothing about a worship of Yahweh that antedates the exodus from Egypt (12:10)—in his eyes it was only then, when in Egypt, that Israel was found (9:10), loved (11:1) and established as Yahweh's people with the help of a great prophet (12:14). He makes a sharp distinction (just as did the Levites generally) between the Yahwistic tradition begun by Moses and the Canaanite Yahwism of the national shrines then in vogue in the northern kingdom. True, the forefather Jacob is mentioned in his book, but only as an example of how to repent (12:3–8), not because of any divine promises made to him regarding progeny or land. Unlike the priesthood he criticizes, at the core of Hosea's religious world was Israel's covenant relationship with Yahweh which, he declares, has now been terminated due to the flagrant violation on every hand of its fundamental precepts (1:9; 4:1–3; 8:2).

This message must have been a shock not only to the priesthood of Bethel, but to the members of his own Levite community. That the covenantal relation with Yahweh could be broken and terminated was regarded as a possibility, but that this had *in fact* happened could not be known for certain except by prophetic revelation, for only Yahweh himself could say when his patience and mercy had been exhausted. The core of Hosea's proclamation was to reveal that this point had been reached (1:6) and Israel (the northern kingdom at least) could no longer assume it was still Yahweh's people (1:8–9). The question thereby posed was what Yahweh would do now that this was the case. It appears that Levite tradition had no ready answer for such a question, for it was only in the wake of new revelations that Hosea himself was able to set aside the prospect that Israel might be totally annihilated as were Admah and Zeboiim (11:7–9) and envision instead a more hopeful future: namely, restoration (after judgment) to the Israelite homeland as a people miraculously renewed (2:16–25; 3:1–5; 14:2–9). Like Amos, he seems to have thought this would happen in conjunction with a renewal of the Davidic commonwealth (Hos. 3:4–5; see also 1:7; 12:1b).

(c) Micah of Moresheth

Another prophet of this period had yet another "word" to say.[7] His name was Micah of Moresheth. Moresheth was another Judean fortress-city (2 Chron. 11:5–12). Speaking somewhat later still (perhaps as late as the Assyrian invasion of 701), his focus was on an imminent Assyrian onslaught that he believed would sweep through Judah right to Jerusalem (1:8–16) and destroy both it and its temple (3:12). He did not share the convictions of those he addressed, that "Yahweh is among us" and therefore "no disaster is going to overtake us" (3:11), or that the "House of Jacob" cannot be accursed, or that true prophecy can only be favorable so far as Jerusalem is concerned (2:7). His theological home, rather, was identical to that of Amos and Hosea: to hate what is good and love what is evil are viewed as irrevocably breaking the bond that connects the House of Israel with its God (Micah 3:1–4). However, unlike them, he did not shrink from declaring that this truth was now just as applicable to Jerusalem as it was to Samaria (1:5). Like Amos he resided in one of the fortress cities built by Rehoboam at a time when there was an influx of Levites from the northern kingdom (2 Chron. 11:7–9). He is remembered among the elders of Jerusalem a generation later as one of Moresheth's leading citizens (Jer. 26:17–19); perhaps he was one of the Levite elders whose role it was to see that justice was done in his city, as these are described in 2 Chron. 19:5–11.[8]

(d) Isaiah of Jerusalem

The predictions of the Levite prophets of disaster ahead for the northern kingdom because of its deplorable social and religious conditions were fulfilled when Assyria conquered this region in 721. In the mission of Micah we have glimpsed the beginnings of what will become an ever intensifying confrontation between the prophets of this tradition and the Zadokite traditions of Judah–Jerusalem. Right at this juncture, however, within Jerusalem itself, yet another prophet appeared, Isaiah, with a quite different theological orientation and message. His oracles have been heavily supplemented and incorporated into a larger volume that includes several chapters from 2 Kings (Isa. 36–39/2 Kings 18:13, 17–20:19), plus the writings of two later prophets, the so-called Second and Third Isaiahs (chs. 40–55, and 56–66), both of whom were representatives of Levite tradition (see below). The first Isaiah, however, was not so, for he regarded Yahweh as one who "dwells on Mount Zion" (8:18); for him, therefore, Jerusalem was a city that Yahweh would never abandon or allow to be totally destroyed (31:5), and the House of David too, in his eyes, was a sacred institution of enduring and enormous potential (9:1–6; 11:1–9). Both are key themes of Jerusalem–Zadokite tradition.

However, what Isaiah *also* came to believe was that things had gotten so bad morally, religiously and socially in Jerusalem that a purging was needed which Yahweh was now supplying through the

Assyrian invasions (1:25). Unlike Micah, it was Isaiah's belief that these invasions would reach only to Jerusalem's gate and no further; thus, the city itself would be miraculously spared and Assyria would soon thereafter fall (31:8). A religious renewal or revival would then occur that would result in Jerusalem being rid of its false gods and wrong ways (1:21–28) and restored to "the one whom the Israelites have so deeply betrayed" (31:6). At that point, he believed, a truly wise and just-minded king would ascend to the Davidic throne in Jerusalem, bringing domestic peace and prosperity (9:3–6; 11:1–9) and, in days to come, a new international order based on dispute settlement by law instead of war (2:1–5; 19:16–25).

The rudiments of this vision were first revealed to Isaiah at the temple in the death-year of Uzziah (6:1), when he "saw" Yahweh enthroned on high, his power and glory radiating throughout the cosmos (6:3). It was from that time onward that he opposed the political stratagems of the reigning Davidic king, King Ahaz. This was the leader who 2 Kings 16:10–12 reports went to Damascus to meet Tiglath–Pileser of Assyria, and sent back a model of an altar he saw there, with instructions for its construction by the Zadokite priest, Uriah, who was then in charge of the Jerusalem shrine. References to this and other religious practices of the era (such as child sacrifice, 2 Kings 16:3) alert us to the novelty of Isaiah's messages within Jerusalem tradition. While his theological outlook was essentially that of the Zadokites, Isaiah challenged their bent toward syncretism (2:6–8), "endless sacrifices" (1:10–15), moral indifference (1:17) and shallow, self-serving wisdom (5:21). Many of his fundamental concerns and insights were close to those of the Levites.

It is not difficult to understand why. In the wake of the catastrophic fall of the northern kingdom to the Assyrians in 721, and the death of King Ahaz a short time later (c. 716), Levite influence became powerful in Jerusalem during Hezekiah's reign. The accuracy of the Levite prophets in predicting the destruction of northern kingdom Israel heightened the relevance of their warnings for Jerusalem as well (those of Micah in particular), thereby intensifying the urgency of a reappraisal of this neglected tradition (see Jer. 26:19)—and especially so, in that a prophet of Jerusalem itself, Isaiah, now had very similar things to say. Although differing in theological outlook and tradition, the "words" of all four of these prophets seem to have converged in support of a renewed consideration of "the commandments which Yahweh had laid down for Moses" (2 Kings 18:6) as transmitted and understood in Levite tradition.[9]

2. Prophets of the Second Wave (c. 640–540)

It turned out that the Hezekiah reforms were not enduring and Isaiah's predictions regarding Jerusalem's future increasingly posed problems, for he had said the Assyrian empire would suffer a humiliating defeat soon after it unsuccessfully attacked Jerusalem (10:5–23). It is true that the Assyrians did *not* destroy Jerusalem, as predicted (36–38), but there was no humiliating defeat soon thereafter, as Isaiah had prophesied. Assyria remained a force to be reckoned with for another seventy-five years. Isaiah had also anticipated a spiritual purging and renewal of Jerusalem in the wake of its miraculous deliverance (1:26; 7:17), but this too did not happen (Isa. 22).[10] Rather, after Hezekiah's death religious affairs in Jerusalem became much as they had been during the reign of King Ahaz before the reforms (cp. 1 Kings 21:1–18 with 16:2–4). During Manasseh's long reign, in the first half of the seventh century, religious syncretism flourished in Jerusalem as never before. Altars to the astral deities of Assyria were added in the temple courts to those of a more local vintage (2 Kings 21:3–7).

Against this background, as Assyrian power was waning during the latter half of the seventh century, another cluster of Yahwistic prophets arose. For some of these (those belonging to Zadokite tradition) these events seemed to signal at last the fulfillment of Isaiah's predictions of Assyria's demise and the dawn of the promised new age of Zion's glorious restoration (Obadiah, Nahum, Habakkuk). Others, from the Levite camp, lamented the almost total breakdown of the Hezekiah reforms and saw the necessity of another cycle of devastation for Jerusalem before any genuine renewal could begin (Zephaniah). In tracing the convoluted story that ensued, the prophets Jeremiah and Ezekiel are of paramount importance.

(a) Jeremiah of Anathoth

In and through Jeremiah, "son of Hilkiah, one of the priests living at Anathoth" (1:1), the "voice" of the Levites of Anathoth who had been banned from the Jerusalem priesthood almost three centuries earlier (1 Kings 2:26) was heard again in Jerusalem. Empowered by his prophetic call, he stood and spoke to "the kings of Judah, its princes, its priests and the people of the country" (1:18) like no Levite prophet before or after. From the beginning his message, like that of Micah of Moresheth, was sharply focused on Jerusalem which he believed was now in grave danger of being destroyed by an invasion from the north (1:13–14). Unlike Micah, he felt compelled to bring this message right to Jerusalem itself. As a consequence an unprecedented encounter ensued between Levite tradition and that of the Jerusalem Zadokites. Early in his mission a surprising turn of events occurred that we are not sure he had anticipated or knew how to respond to. When repairing the temple, workmen of King Josiah (2 Kings 22) found the book which we earlier characterized as the Levite reform manual (Deuteronomy) and which had possibly been deposited there in the days of Hezekiah (2 Kings 18:1–8). Despite all the obvious affinities between Jeremiah and the message of this book, there does not appear to have been any direct relation between this event and this prophet. The Levitical historians do not mention Jeremiah in their report of this development, perhaps due to the rift that Jeremiah himself mentions had opened up between him and his own Levite family and village during the course of his turbulent mission (cf. 11:21–23). Nevertheless, there are allusions to this reform in his book that suggest he may, even so, have supported it at first (11:1–8), but soon came to see that its results were superficial (Jer. 5:1–6; 3:10). For that reason he was hardly taken by surprise, when early in the reign of Jehoiakim (Josiah's successor) all pretenses of adhering to its precepts were abandoned (11:9–12).

It was then (at the beginning of Jehoiakim's reign) that Jeremiah began confronting the people of Jerusalem with a passion seldom before seen in prophetic tradition, beginning with a broadside confrontation of the Zadokite priesthood right at the shrine where they had been for centuries the sole custodians (7:1; 26:1). What he said was that this shrine was no less vulnerable to destruction than was the shrine at Shiloh where the ark earlier had been, and that the only thing that could save it from suffering a similar fate would be strict adherance to the code of conduct set forth in the Levite (Deuteronomic) decalogue (7:1–15). Two additional charges against Zadokite theology are synopsized at this same point in Jeremiah's book: (1) his strong protest in 7:16–20 against Zadokite tolerance of other gods and modes of worship; (2) his sweeping critique of the typical Zadokite over-reliance on animal sacrifice, including a frontal attack on the sacrifice of children (7:21–34), a practice which we are suprised to learn was still a prominent feature of Jerusalem tradition even this late in its history (a point confirmed by Ezekiel 20:26; cp. 2 Kings 23:10).

Jeremiah's diatribe against sacrifice was especially troublesome for his Jerusalem temple audience, for with this he specifically contradicted the "claim of the Aaronids that their Torah of offerings was divinely ordained in the wilderness."[11] This is simply not true, Jeremiah states, "for when I [Yahweh] brought your ancestors out of Egypt, I said nothing to them, gave them no orders, about burnt offerings or sacrifices" (7:22). In Jer. 8:4 he goes on to charge this priesthood with falsifying Yahweh's law. "How can you say, 'We are wise, since we have Yahweh's Law'?" "Look," he counters, "how it has been falsified by the lying pen of the scribes!" Referring to the same group, he states (in Jer. 2:8), "Those skilled in the Law did not know me." It is sometimes thought that Jeremiah was here speaking about Deuteronomic law, but Friedman argues that "Jeremiah cannot possibly refer here to the Torah of the Deuteronomists" of which he himself was such a strong defender (see Jer. 6:19; 9:12; 16:11; 26:4; 32:23). What appears instead to be going on is that the Jerusalem priesthood, dissatisfied with the Deuteronomic reforms, was now active in revising and reforming their own priestly traditions.[12] Jeremiah's message was thus a direct attack on traditions being formulated right at this time by Zadokite priests in search of alternatives to the challenge posed by the Levite reforms. It is hardly surprising that they charged him, on the spot, with promulgating heresy for which he deserved to die (26:11).

However, as time passed Jeremiah's prediction that Jerusalem would soon be destroyed by an invader from the north could not so easily be set aside, and especially not when that prophecy was nearly realized through Nebuchadnezzar's conquest and deportation in 598 of 10,000 of Jerusalem's leading citizens (2 Kings 24:10–16). It was then that he began devoting more attention to the question of Israel's longer range future, and with astonishing prescience identified the community of deportees taken to Babylon as the bearers of hope (Jer. 24). It was they, he predicted, whom Yahweh would visit and restore again to their homeland (and whose descendants would eventually return to

Yahweh with their whole heart) in about seventy years (24:8). In his visions of what would then happen, the emphasis seems to lie on the people's inner renewal which in one famous passage he likened to a "new covenant" in which Yahweh's "Law" would be written, not upon stone tablets, but upon the tablets of the heart (Jer. 31:31–34).

Notably muted in his picture of things to come is the temple. Not even the ark of the covenant will be missed or rebuilt, he states (3:16), for in the future it will be Jerusalem itself that "will be called: The Throne of Yahweh," the bearer of Yahweh's name and the place to which the nations of the world will converge (3:17). Joy and praise and pride for all the nations on earth to see will prevail there, and prosperity and peace (33:9). The house of Judah and Israel will be reunited (3:18) under wise, discreet shepherd-leaders of Yahweh's appointment (3:15; 30:21); later sayings specify that these will be of Davidic descent (33:14–16), just as the priests officiating at the temple will be of Levite descent (33:18).[13] In summary, a new era of harmony and unity will prevail as in the olden days of the Davidic commonwealth, but with Levites now again in charge at the temple and their values implanted in the hearts and souls of its citizenry.

(b) Ezekiel of Jerusalem

The other major prophet of this period was a Zadokite priest named Ezekiel, who was deported to Babylon by Nebuchadnezzar after his conquest of Jerusalem in 597, eleven years prior to Jerusalem's fall in 586 (1:2–3). Five years later (Ezek. 1:3) Ezekiel was the recipient of an awesome vision during which he saw Yahweh's "glory" (which he believed resided at the temple in Jerusalem) in the sky over Babylon (1:28; cp. 10:18), and was told to eat a scroll written front and back with lamentations (2:9–10). This document reminds us of the Deuteronomic and Jeremianic scrolls which Ezekiel may have heard read at the temple (Jer. 36:1–3; 2 Kings 23:1–3)—both of which warned of disasters to come for neglect of their messages (Jer. 36:1–3; Deut. 28:25–46). From the moment of this scroll-vision Ezekiel came to share Jeremiah's belief that the Jerusalem temple was fated for destruction, and began announcing this to his fellow deportees with an explanation of why this was occurring.

The importance of this development for the subsequent fate of Israel's priestly traditions is hard to exaggerate. Here a Zadokite priest has joined the ranks of the Levite prophets in declaring that he no longer regards Jerusalem or its temple as indestructible. This must have plunged him into a theological crisis of monumental proportions. Up to this point the belief that Yahweh would be forever present at the Zion temple as a guarantee of its ongoing existence was a pillar of Zadokite theology. This now had to be viewed as mistaken (in the visions of chs. 8–11 Ezekiel is actually forced to "see" or witness Yahweh's departure from that temple). What had gone wrong? Why was this happening? Ezekiel's answer is both alike and different from that of the Levites. He shares the Levite perspective that Israel had gone astray when it adopted norms, laws and traditions of the surrounding peoples and disobeyed Yahweh's laws and traditions (Ezek. 5:5–12; 11:12). Where Ezekiel differs is in his insistence that this is the way it had always been from the very beginning, long before the entry into Canaan. When Jeremiah and Hosea looked back, they could recall a time before the entry into Canaan, when Israel had been faithful to Yahweh (Jer. 2:1–3; Hos. 9:10f.). Ezekiel, in looking back, does not recognize such an ideal time (see chs. 16, 20, 23). Rather, what he emphasizes in his reviews of Israel's history (Ezek. 20), that of Jerusalem (ch. 16) and of the two Israelite kingdoms (ch. 23), is that there never was a time when Israel was not apostate; it was apostate from its very origins in Canaan and Egypt (16:1–5; 20:1; 23:1).

What appears to be happening here is an agonizing reappraisal of Zadokite tradition by a Zadokite priest who had become a prophet under the stimulus of his highly emotional encounters with Levite tradition during the reforms of Josiah, the mission of Jeremiah, and the deportation of his people to Babylon. What emerges as a consequence is a not always tidy cacophony in which the traditions of both priestly houses begin to get blended together into a not completely harmonious whole, but on foundations that are still fundamentally Zadokite in orientation. At no point, for example, does Ezekiel acknowledge the existence or authority of Moses or the Sinai–Horeb covenant, even though in some parts of his book a Moses-like tradition of authoritative law is cited (ch. 18). An interesting comparison of Ezekiel's and Jeremiah's respective traditions is afforded by their parallel references to heroic figures from the past: Noah, Daniel, and Job in Ezek. 14:12–20, as compared to Moses and Samuel in Jer. 15:1–3.[14]

Some of the points incorporated by Ezekiel from Levite tradition (in addition to the conviction that Jerusalem was doomed to destruction) are the following:

> –the absolute necessity of worshiping Yahweh only (Ezek. 14:1–11; cp. Deut. 13:2–6);

> –the need for a quite specific decalogue-like listing of requirements for membership in the people of God (Ezek. 18; cp. Deut. 5);

> –the necessity of inner renewal if this community is ever to live and not die (Ezek. 18:31; cp. Jer. 31:31–33);

> –the importance of each individual making a covenant-like decision as a condition of membership in the people of God (Ezek. 20:37; cp. Ezek. 16:59–63);

> –the hope that Yahweh would bring Israel back to its homeland and restore it as a united people under Davidic leadership, and that when this occurred it would truly be a new beginning (Ezek. 34; 37:15–26a; cp. Jer. 23:1–8).

The main points at which Ezekiel (or his school) showed Zadokite colors, and hence still differed from Jeremiah and the Levites to some considerable extent, may be seen in the more precise details of the prophecies in his book regarding the Second Temple, and the manner in which the peoples of the world are envisioned relating to (and being affected by) that temple (37:26b–ch. 48).[15] Clearly, this new temple is the preeminent feature of the futuristic visions of this book. To it Yahweh will return in his glory (43:1–5) and from it a miraculous stream will flow that will restore paradise conditions to the land (ch. 47).[16] It is through these events that "the nations will know that I am Yahweh the sanctifier of Israel, when my sanctuary is with them forever" (Ezek. 37:28). Who will preside as priests at this temple is therefore also of some considerable importance. Those specified for this role are carefully identified as "the levitical priests, the sons of Zadok, who maintained the service of my sanctuary when the Israelites strayed far from me ..."(44:15). However, we also read here of another temple group, "the Levites who abandoned me when Israel strayed far from me by following its idols" (44:10), and what is said about them is that even though "they may never approach me again to perform the priestly office in my presence, nor touch my holy things and my most holy things," yet, they are to have "the responsibility of serving the Temple ... and for everything to be done in it" (Ezek. 44:14). More specifically, they are to guard the temple gates and "kill the burnt offerings and the sacrifice for the people, and hold themselves at the service of the people" (44:11).

The fact that Zadokite priests are referred to here as "the levitical priests, the sons of Zadok" (Ezek. 44:15), but that "Levites" too are recognized as having an important role to play at the temple, may be a consequence of the authority Deuteronomic teachings now have in Zadokite circles following the reforms of Josiah. In any case, the terminology seems to echo what is written about the priesthood in Deut. 18:1–8, where *both* "levitical priests" (18:1–5) and "Levites" ("the Levite living in one of your towns") are mentioned (18:6–8). Here too it is specified that if a "Levite" should decide "to move to the place chosen by Yahweh," he shall be permitted to "minister there in the name of Yahweh his God like all his fellow Levites ..." (18:7). Looked at in the light of this text, what the priestly legislation in Ezekiel appears to be advocating is simply that the "sons of Zadok" be authorized to continue in the role they have had at the Solomonic temple, but that the excluded Levites should be reinstated as temple servants (44:10–14).[17] Chief among the duties specified for the Levites is that of guarding the temple gates against intrusions by "aliens" or those "uncircumcised in heart and body" (Ezek. 44:6–9, 11). From this it is clear that in Zadokite circles the future temple was not being envisioned as a place to which foreigners would readily come (Isa. 56:1–7), but rather as a domain of atonement, holiness and blessing for Israel (Ezek. 44:15–31), for that is how the nations will eventually come to know who Yahweh is, Ezekiel had prophesied, through Israel's sanctification (Ezek. 37:28).

3. Prophets of the Third Wave (c. 550–450)

The prophets of the third wave were all focused on events and developments related to the restoration of Israel to its homeland that the prophets of the first and second waves predicted would follow the destruction of the two Israelite kingdoms. Beginning with the rise of Persia in 550 these prophets began to interpret events as they unfolded as "fulfillment" of earlier prophecies and added their own insights to the expectations of what would and should happen. Just as there were differing prophetic interpretations of Israel's destiny prior to the demise of the two Israelite kingdoms, so now that the disasters predicted had occurred (and Israel faced what was believed to be a bright new future) the prophets were again in disagreement over the shape of things to come.

Also, as before, these differing visions were related to the diverse theologies and social locations of the priests and priestly traditions out of which (and to which) these prophets spoke. An added factor now was the previously announced hopes of the earlier prophets within each tradition. Sociologically, it was the Zadokites who continued to occupy center stage and remained the dominant force numerically and institutionally during the early Second Temple period.[18] It was they, for example, who took the initiative in reopening a cult of animal sacrifice soon after the return (Ezra 3), and in rebuilding the Second Temple some decades later (Ezra 5:2). As before, the Levites were on the margins, with the consequence that at first their way of relating to the ongoing developments was of necessity a reactive one. Again, through prophecy they made their voice heard in the land outside their own circles. This is why, to grasp the true nature of the Levite hopes during this period (as this comes to expression in the words of their prophets), we must look first at the expectations of those involved in Zadokite tradition.

(a) The Zadokite Vision

For the period under review only one prophet can be identified as a representative of Zadokite tradition, the prophet Haggai[19] —all others must be regarded as representative of the still alienated Levites whose theological point of view remained on the margins of mainstream Israelite thinking right down to the Ezra–Nehemiah reforms. Isolated and brief as it was, Haggai's prophetic mission is exceptionally important for an understanding of the ideals and expectations that were now guiding Zadokite leadership during the crucial early stages of the post-exilic period. It is in Ezra 1–6 that we first learn that heading up the restoration enterprise was both a ruling member of the Davidic dynasty (Sheshbazzar, then Zerubbabel) and a Zadokite high priest (Shealtiel) and that central to their concerns was the rapid reconstruction of the destroyed temple (Ezra 1:5–11). In fact, we are told in Ezra 1:9–11 that right from the beginning, with this end in view, they had brought with them from Babylon 5,400 gold and silver articles from the First Temple. Furthermore, an exceptionally large number of Zadokite priests was with this first wave of returnees, 4,289 in all (Ezra 2:36–39), a tenth of the total population.

Initially "the altar of the God of Israel" was repaired and the whole community gathered for beginning a new era of worship at this holy site. However, once having laid the Temple's foundations during the initial year of their return, the whole enterprise seemingly came to a halt and was not reactivated or completed until the prophet Haggai appeared some fifteen years later (in 522). According to his book, his message elicited an immediate, enthusiastic response from the whole community; this is specified as including the Davidic prince, Zerubbabel, the Zadokite high priest, Joshua, and "the entire remnant of the people." They were *all* roused and "came and set to work in the Temple of Yahweh Sabaoth, their God" (Hag. 1:14). What was it about Haggai's message, we might ask, that was able to activate this audience in this manner? I suggest that of crucial importance is the fact that thirty years earlier Ezekiel had predicted certain things would happen at this historic juncture when Israel was again back in its homeland and living there under Davidic leadership: in its midst would arise a magnificent second temple served by Zadokite priests to which Yahweh would return in his glory; furthermore, Israel's restoration drama would now unfold so magnificently that both Israel and the world would at last come to a recognition of the greatness and sanctity of Israel's God. For Haggai's message to be fully understood and appreciated, it must be seen within the framework of Ezekiel's vision. There were aspects of that vision that remained yet to be fulfilled. The reason for their non-fulfillment, Haggai declared in effect, was the failure of the community to complete the rebuilding of Yahweh's temple. Were this failure rectified, he stated, abundant harvests would follow (1:9–11; 2:15–19), the nations would be shaken, their wealth would pour in and fill this temple with "glory" (2:5–9), the people would be sanctified and blessed as never before (2:10–19), and Zerubbabel would be exalted as Yahweh's chosen world ruler (2:20–23). This is a vision of the future that, like Ezekiel's futuristic scenarios, centers on the glorification of the temple (2:9) and the creation of a zone of holiness and blessing through it (2:10–14). Haggai assures his people that the completion of the sanctuary in and of itself will result in just such events coming to pass. There is nothing in this book that reflects Deuteronomic or Levite influence or perspectives.[20]

(b) The Levite Vision

Another vision of Israel's future came to birth through a sequence of prophets, beginning with a nameless prophet of the Babylonian captivity, the so-called Second Isaiah, whose writings have been attached as a supplement to those of Isaiah of Jerusalem (Isa. 40–55). A number of subsequent prophets in the period under review may be thought of as defenders and elaborators of this vision: the so-called Third Isaiah (Isa. 56–66), Proto-Zechariah (chs. 1–8) and Malachi.[21] Each speaks from the perspective of a theological tradition that is oriented toward the thought of the Levites and envisions a future for Israel more in line with that of the levitical prophet Jeremiah than that of the Zadokite Ezekiel. Malachi's levitical orientation is transparent in his call for a renewal of the Second Temple priesthood along lines indicated by the "covenant with Levi" (Mal. 2:4–7; Deut. 33:9). That Second and Third Isaiah and Proto-Zechariah (chs. 1–8) were from Levite communities may seem less apparent, but their levitical perspectives are evident in the prominence accorded the Levites themselves in the temple they envision (as in Isa. 66:21), as well as in the importance ascribed to Moses (cf. Isa. 63:7–39). For the Levite orientation of Proto-Zechariah (chs. 1-8) note the typical levitical themes in his review of Israelite history (cf. Zech. 7:4–14) and the Levite-type strictures placed upon the Zadokite high priest (Zech. 3:7). It is a mistake to think that Zechariah and Haggai were calling for the rebuilding of the Second Temple from identical perspectives or were members of the same priestly community or tradition. Debate and encounter on the part of these Levite prophets with the Zadokites heading up the rebuilding of the Second Temple became increasingly intense during this period. To get an overall sense of the Levite vision that emerged through these prophets at this time I will approach their messages synoptically and thematically, rather than one by one.

Framing their vision was a concept of the universe derived from Isaiah of Jerusalem, one in which Yahweh is viewed as monotheistically in control of the whole world and as creator and guide of all nations (Isa. 40). This enlarged cosmic framework is a derivative in part of Zadokite tradition (the creation theme, and the emphasis there on Yahweh as highest of all gods) and represents as such an important contribution of that tradition to Levite theology as it unfolded at this time. In the foreground (again as in Isaiah) was the idea of a "plan" (cp. Isa. 37:26) which Yahweh was carrying out in fulfillment of older prophetic oracles (42:9). As Yahweh had acted to punish Israel, by raising up the Assyrians and Babylonians to invade Israel-Judah (Isa. 44:27–28), so Yahweh was now seen as at work once again (and again on an international scale), but this time through Cyrus working for Israel's redemption (Isa. 44:24–45:7). However, it was not just Israel that God was seeking to redeem, but God was seen acting through Israel for the sake of the whole world to bring about international changes (Isa. 45:14–25). In certain respects this vision was not too different from the Zadokite vision: both Levites and Zadokites envisioned Israel's future as now unfolding (in fulfilment of earlier prophecies) as part of a divine plan which would encompass both Israel's and the world's future.

However, in the Levite expectations of *how* this would come about there were a number of striking variations to those enunciated by the Zadokites. First, the focus of their expectations was less on the temple than on a restored *people* living justly, joyfully and at peace in and around Jerusalem, a vision more in line with what Hosea and Jeremiah had prophesied (see Isa. 54:1–10; 61:1–4; 65:17–25; Zech. 1:17). Even Zechariah, who joins Haggai in encouraging the temple's completion, foresees Yahweh's exaltation not in the event of his glorification of the temple itself, but in his restoration of Jerusalem as a repopulated city with large numbers of people (1:8–9), its streets alive with old and young (8:4–5), its populace a true people of Yahweh, just and law-abiding (8:7–8). In Malachi, where there is a call for implementing the temple tithe in support of the temple priesthood, it is this priesthood's leadership in *community* building that is emphasized (2:1–3:22).

Secondly, the temple was visualized differently in the two prophetic traditions. Too much emphasis on animal sacrifice and for-

malistic fasting without a corresponding concern for heartfelt reverence and just laws appears to be one of the issues that resurfaced in the
early post-exilic period (Isa. 58; 66:1–2), as did the differing attitudes
toward syncreticistic compromises with local non-Yahwistic cultic
practices (65:1–7). Animal sacrifice was not completely repudiated by
the Levites; however, it does seem to have been significantly recon-
ceptualized in order for the temple to now be referred to as a "house of
prayer for all peoples" (56:7), a characterization that underscores what
happens between the worshiper and Yahweh at a personal level.
Perhaps this is why Malachi can call for a total shutting down of the
temple where such personal piety and reverence are lacking (Mal.
1:14).

Thirdly, the institution of Davidic kingship was also radically
rethought and devalued in this tradition. In the whole of Second and
Third Isaiah there is not a single reference to the reconstitution of the
Davidic dynasty, and only once, in 55:3b, are the "favors promised to
David" even mentioned. The suggestion is made that Yahweh is about
to fulfill this promise by recreating "an everlasting covenant" with the
people about to return to their homeland; that is, he is going to empower the people as a whole (as he had promised to empower the Davidic
dynasty), not to become world rulers, but to be "a witness to peoples, a
leader and lawgiver to peoples" (Isa. 55:4).[22] This should not be interpreted to mean that the Levite prophets were in principle opposed to a
reconstitution of the Davidic commonwealth. Zechariah joined in
encouraging Zerubbabel's participation in the rebuilding of the Second
Temple (4:7–10; 6:13), and also supported him governing the community with the aid of Yahweh's spirit (Zech. 4:6b). Surely, some of the
Levite prophets would have been glad to see a branching forth of the
Davidic dynasty in this new era (Zech. 6:11; cp. Jer. 33:14–18). But as
Second Isaiah's and Malachi's oracles also indicate, they had no diffi-
culty envisioning Israel's future without this institution.

Fourthly, that this was the case is partly related to their different
conception of how Yahweh would eventually reveal himself to the
world. While they too envisioned this happening through remarkable
events that would impress the nations of the reality and power of
Israel's God (the Cyrus event, for example), it appears they were more
deeply engaged with the issue of how these nations would come to
deepened knowledge of the *Torah* or teaching of their God than were

the Zadokites. An important insight of Second Isaiah was that Yahweh was calling him not only to win back and reunite Israel, but to be "a light to the nations so that my salvation may reach the remotest parts of the earth" (Isa. 49:1–7). Likewise, his prophetic successors saw the world being transformed as people from every nation and language who survived the upheavals of the time became converts to faith in Yahweh and in turn converted others whom they brought "as an offering to Yahweh" at his holy mountain (Isa. 66:18–22). In this manner, it was anticipated, the temple of Yahweh at Jerusalem might one day become "a house of prayer for all peoples" (Isa. 55:7). Such a vision was new to Levite tradition, but it was picked up and endorsed by Zechariah and Malachi, each in his own way (cp. Zech. 2:15–16; Mal. 1:11; 3:12). The triumph of Yahweh's revelation of himself to the nations, these texts suggest, is going to occur not so much through the reconstitution of the Davidic commonwealth or temple (the Zadokite vision) as by means of the witness of prophet-like messengers going forth in the power of God's spirit from a Yahweh worshiping people restored to their "holy land" (Zech. 2:15–17).

At the core of the Levite vision of a renewed Israel and world was, finally, a quite different conception of the nature and role of the priesthood than that which prevailed among the Zadokites. In his address to the Zadokite high priest the prophet Haggai said nothing regarding his *character,* but precisely that was *Zechariah's* chief concern (Zech. 3:7); nor did Haggai have anything to say regarding deficiencies in the teaching role of temple priests, yet that was *Malachi's* foremost concern (2:6; cp. Isa. 65:16). No doubt, Zadokite priests of the Second Temple were expected to be upright and teach, but what Zadokite tradition in Ezekiel envisioned as priorities in this aspect of their role was that their teachings should clarify "the difference between what is sacred and what is profane and ... between what is clean and what is unclean" (Ezek. 44:23). By contrast what Malachi emphasizes is that the lips of an ideal priest should "safeguard knowledge; his mouth is where the law should be sought, since he is Yahweh Sabaoth's messenger" (Mal. 2:7). The divergent roles of priest and prophet begin to merge in this new priestly concept, for "messenger of Yahweh" was precisely the function that the prophets of this tradition were until now seeking to serve. "The teaching of truth was in his mouth and nothing false was on his lips; he walked in peace and justice with me and he converted many from sinning" (Mal. 2:6). These words, which Malachi states, epitomize the covenant of Levi, characterize authentic priests as a guild of prophet-like teachers.

Malachi went on to embody this role in his own mission in the trenchant way he critiqued the misguided marital practices of his generation (intermarriage and divorce; 2:10–16). The purging, renewal and support of such a prophet-like priesthood, he states at the conclusion of his book, is the essential next step that Israel must take if it is ever to realize the goal Yahweh has set for it: namely, to be so blessed it will be a blessing to the whole world (Mal. 3:1–12). It is on this point especially (the differing ideas of what priests ought to be doing) that the ideals, aspirations and realities of the two groups, the Zadokites and Levites, seem to have become most dangerously strained and headed for a split. Malachi calls for a virtual shutting down of the Second Temple unless and until the Zadokite priesthood can be purged and renewed in accordance with the ideals he outlines.

Zadokite reaction to his challenge, as indicated in the responses he quotes, is one of sheer incredulity. They do not seem to know what he is talking about or even care to know (see especially Mal. 1:6–7, 12; 2:2–3, 17), a situation whose hard reality we shall encounter again as we turn to the Ezra-Nehemiah reforms and learn more of the enormous difficulties these reformers encountered right at this point. In other words, with Malachi an impasse appears to have been reached in the long history of these two priestly traditions, an impasse that prophecy alone was powerless to resolve. On the threshold of a new era, with the Second Temple now rebuilt and functioning, the Levites were once again in grave danger of being shunted aside and denied a place at the center of the life of this people.[23] Were this to happen, Israel might live on for a few more years, or decades, or centuries, but as a wounded, divided people—a far cry from the destiny and fulfillment of Yahweh's plan and purposes which the prophets themselves had envisioned.

Chapter Six

THE EZRA–NEHEMIAH REFORMS AS A RESPONSE

While maintaining the Zadokites in their traditional priest-
ly roles, the Ezra-Nehemiah reforms also fully endorsed
the tradition and vision of the Levites and made room for
them again at the temple as liturgists and teachers of a
growing collection of authoritative scriptures.

We have arrived at a critical juncture in our reconstruction of the story of how the Hebrew scriptures were compiled in the form they had when the Christian Bible was formed. This happened, it has been suggested, as part of a response of certain leaders to the confusion and despair that were threatening to destroy the Israelite people during the century following the rebuilding of their Second Temple in Jerusalem. It was at this time (c. 450 BCE) that certain reforms were enacted that laid the foundation for the survival and continued existence of this community. A significant feature of these reforms was the compilation of authoritative scriptures, together with procedures for studying and relating them to the life of the community.

In our search for a better understanding of these reforms (hence also of the scriptures compiled at this time), we have asked why such reforms were necessary and have just completed our survey of some of the immediate and long-standing problems that beset this community. What we have discovered is that a long and complex history lay behind the tensions and confusions of the period leading up to the Ezra-Nehemiah reforms. An accumulation of unresolved problems which had gradually reached crisis proportions confronted this community. Before turning to an analysis of the reforms themselves, it may be useful to recall briefly what a few of these problems were. First and most urgently was how to reconcile Israel's rival priestly traditions. Available records indicate that only for brief periods during the reigns of David, Hezekiah and Josiah were Zadokites and Levites even superficially united. A more specific form of this problem arose during the reign of Josiah when a major document of the Levites, Deuteronomy, was found at the temple. The perplexity that greeted its discovery by the Jerusalem Zadokites is a sure sign of how little Levite traditions and beliefs had penetrated their realm. To compound their dilemma, during the period of the cataclysmic destruction of the two Israelite kingdoms and the restoration of a remnant of Judeans to their homeland, prophets had appeared from within both priestly communities who had interpreted these developments in contradictory ways. Which prophets were to be believed as true messengers of Yahweh? The question became especially acute at the point the temple was rebuilt and hopes for a resurgence of the Davidic commonwealth were dashed to the ground. It was in the wake of this disappointment that Malachi issued his strident call for reforms.

How to reconcile Israel's rival priestly traditions? What status to accord the recently adopted Levite Reform Document, Deuteronomy? How to understand God's plan for Israel now that it was back again in its homeland? What to do in the wake of the demise of the Davidic commonwealth? These are a few of the issues and challenges facing the Israelite people on the threshold of the Ezra-Nehemiah reforms.

A. THE EZRA-NEHEMIAH REFORMS: SOURCES AND OUTLINE

Turning to the reforms themselves, the primary sources of information regarding them are two works which it is believed the reforming groups themselves may have compiled as a kind of authorization and documentation of their endeavors. These are Ezra-Nehemiah and the two books of Chronicles. In Ezra-Nehemiah the reforms are described in narrative fashion. A major goal of the two books of Chronicles appears to have been to articulate, encode and authorize the theological perspectives and rules that were put in place as a basis for uniting priests and Levites in the service of a single unified people.[1] For an account of the reforms as such we are thus dependent on a single volume, Ezra-Nehemiah, and more particularly on the data provided from Ezra 7 onward to the end of Nehemiah. A quick overview of these chapters suggests that those who compiled them made use of older sources which, for the most part, were arranged chronologically, with Ezra's mission coming first (seventh year of Artaxerxes, Ezra 7:7–9), followed by that of Nehemiah some twelve or thirteen years later (twentieth year of Artaxerxes, Neh. 2:1).[2]

While there is no compelling reason to question this chronology overall, one event has obviously been changed from its place at the forefront of Ezra's mission to the end of Nehemiah's. This is the account in Neh. 8–10 of a great assembly which was presided over by Ezra and where scriptures were read and responded to in a covenant-renewal type ceremony. This eventful gathering, which is dated to the *seventh* month (Neh. 7:72b) and located at the book's end for compositional reasons (from the editorial point of view it was the climactic event), would more likely have occurred soon after Ezra's arrival at Jerusalem in the *fifth* month (Ezra 7:7), prior to Ezra's marriage-reforms in the *ninth* month of that same year (Ezra 10:9).[3] The sequence of events alluded to in Ezra 7–10 and Neh. 8–12 belong, therefore, to the fifth, seventh and ninth months of the initial year of Ezra's mission. This would indicate that well before Nehemiah's arrival Ezra and his entourage had carried out a significant program of covenant renewal based on certain scriptures (Neh. 8–10), and had also initiated marriage reforms (Neh. 8–10). It was only in the wake of these events that Nehemiah came to this community and gave leadership to the rebuilding of Jerusalem's walls (chs. 1–6), repopulated the city (chs. 7, 11), reformed its economy (ch. 5) and drafted protocol for the collaboration of priests and Levites (see Neh. 12–13).

B. The Ezra-Nehemiah Reforms: Filling Out the Picture

This implies that the Ezra-Nehemiah reforms unfolded in two interrelated stages: there was an initial reform begun by Ezra in which scriptures were put in place and agreed to as guides for the life and institutions of this community; this was followed by a second consolidating stage of reform under Nehemiah's leadership in which Ezra's initial efforts were carried forward into new areas and given much needed social and institutional backing.

1. The Reforms of Ezra and His Co-Workers

Virtually everything we know about Ezra is related in chs. 7–10 of Ezra and chs. 8–10 of Nehemiah. About half of this material is in the form of first-person narratives (7:27–9:15); the rest is a third-person account which may have been rewritten or abstracted from other first-person memoirs (7:1–11; ch. 10; Neh. 8). It is possible that the original memoir was Ezra's report to the Persian monarch Artaxerxes who had authorized his mission. What do we learn from these documents about Ezra and the reforms he undertook?

The opening genealogy (Ezra 7:1–5) identifies Ezra as a Zadokite-Aaronite priest. More remarkable, then, is the fact that he is immediately thereafter characterized as a "scribe versed in the Law of *Moses,* which Yahweh, the God of Israel, had given" (Ezra 7:6), and not only did he study this "Law" but he taught and applied "its statutes and rulings" (Ezra 7:10). This notification that a Zadokite priest was engrossed in this manner with the "Law of Moses," seen against the background of the prior Levite history in Samuel and Kings, is shocking. It was obviously meant to signal the beginning of an unprecedented development. While several Judean *kings* had earlier been identified by Levite sources as having launched reforms based on such a "Law" (Hezekiah and Josiah), never before was it said or even implied that a *Zadokite priest* had done the same. The epochal significance of Ezra's endeavors stands out right at this point: for the very first time in the biblical accounts of Israel's long history we are introduced to a Zadokite priest who openly embraces and teaches the "Law of Moses" as though it was his very own.

Is there any explanation for this? Perhaps there is meant to be a hint of an answer in Ezra's genealogy where it is stated that his great-grandfather was Hilkiah (Ezra 7:1)—this *may* be intended as a reference to the Zadokite High Priest who found the "Book of the Law" which served as the basis of the Josiah reforms (2 Kings 22:8). If so, we can imagine this scroll, which we believe was Deuteronomy, being treasured by at least some Zadokite priests from this time onward, especially so since its teachings had been authenticated as Yahweh's "word" to the nation not only by a Jerusalem prophetess (2 Kings 22:11–20), but by the catastrophic events which soon followed its neglect and rejection by Judah's last kings and the population they governed.[4]

Ezra is also introduced as an employee of the Persian monarch Artaxerxes with whom he obviously had great influence. It is said that the king "gave him everything that he asked for" (Ezra 7:6). This and Artaxerxes' subsequent letter authorizing him to take leadership in implementing cultic and legal reforms in Jerusalem and the Transeuphrates (Ezra 7:11–26) can be seen as an expression of the Persian monarch's concern for the welfare and loyalty of a strategic part of his empire at a time when its western borders were under attack from the Egyptians and Greeks. For the discharge of his responsibilities Ezra is given full administrative backing of the empire, "whether it be death, banishment, fine or imprisonment" (Ezra 7:26).[5] Rarely, however, do we see him using such coercive measures (Ezra 10:7). His approach, rather, is that of a religious leader concerned for the spiritual rejuvenation of his people and conscious of the historic opportunity that had been afforded him for doing something helpful to that end.

From the sources available, three distinct and important phases in the reforms he subsequently undertook may be identified: the return journey to Jerusalem, enlistment of Levites and beautification of the temple; the initiation of a new covenant (or constitution) for his people, based on the study and application of certain scriptures; his leadership in the dismissal of foreign wives.

a. Phase One: The Return to Jerusalem

The narrative accounts of Ezra's departure from Babylon and return to Jerusalem (in Ezra 7–8) testify clearly to the goals that were his as he began this mission. Four items stand out as of special importance during this opening stage of his crusade.

i. A Second Exodus

His hope had been to depart Babylon on the first day of the first month (7:9), the month of the exodus from Egypt (Exod. 12:2). This notification, together with the allusion in Ezra 8:21 to a "straight path" which he prayed Yahweh would provide him on this journey, suggests that Ezra viewed this return to Jerusalem as a second Exodus not unlike that referred to in the prophecies of Second Isaiah (Isa. 43:16–21). It would appear that for Ezra, Israel's rebirth from the ashes of judgment and destruction was consummated not with the Edict of Cyrus (Ezra 1:1), but with the decree of Artaxerxes (7:12–26). It was in this way (and at this propitious moment) that "the beauty of the Temple of Yahweh in Jerusalem" was about to be restored (Ezra 7:27), just as the prophets had predicted (Isa. 60:7, 13).[6] Ezra's lofty sense of destiny in carrying out this mission is also revealed in the fast that was celebrated just before leaving (Ezra 8:21–23), and in his decision to place his considerable company and its belongings under the protective care of God alone, as during the Moses-led exodus from Egypt (Ezra 8:20).

ii. Enlistment of Levites

As it turned out, however, when Ezra and his party gathered to begin this momentous journey, a significant deviation from the announced date of departure became necessary, due to the discovery that among those assembled were laity and priests, but not a single Levite (8:15). That this fact would halt the departure and require immediate measures to rectify it is revelatory of Ezra's goals in this venture: this journey, which marks the beginning of a new era for Israel, *dare not* begin without a contingent of Levites. Men of rank were promptly dispatched to a place called Casiphia with the request that the Levites who lived there should consider leaving their homes at once to help "serve the Temple of our God" (8:17). Responding on such short notice were thirty-eight Levite notables of this community, including "a wise man of the sons of Mahli son of Levi, son of Israel," named Sherebiah, together with a certain Hashabiah (both of whom were destined to play leading roles in Ezra's reforms). Interestingly, those sent on this mission by Ezra were also able to recruit from this same region "two hundred and twenty temple slaves" who were descendants of those whom David and his entourage had once assigned as assistants to the Levites, "all of them designated by name" (Ezra 8:20). This incident affords us confirmation of how intact, yet alienated, the Levite communities of Israel still were at this point from any serious involvement in the restoration enterprise, and how serious were Ezra's intentions to remedy this situation.

iii. Levites and Priests Together

Dramatic confirmation of this latter point (Ezra's determination to rectify the Levite alienation from Second Temple affairs) was given when, just before leaving Babylon, he chose twelve of the leading Zadokite priests, *but also* twelve Levites (among whom were Sherebiah and Hashabiah), the intention obviously being that this group of twenty-four priests would *together* bear responsibility for "the silver, the gold and the untensils which the king and his counsellors, his notables and all the Israelites there present had made for the Temple of our God" (Ezra 8:24–25). Too little attention has been paid to the fact that in this highly symbolic manner Levites were initially accorded exactly the same priestly status and honor as were the Second Temple Zadokites, for to both groups Ezra declared (as he vested them with responsibility for this task): "You are consecrated [as priests] to Yahweh" (8:28).

iv. "All Israel" at One Temple

The first action of "the exiles" upon their arrival at Jerusalem was the handing over of these gifts, and then the offering up of a burnt offering of "twelve bulls" on behalf of "all Israel" (Ezra 8:15). This was followed by the transmission of orders to the surrounding satraps and governors that would secure their ongoing support for this Temple. In this we glimpse again Ezra's goal of uniting "all Israel" as one people in the service of a "beautifed" Temple.

b. Phase Two: Covenant Renewal

Nothing we read in Ezra 7–8 quite prepares us for Ezra's subsequent actions in Jerusalem as these are described in Nehehiah 8–10 (the chronological sequel). Here we are told of reforms that went beyond the unification of priesthoods or beautification of the Temple. The only precedents in biblical history for the manner in which Ezra is here portrayed functioning are the accounts in Deuteronomy of Moses as covenant mediator, or, perhaps, of Josiah in 2 Kings 23 performing a similar role during the Josiah reforms. Precisely as specified in the instructions of Moses in Deut. 31:11–13, Ezra is portrayed summoning an assembly of "all the people as one" (and not just the men, but men, women and children old enough to understand), to have read to them "the Book of the Law of Moses which Yahweh had prescribed for Israel" (Neh. 8:1–8). This assembly was followed, on the second day, by a session of study in which heads of families, together with the priests and Levites, gathered around Ezra to deepen their understanding of this "Book" (Neh. 8:13). While doing this, a third event transpired: the discovery and subsequent celebration of the feast of shelters, the "feast of the seventh month" (Neh. 8:13–18; cp. Lev. 23:39–44), with "the whole assembly" participating, "all who had returned from captivity … " (Neh. 8:17). "Each day, from the first day to the last one," Ezra read from "the Book of the Law of God" (Neh. 8:18).

By the arrangement of texts we are led to believe that two additional developments came on the heels of this festival. The first, described in Neh. 9, was yet another assembly like the one portrayed in Neh. 8, except that this time it was led, not by Ezra, but by certain Levites, who (it should be noted) had figured prominently as Ezra's assistants in the initial assembly of ch. 8 (see Neh. 8:7, 9, 11–12). Also, the company of those assembled on this occasion is characterized somewhat differently than before, as "those of Israelite stock who had severed relations with all foreigners" (Neh. 9:2).[7] The meaning seems to be that they were now constituted as a self-consciously distinct religious community. The occasion was a fast for "the confession of their sins and the iniquities of their ancestors" (9:2). Once again "the Book of the Law of Yahweh their God" was read, but this time by each person ("standing each man in his place"), and only for a quarter of the day, with the second quarter-day being taken up with worship and a lengthy "Blessing of Yahweh" recited by the Levites (Neh. 9:5–37). This recitation is the most comprehensive compendium of biblical history and theology to be found in the whole of the Hebrew scriptures and will be discussed further as we proceed. Both assemblies (the one in Neh. 8 and this one in ch. 9) are evidence for the birth of a people who are now progressively defining themselves as a distinct apolitical religious community within the wider Persian commonwealth.

In Neh. 10 we are informed that the ceremony described in Neh. 9 was concluded by a covenant in which "all those who had severed relations with the people of the country" (together with "their wives, their sons, their daughters, that is all those who had reached the age of discretion") thereupon solemnly agreed by oath and in writing "to follow the law of God given through Moses … and to observe and practice all the commandments of Yahweh …" (Neh. 10:1, 29–30). As tangible proof of their resolve on this occasion, it is said, they compiled a list of specific obligations to which they pledged themselves: not to intermarry with the resident peoples of the land, not to buy or sell on the Sabbath, to abide by the rules for the seventh year, to provide support for the Temple services by bringing both an annual sum of money and deliveries of wood, as well as the traditional tithes and first-fruits for the Levites (Neh. 10:31–39).

The reforms to this point appear to have been modeled on those of Josiah and the instructions of Deuteronomy, and in that sense were not totally novel. However, what *was* unprecedented about all this was that a *Zadokite priest* was leading out in these initiatives and was intent upon strengthening the hands not only of his own priestly group, but of the *Levites* as well. So far as we know, this was the first time since the expulsion of the Levites by Solomon that a serious effort was actually put forth to reenlist them as active participants in the liturgical activities of the Jerusalem temple.[8] Equally notable is the fact that in these reforms, not just the Levites themselves, but their *writings* too were given pride of place in this community's deliberations. Evidence of this is found not only in the repeated references in the accounts of these reforms to the important role played in them by the "Book of the Law of Moses," but in that remarkable recitation in Neh. 9 in which for the first time, so far as we know, Levite theological perspectives were added to those of the Zadokites to form a single worldview. Here, themes unique to Zadokite tradition (Yahweh's attributes as creator, his promises to the forefathers, his deliverance of Israel from Egypt) are supplemented with an account of Moses and the Sinai covenant (Neh. 9:13–14) and the tragic history that followed when despite the warnings of many prophets Israel rejected that covenant and was humiliated and destroyed by international superpowers (9:15–31). For the first time in the Hebrew scriptures, the theological perspectives of the Levites were firmly linked to those of the Zadokites to form a single ecumenical theology.[9]

c. Phase Three: Dismissal of Foreign Wives

Ezra's highly emotional reaction (recounted in Ezra 9) upon discovering in the ninth month of his return how entrenched the practice had become of contracting marriages with foreign wives (and his support of the drastic action of terminating such marriages) provides additional evidence of the degree to which he had now embraced Levite perspectives on matters of this kind, for it was right on this point that Levites and Zadokites had earlier gone separate ways, with the Zadokites taking a far more permissive attitude toward relating to (or even marrying) adherents of other religions than had the Levites. Once again the community was deeply divided on this issue, for at first, we learn from our sources, it was only those who "trembled" at God's words who gathered to Ezra's side (Ezra 9:4) and stood firmly with him in his deep concern about these mixed marriages (Ezra 10:3). It has been conjectured that the "tremblers" and God "fearers" of whom we read here were members of the same sub-communities as those "tremblers" and "fearers" referred to elsewhere in the books of the Levite prophets of this period (see Isa. 66:2, 5; Mal. 3:16–21).[10] In any case, Ezra's prayer, permeated as it is with anxiety that this community might be abandoned *forever* should it now, a second time, lose its way through intermarriage with people of a decadent religion (Ezra 9:14), reflects how deeply he had now drunk of Levite tradition. It affords us as well a piercing insight into the motivations behind both the reforms *and* the scriptures that were being assembled at this time to serve as a protective wall against precisely such a tragic eventuality. In summary, Ezra's reforms, while maintaining the Zadokites in their traditional role as custodians of the temple, seem at the same time to have fully embraced the Levite vision of what at heart Israel in this next period of its history was meant by God to be and do.

2. The Reforms of Nehemiah and His Co-Workers

How long or in what capacity Ezra stayed on in Judea after the reforms initiated during the first year of his return is nowhere stated. There is no substantive evidence that would permit us to say with certainty that he was there when Nehemiah came to this community twelve years later (Neh. 1:1; 2:1), or that he collaborated directly in any way with Nehemiah during either the twelve years of his initial mission to this community (Neh. 5:14), or when Nehemiah returned for a second visit some time later (13:6).[11] Rather, the reforms of Nehemiah appear to have been carried out at his own initiative independent of Ezra, although not necessarily without some awareness or appreciation of what Ezra had accomplished. How significantly the interests and concerns of the two reformers dovetailed and complemented one another seems to have become fully evident only in retro-spect.

Nehemiah's journal (in ch. 1 of his book) opens with a report of the news that prompted his mission. Judah, he was told by citizens of Judah who visited him, was still largely in ruins and the people living there were demoralized (1:1–3). The prayer reportedly offered on this occasion (whether verbatim or not) is our best clue as to why he react-ed to this news as he did. It identifies him as someone who shared the ideals of the Ezra reforms, insofar as these were based on "the Book of the Law of Moses," or Deuteronomy, especially those teachings now found in the latest additions to this book. In these the warning that dis-obeying Yahweh's torah will lead to destruction and dispersal is enlarged to include a promise for those so dispersed: *if* they are obedi-ent, they will be gathered again to their homeland (Deut. 30:1–5; cp. Jer. 29:13f.). Thus, when Nehemiah is said to have called upon Yahweh to honor this promise and attend to the needs of those who revere his name and are his servants (Neh. 1:5–11), his theological home in this tradition is clearly revealed. The place of the promised ingathering was to be Jerusalem, but its deplorable conditions posed a wrenching theological contradiction for Nehemiah: the *blessings* promised by Yahweh to those who obey his Torah were not at all in evidence there (Neh. 1:3). This would suggest that the motives that prompted Nehemiah in the reforms he subsequently undertook were as deeply religious as the reforms of Ezra, but were somewhat differently focused: on rebuilding the institutions of a *people* rather than "beauti-fying" the temple per se. More specifically, Nehemiah's subsequent contributions to these reforms (as we learn of these in his book) were predominantly in three areas: restoring Jerusalem, socio-economic reform and strengthening and consolidating Levite participation in the community's central institutions.

a. Restoring Jerusalem

Nehemiah's first target for reform was repairing and rebuilding Jerusalem's walls soon after returning there (Neh. 2–4). This had to be done in the face of considerable internal and external turmoil and opposition. The charge of his opponents that in undertaking this endeavor he was aiming at restoring the Jewish commonwealth and having himself proclaimed as its king was vigorously denied (Neh.

6:1–9). While he may have been trying to recover for Judah-Jerusalem the status of an administrative unit within the Persian empire that it earlier had and lost (see Ezra 4:6–23), more important by far was his goal of strengthening his people's religious identity, as the joyful celebrations (12:17–23) and elaborate plans for repopulating the city (ch. 11) would seem to indicate. In other words, paramount for Nehemiah was *not* Jerusalem's status as a fortified city only, but its future as a place where people could live under the blessing of God with the kind of happiness, normalcy and vitality envisioned by the Levite prophets (cf. Zech. 8:1–8).

b. Social Reforms

Consistent with this ideal was Nehemiah's act of calling a "great assembly" to deal with the more flagrant socio-economic problems of this community (Neh. 5:7). This was occasioned by "a great outcry from the people, and from their wives, against their brother Jews" (Neh. 5:1). An underclass was becoming increasingly impoverished and enslaved because of indebtedness to a group of wealthy nobles and officials (5:6; cp. 6:17).[12] Nehemiah's response to this crisis highlights the differences between himself and Ezra. Ezra had introduced authoritative scriptures to this community, but in their application seems to have focused on sacral matters primarily (support of the temple, renewal of religious festivals, the ban on intermarriage). By contrast, after having completed the rebuilding of Jerusalem's walls, Nehemiah turned his attention to the economic disparities that plagued this community. As he viewed it, the practices that had led to these disparities (high interest rates, loss of property and indentured servanthood for non-payment of debts), though legal, were incompatible with "fear of Yahweh" and the common decency due fellow Jews so recently liberated (Neh. 5:8f.). In this action he reflects traditions and principles central to Levite tradition through the centuries (Amos 5:24; Isa. 58; Deut. 15:1–11).

(c) Strengthening and Consolidating Levite Participation in the Community's Central Institutions

Nehemiah's crowning achievement was the step he took to consolidate and strengthen the role of the Levites at the center of the institutional life of his people. Ezra had prepared the way for this when he made sure that a contingent of Levites should accompany him on his return to Jerusalem, and also when assigning them equal status with the Zadokites in bringing gifts that would enrich and beautify the Jerusalem temple. Remember too how Ezra had relied on Levites for assistance when inaugurating a renewed religious covenant and during the study process that was such a hallmark of his reform efforts. But there is no indication that, with all this, Ezra had in fact re-established the Levites in an institutionally secure role in temple affairs, or had worked out specific agreements with the Zadokite establishment for such a development. It would appear, therefore, that despite Ezra's efforts at reintegrating the Levites into the life of the Second Temple community, they remained institutionally marginalized and alienated.

Seen against this background, several of Nehemiah's actions on behalf of the Levites take on fresh significance. Noteworthy to begin with is how carefully he is said to have enlisted not only Zadokites but Levites too, when rebulding Jerusalem's wall (Neh. 3:1, 17). Also when celebrating the *completion* of the walls, it was to the Levites that Nehemiah turned in a special way for help in enhancing this event through music and song (Neh. 12:27–30). This action, the account of which has been placed at the very end of the story of his reforms, may have marked a new stage in Levite involvement in the worship-life of this community. While Ezra may have been the first Zadokite priest to enlist Levite help in liturgical reading and teaching (Neh. 8–9), it was Nehemiah apparently who assigned them an expanded role in hymnology and music. That this new role and status (as Temple liturgists) was meant to be a substantive and enduring one is suggested by the *numbers* of Levites Nehemiah summoned to Jerusalem at the point when the city was resettled. Initially, the ratio of Zadokites to Levites in the community at large is reported to have been one Levite for about every sixty Zadokites (Ezra 1:36–40); now their numbers were to be (in Jerusalem at least) one Levite for every two priests (Neh. 11:12–16). Furthermore, it was Nehemiah's intention that Levites too should be fully supported for their duties (and not just the priests) by "contributions, first-fruits and tithes" commensurate with the temple duties of each, just as in "the days of David and Asaph," it is added (Neh. 12:44–47). This implies that the models that guided these new institutional initiatives were taken from the era of King David, which was the only age in Israelite history when these two priestly groups had functioned harmoniously at the same shrine.[13]

With these steps not just the Levite scriptures, but the Levites themselves were at last given a more clearly defined and established role within Second Temple Jerusalem. How precarious this role still was, however, is illustrated by another cluster of events that occurred during the interval between Nehemiah's first and second missions to Jerusalem (Neh. 13:6). It was at this time, we learn, that proscribed alliances between the Temple high priest and the leaders of the surrounding peoples were reconstituted. These included the contracting of a marriage between the high priest's own son and the daughter of Sanballat the Horonite governor of Samaria (13:28), and the provision of a room right in the Temple compound itself for a certain Tobiah governor of Ammon (13:4–9; cp. 2:10). Furthermore, the Levites whom Nehemiah had arranged to settle in Jeursalem during his first mission were harshly harassed by being deprived of their food and sustenance, so that they had to leave the city en masse and return to their farms (13:10). Simultaneously, there was a resurgence of interethnic and interreligious marriages among the populace generally (13:23–27) and a breakdown of Sabbath day observances (13:15–22). In this cluster of reported developments one can readily discern the resurfacing of the centuries-old struggle between Levites and Zadokites, with the Zadokites once again gaining the upper hand to the exclusion and detriment of the Levites.

Nehemiah's response to these developments upon returning to this community on his second mission was vigorous: the furniture in Tobiah's room at the temple was thrown into the street and the room purified and rededicated to its proper temple use (Neh. 13:8–9);[14] the High Priest's son, who had married Sanballat's daughter, was summarily dismissed (13:28); most importantly, the Levites who had returned to their farms were all brought back and reinstated to their Jerusalem posts, with a new committee assigned to guarantee them their legitimate support (13:11–14); orders were given for closing the gates of Jerusalem on the Sabbath and Levites were posted as guards to insure that these orders would be followed (13:17–22); finally, those who had intermarried were chastised and warnings were given of the tragic consequences that would result from a continuation of this practice (13:25–27). Few as they are, the verses describing these events shed a great deal of light on the nature and contents of Nehemiah's reforms. While fully accepting the Zadokites as the duly appointed priests in charge of the temple, he most vigorously opposed their syncretistic outlook, their *Torah* laxness and cavalier attitude toward the Levites. "Why is the temple of God deserted?" he asked the officials upon discovering that the Levites had been dismissed from their liturgical posts. For him the flight of the Levites from Jerusalem was tantamount to "the temple of God" being deserted.

SUMMARY

With the reforms of *Ezra,* the scriptures of the Levites were restored to a place of primacy in the life of this community and the Levites themselves deployed as teachers of those scriptures; with *Nehemiah*, Jerusalem was restored as a liveable city with the Levites once again at home there and functioning (as in the days of David) as temple musicians and liturgists as well as teachers. In this light the report in 2 Macc. 2:13, which states that Nehemiah had also at about this same time created a library in this city where the scriptures were housed that would serve as the constitutional and pedagogical foundations of this community, is highly credible. It may also be assumed that the Levites were put in charge of that library. Thus, the Levites were now playing diverse roles as liturgists, musicians, teachers, and custodians of a library of authoritative scriptures.[15]

The question remains as to how these developments would meet the challenges confronting this community as outlined at the beginning of this chapter. A more precise analysis of what the Levites actually did and taught, and what the scriptures were which they now began to assemble, will be the subject of the following chapters.

Chapter Seven

THE BIRTH OF A
SCRIPTURE BASED COMMUNITY:
THE LAW AND THE PROPHETS

During and after the Ezra-Nehemiah reforms the religious
traditions of rival priesthoods at war with one another for
centuries were at last combined in a manner that left the
most essential and important truths of each intact for the
enrichment of the other.

We have been searching for answers as to when, why, and by
whom the Hebrew scriptures in their tripartite form were assembled
and how it was that they eventually became authoritative for the
Jewish people of the Second Temple period. We have come to see that
this began happening at a time of division and discouragement in the
community of those Israelites who had returned in the latter part of the
sixth century to Judah from Babylon after their captivity there. At first
led and inspired by mostly Zadokite priests and prophets, it was
expected that this homecoming would be a time when the Davidic
commonwealth and Jerusalem temple (now in ruins) would be so magnificently restored that all nations would come to know that Yahweh
their God was truly God. It was in part the precipitous collapse of
these hopes at the time of the completion of the Second Temple that
led to the despair of which we read in the literature of this period.

However, there was another priestly and prophetic tradition alive
in this community, that of the Levites, and from this sector a somewhat
different vision of Israel's future had emerged and was now being vigorously put forward: one unshaken by the demise of the Davidic kingdom, but focused instead on the formation of covenant assemblies like

those Moses had presided over, where the emphasis was on religious and social values. It would be in this way, through loyalty to the teachings of Moses, that Israel would realize its destiny and all nations would come to share in the consequent blessings. Yet, because of the long-standing tensions between themselves and the priesthoods in charge of the national shrines, this Levite vision had for centuries been excluded by the top echelons of leadership, and remained so in the first stages of the post-exile as well.

What has now become evident is that it was the introduction of the Levite scriptures and the Levites themselves into the Israelite mainstream that constituted one of the most significant aspects of the Ezra-Nehemiah reforms. From this fact alone one might expect that in the scriptural library assembled as an important feature of these reforms the traditions of the Levites would at last be included and respected along with those of the Zadokites. Furthermore, on the basis of the important liturgical and pedagogical roles the Levites are reported to have begun to play at this time, it may also be conjectured that their own involvement in the collection and care of these scriptures would be significant. It will be my goal in what follows to show that both hypotheses are true. More specifically, what I hope to indicate is two things: (1) first, that it was in fact in the context of the Ezra-Nehemiah reforms and their immediate aftermath that the books later known as "the Law and the Prophets" began to be assembled, and that this was indeed a collection in which the traditions of both Zadokites and Levites were united in such a way that they could serve as the ideological and pedagogical foundation for a *united* Israel; (2) second, that at this time the Levites did in truth begin functioning as the custodians and teachers of this growing library of authoritative scriptures, and that in this role they added yet "other writings" to it. The first of these topics will be the focus of this chapter, the second of the two chapters to follow.

A. THE BIRTH OF A SCRIPTURE BASED COMMUNITY: INTRODUCTORY COMMENTS

As noted earlier (in Chapter 2), explicit support for the idea that the library of scriptures later known as "the Law and the Prophets" were compiled in the wake of the Ezra-Nehemiah reforms may be derived from at least one ancient text. In the *Memoirs of Nehemiah* (quoted in 2 Macc. 2:13) it is stated that Nehemiah founded a library of writings about "the kings and the prophets, the writings of David and the letters of the kings on the subject of offerings," an allusion perhaps to a library of Hebrew scriptures not unlike the one in use among Jews and Christians today.[1] To entertain the possibility that Nehemiah might in fact have undertaken such an initiative is important for visualizing how these scriptures were first assembled and came to be regarded as authoritative by the wider Jewish community. It suggests not only *when* such a collection might have come into existence (in Nehemiah's time), but *where* (in Nehemiah's library), and *how* (through the initiative of those put in charge of this library).[2]

I now want to show that the actuality of some such library having come into existence in this general period can be supported and illuminated by a substantial body of evidence from *within* the Hebrew scriptures themselves. The biblical data relevant to this issue is of several types: (1) there is, first of all, the way in which the books we now call "the Law and the Prophets" are used and referred to in "the Chronicler's History," (a set of documents written not long after the Ezra-Nehemiah reforms); (2) secondly and more specifically, there are the remarkable overviews of the contents of "the Law and the Prophets" in several synoptic prayers or confessional recitations which are strategically placed in "the Chronicler's" report of these reforms; (3) thirdly, there are innumerable editorial features of the books of "the Law and the Prophets" themselves that point to the compositional history of this collection (when, how and to what end it was assembled). It is these several clusters of evidence that will be the focus of the remainder of this chapter.

B. "THE LAW AND THE PROPHETS" IN "THE CHRONICLER'S HISTORY"

For ascertaining the reality, scope and format of the scriptural library that was put in place in Jerusalem in the aftermath of the Ezra-Nehemiah reforms, a quick look at the so-called "Chronicler's History" in Ezra-Nehemiah and Chronicles is especially instructive.[3] These volumes frequently allude to, quote from and interpret a prior body of revered writings which it soon becomes evident are none other than those later known as "the Law and the Prophets." It follows that when the Chronicler's History was being written this collection of books must have already existed and been regarded as authoritative in some sense. Precisely when this History was composed is uncertain, but it is noteworthy that the priestly and royal genealogies cited in its pages terminate abruptly at about 400 BCE (Neh. 12:2; 2 Chron. 3:17–24), suggesting it may have been completed about this time.[4] Recalling that Nehemiah was possibly still active as governor in this community as late as 430 BCE (see Neh. 13:6), it is then evident that the Chronicler's History might well have been composed and completed during the period immediately following.

What more specifically are the references and allusions to older scriptures to be found here? One discovers, to begin with, that a body of writings called "the Book of the Law of Moses" or "the book of the Law" or simply "the Law" is repeatedly mentioned in this History.[5] Specific pentateuchal laws are also frequently cited and discussed.[6] From an examination of these various citations and references alone the conclusion has been drawn that those who wrote and compiled the Chronicler's History had before them a collection of scriptures "well on the way" to becoming the Law or Pentateuch as we now have it.[7] However, not just *pentateuchal* laws or sources were known and available to the compilers of this History, but books later known as "the Prophets" as well, for what we discover when the books of Chronicles are placed side by side with the books of "the Law" *and* "the Prophets" (as we now have them), and the two sets of volumes compared, is that from the opening chapter of 1 Chronicles through to the end of 2 Chronicles, in text after text, the entire library of Hebrew scriptures from Genesis to the end of 2 Kings was appropriated, adapted, interpreted and supplemented by the authors of Chronicles.[8] In addition, the scrolls of the Prophets in one form or another may also have been accessible to these authors, for the prophecies of Jeremiah are given pride of place at the forefront of Ezra (Ezra 1:1–3) and the end of Chronicles (2 Chron. 36:22–23), and there are allusions to prophetic scriptures elsewhere in the body of these volumes.[9] In summary, older scriptures are referred to and used in the Chronicler's History in a manner that points to the existence of a library of authoritative writings very much like the collection later known as "the Law and the Prophets."[10]

C. "The Law and the Prophets" in Nehemiah 9:5–37 and Ezra 9:6–15

To ascertain the *purposes* for which this library was assembled, few texts of the Bible are as important as the prayers of confession and lament in Nehemiah 9:5–37 and Ezra 9:6–15. The longest of these, the prayer in Neh. 9:5–37, occupies a quite special place of honor within the library of Hebrew scriptures. Ezra-Nehemiah brings the biblical story of Israel's origins, rise and fall as recounted in the older Levite History (Deuteronomy through Kings) to a climactic *new* conclusion: here are described the travails and triumphs of that new community born of the edict of Cyrus in fulfillment of the prophecies of Jeremiah (see Ezra 1:1)—and the point at which *this* story culminates is the report in Neh. 8–10 of a sequence of events in which an entire community ("all those who had reached the age of discretion") joined "in a solemn oath to follow the law of God given through Moses ..." (10:29). Just prior to making this oath, we are informed, was a gathering of all who "had severed relations with all foreigners."[11] These rose "and confessed their sins and the iniquities of their ancestors" (Neh. 9:2), then listened as Levites in "ringing tones" summoned them to "bless Yahweh" with the words recorded in Neh. 9:5–37.

It is in this passage (Neh. 9:5–37) that we can discover at a glance *the unprecedented scope* of the scriptural story that was now at the disposal of this community. Here are synopsized and brought together in a single recitation (for the first time, so far as we know) themes that we have come to recognize in our prior study as belonging to the disparate traditions of the Zadokites and the Levites.[12] At the recitation's beginning are the Zadokite themes of creation (9:6), unconditional promise of land and progeny (9:7–8), and the miracle of the exodus from Egypt (9:9–12); these are followed by the Levite themes of Yahweh's revelation at Sinai (9:23) where right rules and reliable laws were given through Moses (9:13–15), laws which are then described as having been rejected despite the warnings of prophet after prophet (9:16–31), with the tragic consequence that from the time of "the Assyrians" to "the present day" (9:32) great hardships befell this people. Here in a single recitation Israel's story from creation to the destruction of the two Israelite kingdoms is synopsized in a manner that reflects and exactly parallels the history recounted in "the Law and the Prophets."[13]

However, it is not only the *contents* of the biblical library now in place that are indicated in this chapter, but the broader theological *perspective* from which that library was now being read and interpreted. This is brought out in the way the recitation is organized. While the promises of a homeland to Abraham are given pride of place at the beginning of this recitation, central to its middle and end is the theme of the terrible consequences that befell Israel for having forsaken and forgotten the right rules given through Moses. In other words, looked at as a whole this recitation appears to have been designed not so much to assure Israel of the validity of past promises as to bring about a recognition of how, despite these promises, disastrous consequences can ensue. Only a wholehearted return to the Torah of Moses can reverse the misery this community has experienced since the days of the Assyrians (9:32)—this appears to be the rationale behind its concluding confession of guilt (9:33–35) and lament (9:36–37), and this too is why this recitation was followed by an oath-making ceremony in which those involved declared themselves ready to live by this Torah (Neh. 10:28f.). Thus, it may be concluded that Zadokite and Levite themes are here combined in the service of a single goal: to bring about awareness of "the sins and the iniquities" of the ancestors (Neh. 9:2) and a renewed sense of the importance of being faithful to the teachings of Moses (Neh. 10:29).

How urgently those involved in this reform effort felt about this matter, and why, is poignantly expressed in the prayer Ezra is reported to have uttered on the occasion of discovering that intermarriage with foreigners was rife in the restoration community, even among the highest ranks of its officials and leaders (9:1–15). As in the recitation in Neh. 9, here too Israelite history "from the days of our ancestors until now" is briefly reviewed and Israel's experience of being handed over to "the kings of other countries" is recognized as a consequence of the "iniquities, we, our kings and our priests" were guilty of (Ezra 9:7). However, the prayer goes beyond the recitation in Nehemiah in the precision and passion with which it describes the precarious nature of the present circumstances of restoration under Persia. In the longer recitation in Nehemiah the restoration is viewed as a continuation of the "enslavement" that had begun when Israel was handed over to "the kings of other countries" because of its sins (Neh. 9:36f.), but in Ezra's prayer something new and promising is said to be happening as well.

"For a brief moment," Ezra prays, "the favor of Yahweh our God has allowed a remnant of us to escape and given us a stable home in his holy place, so that our God can raise our spirits and revive us a little in our slavery" (9:8). Then he goes on to emphasize the uplifting truth, that

> God has not forgotten us in our slavery; he has extended his faithful love to us even under the kings of Persia and revived us to rebuild the Temple of our God, restore its ruins and provide us with a refuge in Judah and in Jerusalem (Ezra 9:9).

What this suggests is that the restoration to the Judean homeland was viewed by Ezra and his colleagues as a time not only of continued enslavement, but also of partial fulfillment, a time during which God had "extended his faithful love to us even under the kings of Persia." At the same time, what had happened so far cannot be regarded as the *full* realization of earlier hopes, for this community was still subject to foreign rule because of past sins.

It is precisely this that makes the present moment such a precarious one, the prayer goes on to suggest. How tragic it would be if right at this juncture of partial recovery and fulfillment Israel would *again* suffer a relapse into those very same iniquities that had resulted in its past and still present state of slavery. Thus, Ezra prayed on:

> After all that has befallen us because of our evil deeds and our deep guilt ... are we to break your commandments again and intermarry with people with these disgusting practices? Would you not be enraged with us to the point of destroying us, leaving neither remnant nor survivor? (Ezra 9:13–14).

A more precise indication of the sociological and theological perspectives that motivated those involved in the Ezra-Nehemiah reforms could hardly be hoped for. In these questions (addressed to God) we encounter the raw religious passions that gave birth to both these reforms *and* the scriptures that would thereafter become authoritative for this community. These scriptures were fashioned as a warning of what *had happened* to bring this people to the brink of extinction and of what *might happen* were they to persist in the older course of action. A future and a hope awaited this people, but only if they were obedient to the Torah of Moses—such was the message enshrined in the library of "the Law and the Prophets" as reviewed in this climactic prayer.

D. EDITORIAL FEATURES OF "THE LAW AND THE PROPHETS"

There is a third line of inquiry that can shed light on the origins and goals of "the Law and the Prophets": within this library itself are numerous texts and editorial features that hint at both when and how this library was compiled and what the intentions of its compilers might have been. A great deal of study has been (and is now being) devoted to this subject—the extent and complexity of the relevant data can be daunting. In the following somewhat randomly selected probes I will try to convey some of the evidence that has led me to believe that the books of "the Law and the Prophets" were assembled in a four-stage process: (1) at the beginning of the compositional history of this collection were Deuteronomy and the Deuteronomistic History; (2) to this core the four scrolls of the prophets were attached; (3) then Exodus, Leviticus and Numbers; (4) and finally, as a prologue to the whole, the book of Genesis. We may diagram this as follows:

Stage four: Prologue to the whole collection: GENESIS	Stage three: The prior period from Egypt onward: EXODUS, LEVITICUS, NUMBERS	Stage one: The core collection: DEUTERONOMY and THE DEUTERONOMIS-TIC HISTORY	Stage two: The four prophetic scrolls added: JEREMIAH, EZEKIEL, ISAIAH, and THE TWELVE

1. Stage One: Deuteronomy and the Deuteronomistic History

We have already cited evidence for believing that an initial version of the book of Deuteronomy (Deut. 4:44–28:68) was first embraced as an authoritative document for the Israelite people during the reign of Hezekiah (2 Kings 18:1–5), but that its discovery during the reign of Josiah and its authorization by a Jerusalem prophetess are what led to its acceptance within certain circles of the Zadokite priest-hood of Jerusalem (2 Kings 22–23; see Chs. 3, 4, 6). This, therefore, was the first of the books of "the Law and the Prophets" to be accept-ed as authoritative in some sense by both Levite and Zadokite priestly groups. A first edition of the Deuteronomistic History (Joshua, Judges, Samuel and Kings) was likely produced in this same era as well, but not, in my opinion, during the reforms of *Josiah* (as Cross and Friedman have suggested),[14] but during the reforms of *Hezekiah,* of whom it is said that "no king after him can be compared with him—nor any of those before him" (2 Kings 18:5). This is hardly how he would have been described were the account of *Josiah's* reforms already part of this history, for the implication there is that Josiah was the preeminent reformer ("No king before him turned to Yahweh as he did"; 2 Kings 23:25). Furthermore, there is a clearly marked cli-max and full stop in the flow of this history in the brief synopsis in Kings 18:9–12, of why Samaria fell at the conclusion of the account of Hezekiah's reforms in 2 Kings 18:1–8, right after the earlier unusu-ally long report and analysis, in 2 Kings 17:5–41, of why northern kingdom Israel was destroyed. "This happened," we are told in the brief synopsis that closes off this account, "because they had not obeyed the voice of Yahweh their God and had broken his covenant, everything that Moses the servant of Yahweh had laid down. They neither listened to it nor put it into practice" (18:12). Thus were ful-filled the prophecies uttered some two centuries earlier regarding the destruction of Bethel and the shrines of the high places in the towns of Samaria (1 Kings 13:1, 3–34).[15] From this one gathers that the *ini-tial* purpose of this multi-scroll history may have been to trace the steps that led to the destruction of northern kingdom Israel, with the goal in mind of warning the people of Judah not to let a similar fate befall them. It is possible, therefore, that Deuteronomy and the Deuteronomistic History were initially drafted to serve a common purpose, that of supporting reforms that would turn Judah-Jerusalem away from the path of destruction followed by both Judah and the northern kingdom after the Levites were excluded from the priest-hoods in charge at the national shrines and the Torah of Moses was no longer revered as normative.[16]

A second edition of this history may have been produced during the reforms of Josiah a century later, although, in my opinion, it is more likely that this happened after the fall of Judah-Jerusalem, either among Levites deported to Babylon (2 Kings 25:21), or among those who fled to Egypt (2 Kings 25:26). The main purpose of this second edition was to explain why, despite the noble reform efforts of Josiah, Yahweh had decided to stretch the same "measuring line" of destruction over Jerusalem as the one he had earlier stretched over Samaria (2 Kings 21:13; 25:27). The conclusion arrived at was that this happened primarily because of "the provocations which Manasseh had caused him" (2 Kings 23:26) by misleading his people "into doing worse things than the nations whom Yahweh had destroyed for the Israelites" (2 Kings 21:9).[17] It is important to observe, however, that this second and final edition does not end on a note of tragedy, but of hope, by virtue of a fairly late addendum (2 Kings 25:27–30) that was attached after the death of Jehoiachin, king of Judah, who was deported to Babylon in 586 (see 2 Kings 24:15). The report in this text of his release from prison in the thirty-seventh year of his exile and of how he was treated kindly and allotted "a seat above those of the other kings who were with him in Babylon" (and the added comment that for the rest of his life he "always ate at the king's table") was obviously meant as a signal of hope, as if to say: the story is not finished yet; God's favor still rests on David's dynasty (2 Sam. 7:16); a day may be dawning when Davidic kings will again reign in Judea.[18]

Turning back to the book of Deuteronomy, we can observe a similar note of hope in the sections of this corpus that many believe were added to this book at about this same time (see, for example, Deut. 4:25–31; 29:22–30:20; and especially 30:1–5). In these the theme expressed is not only that disobeying the teachings of Yahweh as revealed to Moses will result in destruction and being scattered among the nations, but that those who have been so dispersed "from there" (Deut. 4:29) may start searching for Yahweh once again with the sure hope of finding him and being gathered "even from there" and brought back to the country of their ancestors (30:4f.). In these passages those addressed are explicitly identified as a people whom "Yahweh has torn from their own country and flung into another country, where they are today" (29:28). With these additions (both the ones in Deuteronomy, and the new ending to Kings) Deuteronomy and the Deuteronomistic History have been transformed from being primarily a literature of warnings for those who disobey the teachings of Moses, to being a message of hope for those who suffer such a fate. The theological perspective here is still essentially that of the Levites, so one imagines this core set of books was circulated and studied within the Levite communities of the Babylonian diaspora and early Persian period. In any case, this is precisely what we are told Nehemiah believed, in the opening text of his journal, and that this is what motivated him, as he began his mission (see Neh. 1:5–11):

> Remember, I beg you, the promise which you solemnly made to your servant Moses: "If you are unfaithful, I shall scatter you among the peoples; but if you come back to me and keep my commandments and practice them, even though those who have been banished are at the very sky's end, I shall gather them from there and bring them back to the place which I have chosen as a dwelling-place for my name" (Neh. 1:9).

2. Stage Two: Adding the Scrolls of the Prophets

When and by whom were the scrolls of the prophets compiled and added to this library? One thing seems certain: they were compiled to serve as a supplement and companion to Deuteronomy and the Deuteronomistic History. This is most evident in the *headings* at the forefront of the four major prophetic scrolls, Jeremiah, Ezekiel, Isaiah and the Twelve. In each case their headings link them to the final volume of the Deuteronomistic History, the book of 2 Kings, by dating them in the reigns of one or another of the Kings mentioned there. Thus, Isaiah is dated to "the reigns of Uzziah, Jotham, Ahaz and Hezekiah kings of Judah" (Isa. 1:1), Jeremiah to the reigns of "Josiah son of Amon, king of Judah ... until the end of the eleventh year of Zedekiah son of Josiah, king of Judah, until the deportation of Jerusalem, in the fifth month" (Jer. 1:2–3), Ezekiel to "the fifth year of exile for King Jehoiachin" (Ezek. 1:3), and Hosea, the first prophet in the Scroll of the Twelve, to "the reigns of Uzziah, Jotham, Ahaz and Hezekiah, kings of Judah, and of Jeroboam son of Joash, king of Israel" (Hos. 1:1); Amos, Micah, Zephaniah, Haggai and Zechariah, in the Scroll of the Twelve, are also dated in this manner as well.[19] Notable too is the correlation of significant place-names in the respective volumes (Zion, Samaria, Anathoth, Shechem) and the way large blocks of narrative from Kings were sometimes utilized verbatim in the compilation of the Isaiah and Jeremiah scrolls (2 Kings 18:13, 17–20:19 in Isa. 36–39; 2 Kings 24:18–25:30 in Jer. 52). With these headings and editorial embellishments the editors of these books clearly indicate their intention that they be read and studied in close conjunction with the account of Israelite history related in the prior volume, especially that having to do with Assyrian and Babylonian invasions and the decline and fall of the two Israelite kingdoms.

This in itself suggests that those who compiled these volumes in their final form were simultaneously custodians of Deuteronomy and the Deuteronomistic History. As just noted, however, the Deuteronomistic History ends with an account of the destruction of Jerusalem and the deportation of its surviving citizens to Babylon (2 Kings 25), whereas all four of the scrolls of the prophets (as now edited) address issues pertaining not only to these catastrophic developments, but to the period thereafter, especially those events that occurred at the time of the rise of the Persian Empire and the restoration of Judeans to their homeland. It may have been in part to fill in this gap that Ezra-Nehemiah was composed. As such, the Ezra-Nehemiah chronicle constitutes a "next chapter" (indeed, a culminating chapter) to the story related in 2 Kings 25, and the interrelationship between it (Ezra-Nehemiah) and the four scrolls of the prophets would appear to have been every bit as important to its compilers as was the relationship of the prophetic scrolls to the Deuteronomistic History. In other words, the four scrolls of the prophets appear to have been edited to be read and studied in conjunction not only with the Deuteronomistic History, but with the Chronicler's account of the restoration and the reforms of Ezra and Nehemiah. In brief, these four prophetic scrolls are oriented both backward to the judgments that came upon the two Israelite kingdoms in 721 and 587, but also forward to the new beginnings that began occurring after the restoration of Israelites to the Judean homeland in 537.

This bipolar orientation of the collection is evident in other ways as well. In both individual prophetic books, as well as in the four prophetic scrolls as a whole, a pattern of oracles of judgment followed by oracles of hope is apparent.[20] In each of the four scrolls, oracles of critique and destruction are predominant in the first half, followed by oracles of hope in the second (Ezekiel is the prime example of this, with Ezek. 24 forming the bridge between the two orientations). There is also a discernible chronological and theological development in the four scrolls, taken as a whole, if one follows the talmudic listing in Baba Bathra 14b, where Jeremiah comes first, then Ezekiel, Isaiah, and the Twelve. In this order, the end of each of these books carries the reader a few decades further down the road of history, from a point just after the destruction of Jerusalem (Jeremiah), to a point deep into the Babylonian captivity (Ezekiel), then to the threshold of the restoration to Judah under Persia, and the first decades after the return (Isaiah), and finally to the period just prior to the Ezra-Nehemiah reforms (the Twelve). In fact, the last book in the Twelve (Malachi) seems to serve as a bridge from the prophets to the reformers, with it's predictions of a "messenger" who will appear suddenly, purge the priesthood (Mal. 3:1–5) and bring about repentance of old and young alike in advance of the Day of Yahweh (Mal. 4:6 [Hebrew 3:24]).

Near the end of this collection of four prophetic scrolls there stands a text that calls upon the reader to "remember the Law of my servant Moses to whom at Horeb I [Yahweh] prescribed decrees and rullings for all Israel" (Mal. 4:4 [Hebrew 3:22]). With these words these final books are linked editorially to the beginning of the Deuteronomistic History, Deut. 5:1–5 in particular. The reference here is not to the Moses of the Tetrateuch, who is often accompanied by Aaron, but to Moses alone and to "Horeb" (not Sinai as in the Tetrateuch) and to the "decrees and rulings for all Israel"—this is precisely the Moses of Deut. 5:1 who "called *all* Israel together and said to them, 'Listen, Israel, to the laws and customs that I proclaim to you today." This suggests that the prophetic scrolls were added to the Deuteronomistic History prior to the addition of the Tetrateuch. Were this the case, it would help explain how the book of Ezekiel, with its pre-tetrateuchal sketches of the respective duties of Levites and Zadokites at the Second Temple (Ezek. 44:10–31), found its way intact into this collection. It also intimates what the purpose was of this much enlarged collection: the addition of the four scrolls of the prophets was meant to further encourage the wholehearted return to the teachings of Yahweh as revealed to Moses at Horeb.

3. Stage Three: Exodus, Leviticus and Numbers

The oldest core collection of "the Law and the Prophets" exam-ined thus far is predominately Levite in origins and orientation. Was there no room in this library for the traditions of the Zadokites? Our analysis of the Ezra-Nehemiah reforms in Chapter 6 has led us to believe there would be, for at this time a way was found for Israel's rival priesthoods to serve together again at the Jerusalem temple as they once had in the time of David. An examination of the four books that are now included at the forefront of this collection suggests that it is here that the traditions and perspectives of these two groups were combined in a manner acceptable to both. It appears this happened in a two-step process: first the traditions of each group pertaining to the period of national origins beginning in Egypt and up to the entry into Canaan were brought together as we now have them in Exodus, Leviticus and Numbers;[21] then the book of Genesis was compiled as a prologue to the entire collection stretching from Exodus to Malachi. In Leviticus are deposited, relatively untouched (one imagines), large blocks of Aaronite tradition pertaining to the operation of the cult of sacrifice at the central shrine. Some of the more contentious issues that needed to be resolved between the two groups are then dealt with in the books that frame this deposit (Exodus and Numbers), as well as in the manner in which this collection as a whole is connected to the Deuteronomic corpus which follows. In the following exegetical probes it is at these points that I will focus.

(a) Aaronites and Levites in Numbers 16–18

An important clue as to *when* the material in these books was assembled and what some of the institutional conflicts were that accompanied this act is afforded by two accounts in Numbers 16–18 describing the resolution of certain controversies over the respective duties of Aaronites and Levites at the central shrine. In the first of these, Num. 16:1–40, an argument over whether Levites may offer incense before Yahweh at his "Dwelling" (16:1a, 3–11, 16–24, 31–32, 35) has been superimposed on an older account of a rebellion of Reubenites against Moses for having brought them into the wilderness to die (16:1b, 12–15, 25–30, 33–34). The argument over who may offer incense ends with the Levites (and those on their side) being destroyed by earthquake and fire (Num. 16:31–32, 35); subsequently, the bronze censers they had wanted to use for their offerings were hammered into sheets to cover the altar, this to serve as a reminder that "no one not of Aaron's line, may approach and offer incense before Yahweh, on pain of suffering" death (16:40). It is important to note that at issue was not whether Levites were to have any role at all at the sanctuary. Rather, this particular text presupposes and recognizes that the Levites were a group whom God had "singled out" and "called" to be "near him," to serve in his "Dwelling and to represent the community by officiating on its behalf" (Num. 16:9). What the text's authors were *not* prepared to recognize was the legitimacy of Levites offering "incense" before Yahweh. This alone is the point being made: "Levites, you take *too much* on yourselves [by wanting to burn incense]!" (Lev. 16:7b). However, the reason this issue was such a contentious one, the text implies, is that by wanting to burn incense, the Levites were seeking full status as priests: "Now you want to be priests as well" (Num. 16:10). In other words, the Levites were perceived by the priests as wanting equal rights with them in the affairs of the sanctuary.

The only period of biblical history we know of when priests and Levites were locked in this type of argument was in the days of Ezra and Nehemiah when these reformers took upon themselves the challenge of restoring the Levites to service at the Jerusalem temple after four centuries of exclusive Zadokite control.[22] Understandably, there were those who opposed what they were trying to accomplish. The grudging recognition on the part of the priests that Levites too were "singled out" by Yahweh and "called" to be "near him" at his sanctuary testifies to the success the reform efforts already had in uniting these alienated groups. However, ongoing tensions between the two groups are also reflected in this text. The priests are represented as still suspicious of Levite ambitions and fiercely determined to restrict their temple activities to strictly non-priestly duties (cp. Ezek. 44:10–15).

A second group of texts, Num. 16:41–18:1–7, addresses the same set of controversies. Here again the issue being considered is that of the precise boundaries to be drawn between Aaronite authority and activities at the temple and those of the Levites. Through the twin stories of the plague (Num. 16:41–50) and the budding branches (Num. 17:1–11) Aaronite control of priestly affairs at the temple is definitively substantiated against all questioners (Num. 17:5), for it was Aaron who is portrayed as having performed the rite of expiation that stopped the plague (16:48), and his name alone that appeared on the "branch" of Levi that sprouted, indicating that only he and his descendants (not any others from that branch) were chosen by Yahweh for priestly duties. These stories serve as back-up for the Aaronite decrees in Num. 18:1–7 which outline the rules that are from now on to govern the respective roles and duties of Levites and Aaronites at the shrine. These specify that both groups bear a responsibility for offenses against the shrine (18:1), but Levites, as subordinates and servants of the Aaronites, must never "come near the sacred vessels or the altar" (18:3), for Aaronites alone have "charge of the sanctuary and charge of the altar ..." (Num. 18:5). These decrees appear to post-date the reforms of Ezra, who had no compunction against putting both Zadokites *and* Levites in charge of the sacred utensils and gifts he brought back from Babylon (see Ezra 8:24–30); on the other hand, they are tacitly accepted by the authors of Chronicles (as will be noted in Ch. 9). Echoes of the controversies that accompanied the final redaction of the Hebrew scriptures are thus all too apparent in the stories and decrees of these chapters.

(b) The Redaction of the Sinai Events in Exod. 19–34

For additional insight into the theological controversies that accompanied the addition of these books to "the Law and Prophets," a look at the way the records of the events occurring at the beginning of Israel's sojourn at Sinai were compiled and edited is especially illuminating, since (as we have seen) it was regarding what transpired at this juncture of Israelite history that the priestly houses of Israel had been most at odds. Thus, in the one tradition (that of the Levites), the Moses-led exodus from Egypt culminating in the sealing of a sacred covenant at Horeb was central, while in the other (that of the Aaronite-Zadokites) the miraculous deliverance from Egypt culminating in God's presence at a sacred shrine was the preeminent tradition. Furthermore, in the Horeb covenant tradition Yahweh's nature-transcendence (no images) as well as the importance of serving him *alone* were stressed, while in the other tradition there was greater receptivity to Canaanite ways of thinking, such as respect for lesser gods (so long as Yahweh's supremacy was recognized) and the place of the calf-icon. How could two such disparate traditions possibly be combined without compromising their respective visions?

The Exodus redaction of the Sinai events in Exod. 19–34 affords us a striking example of how this was accomplished to the apparent satisfaction of both.[23] It *opens* with a substantial block of Levite traditions, so that the first impression one has when reading Exod. 19:1–24:8 is that what happened at Sinai was the forging of a covenant in which "the people" became "a kingdom of priests, a holy nation," Yahweh's own "personal possession" (19:5), by pledging allegiance (24:3–8) to the decalogue (20:1–17) and Covenant Code (22:22–23:33). In this section of the account Levite theology was given its voice. However, right at the point where the covenant was ratified, the editors created a splice by drawing a distinction between the covenant made with "the people" at the base of the mountain (24:3–8) and what transpired on the *top* of the mountain during an event at which only Moses, Aaron, Nadab and Abihu (sons of Aaron), and seventy of the elders of Israel, were in attendance (24:1–2, 9–11). These alone were privileged to "gaze" on the God of Israel and eat and drink there.

This sets the stage for a two-track redaction in which both groups ("the people" on the one hand, and Aaron, his sons, plus "the elders," on the other) wait while Moses, "with Joshua his assistant," approaches Yahweh to receive "the stone tablets" on which Yahweh promised to write the covenant decalogue (24:12). In what follows the covenant initially consummated in Exod. 24:3–8 is described as being radically challenged by the Aaron-led apostasy with the calf-icon (ch. 32); this covenant was then reconstituted (34:1–5, 10, 27–28) after a fresh revelation of Yahweh's glory (33:18–23), but with "*all* the Israelites" *including* "Aaron and all the leaders of the community" submissive to "*all* the orders that Yahweh had given" to Moses on Mount Sinai (34:31–32). Only now is the stage set for Moses to assemble "the whole community of Israelites" and proceed with the implementation of what had been revealed on the mountain (35:1, 4).

There is thus a movement (in the way the story of what happened at Sinai is told in this redaction) from a covenant made initially with only part of the people to a reconstituted covenant that includes "the whole community of the Israelites" including the Aaronites. In the resulting synthesis of Levite and Aaronite traditions, strategic concessions were made to Levite perspectives. Aaronite readiness to adopt Canaanite religious practices is thoroughly repudiated with the inclusion of the lengthy Levite account of the episode with the golden calf (Exod. 32); also, a radically anti-Canaanite preface (Exod. 34:10–16) has been spliced on to the old Kenite-Aaronite version of the decalogue in Exod. 34:17-26. Furthermore, the preeminence of the Levite version of the decalogue has been retained in both the first *and* second covenant ceremonies: thus, after breaking the first tablets on which this decalogue was recorded (32:19), Moses reportedly "cut two tablets of stone *like the first ones*" and returned to the mountain for God to rewrite the commandments (34:1); the account then ends by stating that after a stay there of forty days and forty nights, the tablets *were* rewritten with the "words of the covenant"—the original "Ten Words" (34:28).[24]

However, a substantial fund of Aaronite tradition has also been spliced into the larger account on the two occasions when Moses was on the mountain, that is, just before and after the incident with the golden calf. Prior to the calf incident, *even before* receiving the two stone tablets on which the original covenant words were written (31:18), it is specified that detailed instructions were given to Moses for building a sanctuary where Yahweh would reside among his people (25:8), instructions which legislate that Aaron and his sons should be the officiating priests at this shrine (28:1). Furthermore, in these splices the Sinai covenant is characterized (quite differently than in Levite tradition) as symbolic of an "eternal covenant" (31:12–17) based, not upon the people's consent, but upon Yahweh's power as creator (of which the Sabbath was to be the sign). Thus, Levite traditions regarding what happened at Horeb remain intact, but room is made for a shrine expressive of Yahweh's unconditional presence, power and readiness to forgive.

The Moses of this enlarged tradition is characterized in its climactic episode (Exod. 34:29–35) as one whose face had become radiant, so that *all* were now in awe of him, Aaron as well as the rest of the Israelites (34:30). Moses is then pictured as summoning *all* to gather before him, and significantly, it is said to be Aaron and the leaders of the community who had previously rejected his teaching (in the earlier incident with the golden calf) who approached him *first,* "after which all the Israelites came closer, and he [Moses] passed on to them all the orders that Yahweh had given to him on Mount Sinai" (34:32). In this carefully crafted conclusion to the preceding redaction of covenant making, covenant breaking and covenant renewal we can almost hear a sigh of relief that at last Israel's rival priestly traditions have been reunited and are again part of a "whole community" (35:1, 4).[25]

(c) The Succession from Moses to Joshua in Num. 27:12–23 and Deut. 34

An examination of the contrasting Aaronite and Levite accounts of the death of Moses and the succession of his office to Joshua affords yet another cluster of insights into how these diverse traditions were reconciled. What especially merits attention is the way the account of Moses' death in Num. 27:12–23 has been modified to make way for the addition of the book of Deuteronomy and a revised account of these events in Deut. 34 (see also Josh. 1:1–9). The chief change introduced at Num. 27:12–23 was the *postponement* of the death itself, for according to the story there (Num. 27:12–23), Moses was then already about to ascend a mountain to view the land of Canaan, before preparing to die (Num. 27:12–13), and in anticipation of this, his successor, Joshua, had been appointed (27:15–23). But to our surprise the story remains unfinished at that point, and not until Deut. 31–34 is it completed. The precise way the *succession* from Moses to Joshua is described in the two stories is also noteworthy. According to the first account, upon being appointed Moses' successor Joshua received only "some" of Moses' authority (Num. 27:20) and as a consequence had to subordinate himself to the authority of the Aaronite high priest (Num. 27:20–21). According to the second account, Joshua "was filled with the spirit of wisdom" when Moses laid his hands on him (Deut. 34:9) and had only to submit himself to Moses' teaching to succeed in what he did (Deut. 31:7–33:29; Josh. 1:6–9). In this manner the supreme authority of the Aaronite high priest in the earlier narrative was superseded by the authority of Moses' Torah (Deuteronomy) in the second account. The subordination of Aaron to Moses appears to be one of the firm principles on which this corpus was compiled (cp. Num. 12). As now edited, the tetrateuchal history climaxes in Deuteronomy, which is simultaneously the point of reference for the Deuteronomistic History that follows.

(d) The Book of Genesis and the Thematic "Architecture" of the Collection as a Whole

A final step in the compilation of "the Law and the Prophets" was taken with the addition of the book of Genesis at its front. John Van Seters has made credible the thesis that those who did this not only had before them Deuteronomy and the Deuteronomistic History, but were also inspired by the world vision of the prophets, the so-called Second Isaiah in particular.[26] In this "Prologue to History," as he terms it, they have created a framework for the narrative that follows, one purpose of which was "to account for the origins of Israel and its neighbors."[27] At a deeper level, the theological theme of sin and judgment ("crime and punishment") that serves as the unifying factor in the Deuteronomistic History has been "extended to the universal domain of God's rule...."[28] In this manner readers and students of Israel's national history are invited to understand it within the setting of a story about the whole world, as they must if they are to take seriously Israel's destiny as expressed in the writings of its great prophets.

Often overlooked in studies of "the Law and the Prophets" is the striking manner in which, with the book of Genesis now in place, this corpus is structured and oriented toward the world of nations, both at its beginning and end—but also in a remarkable panel in its middle which may have been added at this same time. Note, first of all, that in Genesis 1–11 this book is begun, not just with a memorable account of how God created the world and pronounced it good, but with a long, rather bleak follow-up portrait of the human condition fleshed out through stories that focus on the affairs of an ever proliferating and increasingly sinful, confused and divided array of ethnographic and linguistic groups and nationalities (Gen. 4–11).[29] Note too how these nations remain the focus of attention in the immediately following texts in Genesis which recount God's call to Abraham (Gen. 12:1–3). What they state is that if Abraham does God's bidding and goes to the land Yahweh will show him, his descendants will become a great nation through which *"all clans on earth"* will be blessed (or bless themselves). Significant too is the way this promise is repeated in the chapters that follow, with an important clarification as to *how* this plan or calling will be realized: namely, by Abraham's "family after him" keeping "the way of Yahweh" (Gen. 18:19) and obeying his "commandments, statutes and laws" (22:18; 26:5; cp. 16:10; 26:24; 28:15;

35:1–4). A connection is thereby forged between the patriarchal stories and promises of Genesis and the immediately following account of the life of Moses in Exodus, Leviticus and Numbers, which reaches its climax in the liturgies of blessings and curses in the closing chapters of Deuteronomy (cf. 26:16–ch. 28)—as if to say, it is in this manner, by fidelity to these "commandments, statutes and laws" given through Moses, that Abraham's "family after him" will experience God's blessing and be a blessing to all the peoples of the world.

What follows in Joshua, Judges, Samuel and Kings is the history of Israel's sojourn in Canaan from land-entry (Joshua) to expulsion (Kings). In relating this story an important chronological marker has been inserted at 1 Kings 6:1, where we are informed that it was precisely "in the four hundred and eightieth year after the Israelites came out of Egypt" (1 Kings 6:1) that Solomon began building the temple of Yahweh in Jerusalem. This date was seemingly obtained by adding fifty years of the Babylonian exile to the 430 years assigned by the compilers of these volumes to the reigns of the kings of Judah, thus making the time from the Exodus to the building of the first temple exactly equal to the time from the building of the first temple to the reconstruction of the second one. It is hardly accidental, therefore, that right at this juncture texts have been added that strongly emphasize that it was not for Israel's sake only that this temple was built, but for "foreigners from a distant country" who "attracted by Yahweh's name" will come to pray there (1 Kings 8:41). Furthermore, regarding these, the wish is expressed that when doing so (when praying at the temple) their prayers might be answered, "so that all the peoples of the earth may acknowledge your name and, like your people Israel, revere you and know that this Temple, which I have built, bears your name" (1 Kings 8:43). A similar point is made at the end of this section, where we are told how when Solomon had finished offering his prayers, he rose and stood upright and blessed "the whole assembly of Israel" in a loud voice. Not one "of the promises of good" made by Yahweh through his servant Moses has failed (8:56), Solomon declared, and then prayed that God would continue to be with Israel and that Israel would follow his ways, not just so that Israel's cause might be upheld "as each day requires" (8:59), but "so that all the peoples of the earth may come to know that Yahweh is God indeed and there is no other" (8:60).

Seen in the light of these promises at the beginning and middle of this collection, what follows in Israelite history as this is recounted in the remaining chapters of Kings must be regarded as an ironic tragedy, for far from being a people of blessing through whom blessing came to the nations, those nations are reported to have turned against Israel and almost destroyed it because of its sins. Were the book of Kings the end-volume of "the Law and the Prophets," this collection would be a torso. Its thematic architecture requires *another* ending, one which will show how despite the humiliation and destruction suffered at the hands of the Assyrians and Babylonians, Israel one day did or would fulfill its calling of being a people of blessing for the nations. Where is this ending? We have already noted that the four scrolls of the Prophets were compiled and edited with this need in mind. Here is where we learn that the judgment for sin Israel experienced during the destruction of the two Israelite kingdoms was but a prelude to a time when Israel would be renewed and empowered to become what from the days of Abraham God had promised: a light to the nations (Isa. 49:1–6); a place of pilgrimage, reconciliation and prayer for all peoples (Jer. 3:17; Isa. 2:1–5; 55:1–5; Micah 4:1–5; Zech. 2:15–17), a land so blessed that "all nations will call you blessed" (Mal. 3:12). The purpose of "the Law and the Prophets" was, therefore, not just to awaken remorse and renewed fidelity to the Torah of Moses for *Israel's* sake only (themes emphasized in Neh. 9 and the prayer of Ezra in Ezra 9), but to keep alive the vision and hope that through Israel God's salvation will one day reach the whole world (Isaiah 49:6–7).[30]

SUMMARY AND CONCLUSION

In "the Law and the Prophets" we can observe how under Levite supervision and direction, the spiritual legacies of Israel's two major priestly traditions were brought together in such a way that they could begin to serve as the cultic, constitutional and pedagogical foundations of a united Israel.[31] While ready to acknowledge the Aaronite-Zadokites as Israel's only priesthood, its Levite editors were not prepared to accept all that the Aaronites had previously stood for. Yahweh alone must be worshiped, they believed, and his covenant with Israel must be recognized as one that is fundamentally conditional in nature and moral in orientation. Yet, so long as this was clear, the Levites were open to the Aaronite vision of Yahweh's unconditional grace and greatness as creator and wise ruler of the universe and his unswerving promises to Israel. When editing these diverse traditions and combining them, as few changes were made as possible.[32]

A major purpose of the compilation as a whole was to remind Israel of the judgment that had swept over it in the past because of its sins, so that it would resolve never again to abandon the Torah of Moses and suffer such consequences. Beyond this, however, was the goal set before Israel of a "blessing" and a witness that would spread from Israel to the nations, so that the teachings of Israel's God and the benefits to be derived from these would be experienced worldwide. The end product may be characterized as "renewal literature," for it was aimed at helping this community take stock of itself, know who it was and is and what it could hope for, in order that it might survive in the midst of forces that threatened to destroy it. Sobered by the catastrophic destruction of the two Israelite kingdoms, yet enlivened and made hopeful of a better future for themselves and the world, this community was afforded a fresh opportunity to live and not die through this remarkable ecumenical synthesis.

Chapter Eight

CUSTODIANS AND TEACHERS OF THE SECOND TEMPLE LIBRARY

*The expanded library of scriptures which eventually
became authoritative for the Jewish community worldwide
was compiled by a temple guild vested with responsibility
for this task who carried it out with evident goals in mind.*

How were books added to "the Law and the Prophets" to form
the full collection of Hebrew scriptures that eventually became authoritative for the Jewish people worldwide? This question which has been
only touched on so far needs to be looked at more carefully before
turning to a discussion of the books themselves. Current thinking about
this process leaves much to be desired. Many visualize diverse Jewish
"communities" at home or abroad as playing the decisive role. These
are thought to have responded to new books as they appeared, and
accepted or rejected them in accordance with the degree to which they
did or did not address their needs or conditions. It is thus imagined that
books first found acceptance in one or another "community" before
being accepted by the Jewish people as a whole.[1] However, who initiated this process of selection or rejection, or in what way a given book,
once accepted in a certain community, was acknowledged to be authoritative by all and was then added to an already existent library of such
writings, or how this growing library was monitored, cared for and
made accessible to the wider community, is seldom spelled out. Some
believe we will likely never know why certain books and not others
became authoritative,[2] nor ought we even try to find out, since the
Hebrew scriptures themselves, it is claimed, appear to be *deliberately*

vague as to their origins or the principles and procedures that determined their selection and preservation.[3]

A. HOW THE HEBREW SCRIPTURES WERE COMPILED: EXTERNAL EVIDENCE

I hope to show that substantial support for an alternative proposal may be found within the Hebrew scriptures themselves. However, there are also bits and pieces of information relevant to this issue available in other sources as well. I propose to look at these, first of all, beginning with another glance at the statement in 2 Macc. 2:13–15 that Nehemiah had founded a library where scriptures of this nature were compiled and housed. It will be remembered from our earlier discussion (in Ch. 2) that this text was part of a letter purportedly sent from "the people of Jerusalem" to "the Jews in Egypt" (1 Macc. 1:10) and that it went on to report of a "complete collection" of the scriptures of this library that had recently been reassembled by Judas Maccabeus, copies of which were again available to any who might need them and would send for them (2 Macc. 2:15). In these few words we catch a glimpse of how at this time (mid-second century BCE) the sacred scriptures of the Jews were being cared for and disseminated in the wider Jewish world. There was a place in Jerusalem (at the temple, no doubt) where master copies of these scriptures were held in trust for those who revered them. By the simple act of requesting and sending for them, copies of these scriptures could be obtained by Jewish communities elsewhere.[4]

But can we be at all certain that such was the case earlier, perhaps as early, even, as at the time when Nehemiah's library was first founded? If a library of this nature already existed, then who was in charge of it? Who presided over its acquisitions? Who decided what books would be added or rejected? Who cared for these books, and saw to it that accurate copies were made for those requesting them? Unfortunately, regarding matters such as these 1 Macc. 2:13–15 has no answers, but there is another source that may be more helpful. In the opening sentences of the Jewish tractate Abot ("The Sayings of the Fathers"), which the Jewish community of the third century CE produced to account for the origins of its authoritative traditions, there is a brief synopsis of how Jewish traditions were cared for and transmitted during this period.[5] The synopsis begins by stating that the "Torah" Moses received at Sinai was transmitted to Joshua, then to certain elders, who passed it on to the Prophets. It was then, Abot states, that the tradition passed into the hands of "the men of the Great Assembly"; these "men," we are told, were the ones who passed this legacy on from that point in time until the days of Simeon the Righteous, a contemporary of Jesus ben Sira (Sirach 50:1). In other words, responsibility for the transmission of Jewish tradition during the two centuries following the last of the prophets (early fifth century BCE) until the days of Jesus ben Sira (early second century BCE) was in the hands of a guild known as "the men of the Great Assembly." Rabbinic sources go on to state that members of this group were not only traditionists but authors or editors of some of the scriptural traditions they transmitted.[6] What this implies is that the process of initiating, assembling and transmitting the sacred scriptures of the Jews in the period under consideration did not happen in a totally spontaneous manner, but was the task of specific scholars set apart by an identifiable body of people (the "Great Assembly") for that specific purpose. It also raises the possibility that the guild so designated may have been the group put in charge of Nehemiah's library.

But were this the case would we not read of this in other sources? Would not the Hebrew scriptures themselves, if so assembled, contain at least a hint or indication that this was the case? Do they?

B. HOW THE HEBREW SCRIPTURES WERE COMPILED: INTERNAL EVIDENCE

Evidence that the Hebrew scriptures were in fact assembled and cared for in this manner does show up in these scriptures. To be sure, there are no explicit references in these writings to either Nehemiah's library, or to "the men of the Great Assembly" as such. However, plenary "assemblies" *are* mentioned as having played a key role in the Ezra-Nehemiah reforms, and at least one of these is termed a "*great* assembly" (Neh. 5:7). Moreover, a quick survey of what these assemblies were all about suggests that their chief function was not unrelated to that of the "great assemblies" referred to in Abot, for as described, they were plenary meetings of the Torah-loyal peoples of Judah-Jerusalem, either for the purpose of studying the scriptures which Ezra brought to this community (Neh. 8), or to deal with a range of moral and social issues in this light (Neh. 5:7; Ezra 10:7). Most significantly, in the descriptions in Ezra-Nehemiah of what concretely happened at these "assemblies," a quite discrete group of "men" is mentioned who are said to have supported and assisted Ezra on these occasions. In one of the texts these men are somewhat vaguely identified as "all who tremble at the words of the God of Israel" (Ezra 9:4; cp. 10:3), but then, in most other accounts, more explicitly, as "Levites" (Neh. 8:9, 11–12; 9:4–5). In fact, the prominence and involvement of these "Levites" in the affairs of these "assemblies" prompts one to wonder whether they might not be the "men of the Great Assembly" Abot had in mind when detailing how the traditions were cared for and transmitted in the period after Ezra.[7]

Two additional lines of evidence may be noted in support of this proposal: the one has to do with the peculiar placement of Ezra-Nehemiah and Chronicles at the *end* of this scriptural library, the second with the varied roles these concluding volumes report that the Levites were authorized to play in the period after Ezra. Each of these topics deserves our closest attention if we wish to hear what the Hebrew scriptures themselves might have to say regarding the identity of those who compiled them.

1.The Unique Placement of Ezra-Nehemiah and Chronicles

A much neglected topic in studies of how the Hebrew scriptures were assembled is the *order* or sequence in which the books of this library were originally arranged and read. It should be remembered that at this time books were written on separate scrolls instead of being bound together in codexes, as today. It might be imagined that as a consequence their arrangement was of little or no importance. On the contrary, precisely because books were written on separate scrolls (the codex having not yet been invented), specifying and knowing their arrangement could be a matter of even greater importance (if in fact their sequence in relation to other scrolls was a factor in their original design), for that alone was the controlling factor in what sequence they were to be read.[8] That order and sequence *were* essential matters for the *opening* volumes of the biblical library is self-evident in the case of the first five books of the Torah and the next four books of the

Prophets (Joshua, Judges, Samuel, Kings)—all tell a story that continues from book to book in clear chronological order.

However, was sequence important as well in the way the remaining volumes were added to this library? Roger Beckwith's meticulous researching of this subject suggests it was.[9] He begins by reminding us of how important this issue was to the rabbis of the Babylonian Talmud. Their convictions on these matters are to be found in a summary of rabbinic opinion recorded in Baba Bathra 14b, a talmudic text that Beckwith argues might well reflect a quite old tradition.[10] The issue being addressed was the proper arrangement of the books of the second and third sections of the Hebrew scriptures only (that is, "the Prophets and Writings"), not the list or arrangement of "the Law" or Pentateuch, since their arrangement was long established and well known. What "the Rabbans" taught about the order of the books of "the Prophets and the Writings," on the other hand, was apparently in danger of being lost, which is why it needed to be preserved in writing. The text states:

> the order of the Prophets is, Joshua, Judges, Samuel, Kings, Jeremiah, Ezekiel, Isaiah, and the Twelve Minor Prophets ... [and] the order of the Hagiographa is Ruth, the Book of Psalms, Job, Prophets, Ecclesiastes, Song of Songs, Lamentations, Daniel and the Scroll of Esther, Ezra[-Nehemiah] and Chronicles.

The issue of precisely how old this list and arrangement might be will be addressed in Chapter 9 in connection with the closer look taken there at each of the added "Hagiographa" or "Writings."[11] My chief interest here is in what the rationale might have been for this order of books in these two sections ("the Prophets" and "the Hagiographa"), and what appears to be noteworthy in that regard is that, with the exception of Chronicles, the chief consideration determining their arrangement was chronology. As already noted, that this is the case is most obvious in the way the scrolls that make up "the Law and the Prophets" (Genesis through Malachi) are listed, for in this part of the collection each additional scroll clearly takes us a few additional steps down the road of Israelite history, beginning with the creation of the world in Genesis, through Israel's origins, rise and fall, and then, with the books of the prophets, right down to the threshold of the Ezra-Nehemiah reforms (Malachi).[12] It might seem that the arrangement of books in the Hagiographa (or Writings) is an exception to this rule, for here the *initial* volumes predate the last books of the Law and the Prophets—yet, one should note that *within* this final section (just as within the Book of the Twelve) there is again a chronologically determined arrangement. Thus, Ruth (period of the Judges) comes first, followed by works ostensibly from the Davidic and Solomonic eras (Psalms, Job, Proverbs, Ecclesiastes, Song of Solomon), two writings from the exilic period (Lamentations and Daniel), and finally, two more books from the Persian period (Esther and Ezra), with Ezra (Ezra-Nehemiah) being the *chronological* end-point of both this section and the collection as a whole.

From this overview a single exception stands out: only the books of Chronicles are outside this chronologically determined arrangement and *follow* rather than precede Ezra-Nehemiah (as the chronological principle would dictate they should). This is at first puzzling, but hardly accidental, since Beckwith (after an exhaustive review of the data) reports that in virtually all the listings known to us Chronicles always appears at the end of the Hagiographa or Writings.[13] Why might this have been so? A closer look at Ezra-Nehemiah *and* Chronicles may afford an answer. These volumes share a great many themes in common and must have originated among the same circles of writers,[14] yet they are quite different from one another. Characteristic of the first (Ezra-Nehemiah) is the use made of primary sources (personal diaries, letters, official documents, and the like). This is ostensibly for the purpose of presenting a credible account of Israel's new beginnings in its Judean homeland from the time of the edict of Cyrus (Ezra 1), up to and inclusive of the Ezra-Nehemiah reforms (Ezra 7-Neh. 13). In this respect Ezra is much like the earlier Deuteronomic or Levite histories and may in fact be viewed as their sequel. In it the story related in Joshua, Judges, Samuel and Kings (and so abruptly terminated with the account of Jerusalem's destruction and Israel's Babylonian captivity) is picked up and continued by a generically similar account of what happened next: the restoration under Cyrus, the rebuilding of the temple and of Jerusalem, and the climactic Ezra-Nehemiah reforms. Also, and even more importantly, when viewed together (the one as a sequel of the other), it becomes apparent that both histories (the

Deuteronomistic History *and* Ezra-Nehemiah) build toward reforms: the Deuteronomistic History reaches its climax in the reforms of Hezekiah (2 Kings 18) and Josiah (2 Kings 22–23), the accounts in Ezra-Nehemiah build toward their climax in the reforms of Ezra and Nehemiah.

This synchronic feature prompts the reader of these volumes to compare these reforms, and when that is done, I suggest, a special feature of the final reform recounted in Ezra-Nehemiah begins to surface. Each of the three reforms mentioned in these accounts is said to have been based on an identical "law of Moses" (1 Kings 18:6; 23:25; Neh. 8:1), but the earlier two were only temporarily successful (that is, they failed to outlast the kings who initiated them)—it was for this very reason that the two Israelite kingdoms were destroyed, we are told (2 Kings 23:26f.; 24:19f.). Seen against this background, the reforms of Ezra and Nehemiah (as described in Ezra-Nehemiah) stand out as unique. If Israel was not to be destroyed all over again, and perhaps permanently so this time (see esp. Ezra 9:13–15; Neh. 9:32–37), this reform would have to succeed in a way the previous two did not. It will have to endure and be ongoing. But, the reader is prompted to ask: what will it take for that to happen, A prominent feature of the accounts of this third reform as compared to the two that preceded it is the role Levites are said to have played within it. In most other respects Ezra's reforms are similar to those of his predecessors, especially Josiah: both he and Josiah have the "law of Moses" read before a great assembly in Jerusalem; both he and Josiah enlist those assembled in a covenant to obey this law (2 Kings 23:1–3; Neh. 8:1–3; 10:28–29). Where the two accounts differ most strikingly is that Ezra arranged to have his people *instructed* in the meaning and application of the Torah they had just heard read, and was assisted by the Levites in doing so (Neh. 8:7, 9, 10–12; 9:5). There is nothing comparable to this feature of the Ezra-Nehemiah reforms in the accounts of the earlier reforms.[15]

Might this suggest another reason for Ezra-Nehemiah and Chronicles being added to this scriptural library at its very end? Is it possible that when arranging the books of this library Ezra-Nehemiah was placed at the climactic end-point, not only because the reforms described were in fact the culminating episode of the history recited in the scriptures of this library, but also to serve as a kind of "testament" regarding the position and role the Levites now had (and were meant to have) in the perpetuation and ongoing success of these reforms? Improbable as this suggestion might at first seem, a positive answer becomes evident as the connections are seen that bind Ezra-Nehemiah to the immediately following books of Chronicles. As just noted, the climactic volumes of the biblical library are not Ezra-Nehemiah, but Ezra-Nehemiah *and* Chronicles. It is thus only by taking a closer look at what *both together* tell us about the Levites that the true role of these concluding books (and of the Levites) in the Judaism of this period can be fully appreciated.

2. Chronicles and the Levites in Second Temple Judaism

Ezra-Nehemiah and Chronicles are unique among the scriptures of the library of which they are a part in the degree and specificity with which they focus on the activities of the Levites and authorize them to take on a much enlarged role in the life of Israel. From the description of the efforts Ezra himself put forth to enlist them as members of his returning entourage, one gets the impression that it had been his hope that they might even be equals of the Zadokites in the new Jerusalem he was intent upon creating (cf. Ezra 8:24–30). However, that there were obstacles to such a plan becomes apparent from a close reading of Nehemiah (as earlier noted). There we learn that while Levites had been given an ever expanding repertoire of duties in the early stages of the reforms (Neh. 12:44–47), their place in this community remained an extremely precarious one, for after returning to Judea for a *second* term as governor, Nehemiah discovered to his dismay that Levite families he had earlier appointed to temple duties in Jerusalem had been forced to return to their farms for lack of support (Neh. 13:10). As a consequence, we are told, Nehemiah then appointed them to temple duties all over again, only this time making sure they could not be excluded (Neh. 13:10–22). In short, a committee was struck made up of both priests *and* Levites to see to it that support for the Levites would henceforth be forthcoming as required (Neh. 13:13). Furthermore, and most importantly, at the book's very end it is reported that Nehemiah drew up "regulations for the priests and Levites, defining each man's duty" (Neh. 13:30). This concluding information comes as something of a shock, for it suggests that the respective duties of these priestly guilds were *even yet* not entirely specified, and that it was *right at this juncture* that this lacuna in priestly law was filled. That being the case, we are left wondering where in the extant scriptures or traditions of this community such "regulations" might be found? Scanning the Pentateuch (where priestly legislation of all sorts is now deposited) reveals they are not there.[16]

A solution to the conundrum we are left with at the close of Nehemiah is provided by a closer look at the books of Chronicles which immediately follow in the talmudic listing cited earlier. Contained within these books are regulations pertaining to the very matter identified at the close of Nehemiah. Here, the respective duties of priests and Levites are spelled out with a clarity that is evident in no other biblical writings (see esp. 1 Chron. 23–27). Might then at least one of the functions of Chronicles (coming as it does at the end of the biblical library) have been to supply users of this temple compendium (and administrators of the temple) with the requisite guidelines for a proper understanding of the duties of these two guilds? Several recent studies of Chronicles have come to this very conclusion. From a survey of the so-called cult "Regulation Formula" in these volumes (that is, commands of David or the Davidic kings regarding specific matters of ritual or clerical assignment), Simon J. de Vries has come to believe that one of the central purposes of these books was "the legitimation of the Levites as rivals to the priests in the Restoration cult."[17] This was accomplished through the narration of David's status as Israel's new cult founder alongside of Moses.[18] In yet another study with comparable conclusions John W. Wright has noted the very special importance within this literature of the body of cultic legislation ascribed to David in 1 Chronicles 23–27.[19] At the beginning of these chapters David is depicted preparing for the succession of his kingdom to Solomon by summoning "all the leaders of Israel" before him, both priests and Levites" (1 Chron. 23:2). He then outlines the respective duties of these two groups, with particular attention to the duties of the Levites. Wright characterizes these chapters as the "central narrative within the Chronicler's account of David's reign" and "the chief legacy of David within the Chronicler's history."[20] He believes they were meant to serve within the entire corpus of Ezra-Nehemiah and Chronicles as a legitimation for "the proper order of temple personnel, especially in times of national and cultic renewal."[21]

In this light, it seems logical to assume that the placement of the

books of Chronicles at the end of the Hebrew scriptures was intention-
al and purposeful. These volumes follow Ezra-Nehemiah (concluding
the scriptural corpus) because those who compiled this library wished
its readers to know the identity, duties and theology of those who compiled it.[22] In *Ezra-Nehemiah* climactic reforms are described that are
said to have brought the Israelite people into a state of unity and obedience unprecedented in any previous era of reform and renewal. In
Chronicles the duties and theology of the personnel appointed to
implement those reforms are delineated, so that Israel might remain in
just such a condition of obedience and renewal. What those duties
were emerges both in what is said regarding David's specific regulations of the cult just before his death, *as well as* in the descriptions of
the activities and regulations of subsequent reforming kings who followed in David's footsteps. In both cases precedents were established
that must have been viewed by the compilers of these books as valid
and still in effect in their time.

What, specifically, were the duties outlined for the Levites in the
pages of Chronicles? According to 1 Chron. 23:3–5 David assigned
them a fourfold set of tasks:

> –*service of the House of Yahweh,* that is, helping the sons of
> Aaron in the care of the courts and rooms, the purification of
> the holy things, the arrangement of various meal offerings (1
> Chron. 23:28), and oversight of "the treasures" (1 Chron.
> 26:20–28);

> –*service as officials and judges,* that is, taking charge in "all
> matters pertaining to God and the king" in whatever regions of
> the kingdom their services were needed (1 Chron. 26:29–32);

> –*gatekeepers,* that is, "duties just like their brothers' of serving
> in the house of Yahweh" (1 Chron. 26:12);

> –*liturgical musicians,* that is, being "present every morning to
> give thanks and praise to Yahweh, and also in the evening, and
> at the bringing of every burnt offering to Yahweh on Sabbath,
> New Moon or solemn feast, appearing regularly before Yahweh

in accordance with the numbers required of them" (1 Chron. 23:30–31).

Under several reformist kings Levite roles and duties prescribed by David were not simply reactivated, but enlarged and embellished:

–under *Jehoshaphat,* Levites are said to have been dispatched throughout "all the towns of Judah" to serve as instructors in "the book of the Law of Yahweh" (2 Chron. 17:9); they were also active in judicial reforms in Jerusalem (2 Chron. 19:8–11);

–under *Joash,* they were appointed to collect monies for the repair of the temple (2 Chron. 24:4–14);

–under *Hezekiah,* they took leadership in the sanctification of the Temple and in preparations for renewing the people's covenant with Yahweh (2 Chron. 29:3–15); indeed, in this aspect of their duties, it is stated, they proved themselves "more conscientious about sanctifying themselves than the priests" (29:34), with the consequence that in the aftermath of this reform, a fund was created by the citizens of Jerusalem to enable certain ones of them to "devote themselves to the Law of Yahweh" (2 Chron. 31:4);

–finally, under *Josiah,* their role as scholars ("men of understanding") whose expertise was available to "all Israel" was formally acknowledged (2 Chron. 35:3), and Levites were appointed "for each family division" to assist in the preparations for a Passover (35:6) the likes of which had not been experienced since the days of the prophet Samuel (35:18).

What is impressive about this portrait of Levite responsibilities is its communal scope and depth. The Levites are said to be the temple personnel chiefly responsible for giving voice to the meaning and relevance of Israelite faith both inside and outside the temple precincts; the only duties not open to them were those pertaining to animal sacrifices at the altar (1 Chron. 16:39–40) and the "burning of incense" (1 Chron. 23:12–13). Especially noteworthy is the report in 2 Chron. 31:4 that during the Hezekiah reforms a fund was created by the citizens of Jerusalem to enable certain of them to "devote themselves to the Law of Yahweh" (2 Chron. 35:3). The existence of just such a publicly funded scholarly guild at this time already is precisely what would have to be postulated from our prior survey of the redactional history of "the Law and the Prophets" (in Ch. 7) were we not informed of it. Talmudic sources which state that a guild of this kind ("the men of the Great Assembly") also played a role during the Second Temple period in transmitting and teaching Israel's sacred literary traditions thus appear to be more credible than often thought. With this in mind, it is important that we look more closely at the full complement of books in the scriptural library that was eventually compiled.

Chapter Nine

EDITING AND ADDING
"THE OTHER BOOKS"

*The "Writings" appended to "the Law and the Prophets"
were as carefully and purposefully created and added as
were the books of the earlier sections, and with similar
goals in view: to provide resources for Israel's unification
and renewal.*

In addition to Ezra-Nehemiah and Chronicles, nine books were
eventually added to "the Law and the Prophets" to form the third section of the Hebrew scriptures, making eleven books in all. According
to the Rabbis of the Mishna the proper list and arrangement of these
are: Ruth, Psalms, Job, Proverbs, Ecclesiastes, Song of Songs,
Lamentations, Daniel and Esther, Ezra–Nehemiah and Chronicles
(Baba Bathra 14b).[1] In the Foreword to Sirach these volumes are vari-
ously referred to as "the others," "the other books of the fathers," or
"the other books"; in the Talmud they are known as "the Hagiographa"
(Holy Writings), and in Jewish Bibles today, simply as "the Writings."
The nature, purpose and history of this collection will be the focus of
the following discussion.

A. Introductory Comments to "the Writings" as a Whole

The rather fluctuating, nondescript titles used to identify the
books of this section have misled some into thinking that they were of
lesser importance to the custodians of these scriptures than were the
prior books of this library.[2] That this was not the case becomes at once
evident in the careful manner in which they are arranged. This com-

pares with the arrangement of books in "the Law and the Prophets" where each book follows the other on a time-line which, in this case, extends from the period of the judges (Ruth) up to the Persian period (Esther) just prior to the reforms of Ezra and Nehemiah. The impression conveyed is that all of these added "Writings" are related somehow to the ideals and goals of these reforms.[3] That precisely *eleven* scrolls were added to the previous thirteen scrolls of "the Law and the Prophets" may also be significant, for in this way the total library was enlarged to *twenty-four* scrolls. Taking a clue from Ezra's action of consecrating *two* groups of twelve men, twelve priests and twelve Levites (Ezra 8:24), when transmitting the Temple treasures to Jerusalem, and noting too that "twenty-four" is the number of priestly divisions and Levite choirs which Chronicles states were posted for duty at the Temple (1 Chron. 24:7–18; 25:7–31), it seems not impossible that "twenty-four" (the sum of two twelves) was meant to connote the unity of the combined temple guilds. Perhaps from the beginning the plan was to create a library of twenty-four books *in two blocks of twelve,* for "the Law and the Prophets" by themselves, apart from the "Writings," can be viewed as just such a twenty-four scroll collection if the individual booklets of the scroll of "the Twelve" are counted separately. Were that the case, however, the decision to enlarge the collection meant that room had to be created for the additional books by combining the smaller prophetic books into one volume. Likewise, as new scrolls were added (right up to the period of the hellenist persecutions, as in the case of Daniel and Esther), other scrolls also may have been combined or removed to make room for the new ones. In any case, as it now lies before us, the scroll of "the Twelve" is situated in the collection's middle, where it functions as the last of "the Prophets," but also as the first of a second block of twelve scrolls. Thus, as now configured, this scriptural library may be characterized as made up of two blocks of twelve scrolls with the scroll of the Twelve at its center.

1	2	3	4	5	6	7	8	9	10	11	12	1	2	3	4	5	6	7	8	9	10	11	12
G	E	L	N	D	J	J	S	K	J	E	I	T	R	P	J	P	E	S	L	D	E	E	C
E	X	E	U	E	O	U	A	I	E	Z	S	H	U	S	O	R	C	O	A	A	S	Z	H
N	O	V	M	U	S	D	M	N	R	E	A	E	T	A	B	O	C	N	M	N	T	R	R
								G		K			H	L		V	L	G				A	O
												T		M								N	N
												W		S								E	
												E										H	
												L											
												V											
												E											

From these observations the impression grows that "the Writings" appended to "the Law and the Prophets" were as purposefully created and added as were the books of the earlier sections, and with similar goals in view: to provide resources for Israel's unification and renewal along the lines envisioned by those responsible for the Ezra-Nehemiah reforms. This is confirmed by an analysis of the editorial features and contents of these volumes, which indicate that those who edited and added these books were already familiar with "the Law and the Prophets" and were preparing these books for study by an audience likewise steeped in this older literature.[4] This suggests that those who were responsible for this project were members of the same Levite guilds that were custodians of the older library, and that the goal of these additional "Writings" was to strengthen the faith and allegiance of those who had already dedicated themselves to the way of Yahweh set forth there. In the review that follows I will first examine each of the nine "writings" in the order specified in Baba Bathra 14b, attempting to identify what the purpose might have been for adding each one, and then comment on the group as a whole.

B. THE INDIVIDUAL SCROLLS

1. Ruth

It may seem odd at first that this short, beautifully crafted book should follow the Scroll of the Twelve and stand first among the books added to "the Law and the Prophets." However, it is surely no accident that it introduces us to the ancestors of David (Ruth 4:17f), a man whose piety and achievements were of such great importance to the Levite custodians of this library.[5] Furthermore, by revealing that among those ancestors was a Moabitess who had found "refuge" in Yahweh (2:12) and married a leading Israelite citizen, its author (or authors) simultaneously address two issues that were of burning relevance to those who had taken up the cause of the Ezra-Nehemiah reforms: how receptive to be to converts from other nations, and what to do about intermarriage with foreigners. At the time "the Law and the Prophets" were being compiled expectations were running high that the peoples of the world were about to convert to Yahweh (Isa. 56:1–8; 66:18–21; Jer. 3:17; Zech. 2:15; 8:20–23).[6] It also seems apparent from the polemical qualities of a few of these scriptures (Jonah, for example), that some in the community were resistant to these expectations. Not all agreed that Yahweh's temple should one day be "a house of prayer for all peoples" (Isa. 56:7; cp. Ezek. 44:9).

It is hard to avoid the impression that the story of Ruth was meant to address this issue. Both her Moabite identity (1:4, 22; 2:2, 6, 10–13, 21; 4:5, 10) and her conversion are strongly emphasized. Early in the story she is shown beseeching her Israelite mother-in-law to accompany her to her homeland: "... wherever you go, I shall go, wherever you live, I shall live. Your people will be my people, and your God will be my God" (Ruth 1:16). Then, soon after arriving in Israel, in response to Ruth's plaintive question as to why she, "a foreigner," is being so graciously treated, Boaz praises her for her decision "to come to a people" of whom she "previously knew nothing," and prays that Yahweh, the God of Israel, "under whose wings" she has "come for refuge," may richly reward her (Ruth 2:10–12). It is difficult to think that noble words such as these on the lips of a leading Israelite citizen were not meant to encourage greater warmth and receptivity toward converts coming to Israel from other nations.

But as the story unfolds we learn that Ruth is not only warmly accepted in her new-found community, but more astonishingly still, she is taken to wife by the same leading citizen who had at first praised her. As such, this little booklet could be thought of as a hermeneutical supplement and counterpoint to the strictures against marrying foreign women which are found in other parts of this Temple library, most especially Deuteronomy, Malachi, and Ezra-Nehemiah. It should be clearly noted, however, that the issue under consideration in *those* books was the threat posed by intermarriage with foreigners who were still tied to "the disgusting practices" of their native cultures (Deut. 7:3; Mal. 2:10–12; Ezra 9:11–12), whereas Ruth is an example of a "woman of character" (Ruth 3:11; cp. Prov. 31:10) who had undergone a sincere conversion to faith in Yahweh. Noting how carefully the book's authors work with ancient Israelite laws and traditions (for example, the rules governing responsibilities toward a childless widow) to justify this marriage, the conclusion has been drawn that what they were aiming at was to show that marriages such as this should not be automatically stigmatized, no matter what the Torah has to say against Moabites being admitted to the assembly of Yahweh (cf. Deut. 23:3–6).[7] Thus, while introducing us to David, this first of the "the books of the Fathers" (as they are called in the Preface to Sirach) does much more: it encourages greater openness to foreign converts and intimates that even intermarriage with foreign women can be justified if community traditions are fully honored and the person in question is a convert and a "woman of character" like Ruth.

2. Psalms

Gerald H. Wilson believes the traditional idea of the Psalter as "the Hymn Book" of the Second Temple" is "rather unfortunate" in that it "obscures the indications that in its 'final form' the Psalter is a book to be read rather than to be *performed;* to be *meditated over* rather than to be *recited from.*"[8] One such indication of the "intentions" of those who compiled this volume is Psalm 1, where an individual is pronounced blessed who avoids the company of cynics and sinners (1:1) and meditates on Yahweh's Torah "day and night" (1:3); such a person, it is said, stands tall in "the gathering of the upright" and will prosper (1:3–5), for "Yahweh watches over" his path (1:6). Forming an "assembly" of studious Torah-faithful members of this kind was the goal of the Ezra-Nehemiah reforms (Neh. 8, 10; cp. Deut. 17:18f.; 30; Joshua 1:8). The placement of this Psalm at the Psalter's opening suggests that the compilation of prayers, hymns, and teachings that follows was meant as a personal devotional resource for the spiritual formation of just such individuals in such an assembly. The organization of the Psalter's 150 Psalms into a five-book structure like that of the

five books of the Torah (1–41; 42–72; 73–89; 90–106; 107–150) reinforces this impression, as if to say, "here is a volume for the strengthening of individuals and communities who study and live by the Torah
of Yahweh."

But in what sense? How concretely did this book's final compilers imagine it would serve as a resource for someone studying the
Torah of Yahweh? A closer look at the Psalter's contents suggests it
was meant to do this in at least two ways. First of all, reading or praying these prayers helps the Torah-faithful individual persevere in
Yahweh's way in the face of all kinds of troubles and challenges.
More specifically, the many Psalms expressing personal confidence
and trust in Yahweh in the face of adversity teach such an individual
how to pray, how to confess and give thanks, with the same boldness
that David displayed at so many points in his life.[9] Additional Psalms
reinforce the ideal set forth in Psalm 1 of fidelity to the covenant and
of Torah-study as the only true pathway to happiness and blessing (19;
25; 34; 40; 103; 119). Still others, with roots in Israel's wisdom traditions, openly confront the doubts that can arise in the face of glaring
injustices or unmerited sufferings (37; 49; 73). In these and other ways
the resolve of the Torah-faithful individual is strengthened in the face
of the difficulties and incongruities of human existence.

But not just the challenges and problems of *individual* existence
are addressed in these Psalms, but those as well of the *collective* destiny of both Israel and the world. In the light of past sins and judgments is there a future for Israel or the world? Such were the questions
that hung heavy over Second Temple Judaism in the aftermath of the
collapse of hopes for a restoration of the second Davidic commonwealth, and there is reason to believe they grew stronger with the passing of the years. Redactional study of the Psalter has recently brought
to light the remarkable way this compilation addresses these issues
through the placement of key royal Psalms at "the seams" of the first
three books: Psalm 2 at the opening of Book One, Psalm 72 at the end
of Book Two and Psalm 89 at the end of Book Three. These are all
psalms which emphasize Yahweh's covenant or oath to David that his
dynasty will one day inaugurate a reign of uprightness and peace
throughout the world (2:10; 72:11; 89:25) and that Yahweh will *never*
forsake his promise to do this (Psalm 89:19–37). It is Wilson's opinion
that these psalms were positioned in this manner not only to validate or

celebrate this promissory oath, but as a foil for the doubts and questions which it poses, and that Book Three especially, with its climactic sequence of laments and questions as to why Yahweh's "annointed" is so abandoned (Psalm 89:46–51), should be viewed as having been deliberately fashioned to serve as a backdrop for an alternative vision of what to hope for as this comes to expression in the psalms of Books Four and Five (90–150).[10] Others, however, have rightly noted that Book Three reflects an exilic environment and perspective (see Psalms 74, 79, 80, 83, 85:1–8, 89:39–52) and was likely produced and completed in that milieu.[11] I suggest in addition that Books One and Two were compiled even earlier, in the wake of the Assyrian invasions of the eighth century BCE and as part of the Levitical reforms during the reign of Hezekiah that produced first editions of Deuteronomy and the Deuteronomistic History and an early edition of the book of Proverbs.[12] This would explain the chastened, but still vibrant confidence in this part of the Psalter that David's dynasty will yet become the instrument of God's universal rule (Psalms 2; 72) and that Zion will survive and endure (even in the midst of international turmoil) as a place of security and blessing for God's people (Psalm 46, 48), so long as they are faithful to his covenant (Psalms 44; 50). In other words, Books One and Two reflect the thoughts and expectations of those Levitical circles responsible for initiating the Hezekiah and Josiah reforms in the wake of the fall of the northern Kingdom, and Book Three gives voice to their still tenaciously held conviction that the restoration of Davidic rule in Jerusalem was something yet to be fervently hoped and prayed for, despite the passage of time since the destruction of Jerusalem by the Babylonians and the humiliation of Yahweh's "annointed" (Psalm 89:51).[13]

It does appear from a careful reading of Books Four and Five that this hope was modified during the final editing of the Psalter in the period following the reforms of Ezra-Nehemiah. There are no Psalms in Book Four (90–106) that evoke the kind of regal expectations alluded to in Psalms 1, 72 and 89, although in one instance the profile of an ideal Davidic ruler is sketched (Psalm 101). Rather, beginning with Psalm 90 (the only Psalm in the Psalter attributed to Moses), what is emphasized instead is the universal and ageless rule of Yahweh alone (Psalm 90–100), and his tender father-like love toward those who fear him and are faithful to his covenant (Psalm 102), More concretely what

is emphasized is the hope that *Zion* will yet play a role in the glorification of Yahweh's name among the nations (Psalm 102:12–17) and that
the God who so wisely cares for the whole creation will yet be mindful
of his promise to Abraham and gather his people "from among the
nations" that they might give thanks and honor to his holy name
(106:45–47). In the rich collage of theological motifs assembled here,
Zadokite and Levite traditions appear to have been artfully combined
to evoke a new vision of the future that both embraces and transcends
the one fomerly associated with the Davidic dynasty. In this respect
the theology of this final section of the Psalter appears to be similar to
that of Isaiah 55:1–5, where "the favors promised to David" are recon-
ceptualized as a new and "everlasting covenant" with the people as a
whole, so that now Israel collectively is called to be "a witness to the
peoples, a leader and lawgiver" to foreign nations who will "hurry to
you for the sake of Yahweh your God, because the Holy One of Israel
has glorified you" (Isa. 55:5; cp. Psalm 102:21).

It seems no accident, therefore, that in Book Five the three
strategically placed royal Psalms (Psalm 110; 132; 144) are surround-
ed and followed, not by words of lament (as at the end of Psalm 89),
but by a symphony of gratitude and praise (133–136)—and in two
instances, by acrostic poems (the last of these attributed to David himself) extolling Yahweh *alone* for his "deliverance" of his people
(Psalm 111) and his "mighty deeds" to all the children of Adam
(Psalm 145). Prominent too in this *final* Book is the *unity* of the House
of Israel under the leadership of Aaron *and* Levi, who together with all
who "fear Yahweh" sing praise to Yahweh (135:19–20). It is from this
united community that the invitation goes out to "all nations" to join in
this "alleluia" chorus (117). Thus, thanks and praise rise to a crescendo
of universal worship in the Psalms of this section, especially from
Psalm 145 onward.[14] Looked at in the light of this ending, the goals of
this volume become even clearer. Those who compiled it were intent
not only on strengthening isolated individuals, but the individual as a
member of the covenanted "assembly" (cf. Psalm 111:1)—and their
goal was not just that Israel might prosper and be saved, but that the
whole world might eventually join in worshiping Yahweh, thereby fulfilling the hope of a universal rule of God on earth first glimpsed in
connection with the Davidic royal covenant. The theological architec-

ture of the Psalter and that of "the Law and the Prophets" are in this respect remarkably similar.[15]

3. Job

One might say that the conviction that Yahweh "acts only in faithful love" toward "all who call on him from the heart" (Psalm 145:17; Deut. 32:4) was at the core of the scriptures the Levites assembled (their foundational credo, so to speak). But is this belief true to life, true to reality? Doubts that it is are not infrequently voiced in these very same scriptures. "There is a tradition for such questioning at the heart of Israel's faith," writes Roland Murphy.[16] The addition of the book of Job to the temple library, a large scroll devoted to this very issue, bears testimony to the intensity with which these doubts were openly debated among the guilds who compiled these scriptures. The book's chief persona is a non-Israelite hero of proverbial goodness otherwise unknown except for the writings of the Zadokite prophet Ezekiel (14:14, 20). Job experiences a series of catastrophes, and the point of view of Job's friends is that since sin leads to suffering, uprightness to health and prosperity, Job must have sinned and should repent. Job does not deny that he has sinned, but questions the proportionality of his sin to his suffering, or that all that happens in life can be so neatly explained in this manner. As such, Job may be viewed as giving voice to Zadokite questioning of Levite theology: can this theology which places such a high premium on the links between sin and suffering, obedience and blessing be superimposed on the realities of the world without severely distorting or misconstruing them?

Job's passionate probing of these issues is affirmed by the speech of Yahweh in the book's final chapter: Job, not his friends, was in the right (42:7). And yet, Job's fortunes *are* restored (42:10–17), proof that persistent goodness is rewarded after all! Looking at the book as it now lies before us, one has the impression that an attempt was being made to accommodate and reconcile contradictory perspectives. At issue was not just theodicy (justifying the ways of God), but also the role *wisdom* may legitimately play in unraveling life's *ultimate* enigmas.[17] Job's search is affirmed, but not without qualification. A mere mortal can only fathom so much and no more, this book seems to be saying. There come points when further progress in our quest for meaning can be made only if the one who created us himself addresses us (Job 38–42).

In one especially notable chapter (breaking sharply into the book's flow) the question is posed: "But where does wisdom come from? Where is intelligence to be found?" (28:12). The answer given is that wisdom of the kind Job is striving for (wisdom about the whys and wherefores of *everything* that happens under the sun) is inaccessible: "No human being knows the way to her" (28:13). Only God knows the path of wisdom, because only he (as creator) is fully conscious of the complexity of the world in its totality. The conclusion drawn is that those too are wise who know the limits of human wisdom and in humility "turn from evil" and "fear Yahweh" (28:28). Job is portrayed as having himself reached that point in the course of his epic quest (42:6). The book of Job has the appearance of an unfinished symphony.[18] That it was preserved in its present somewhat chaotic, incomplete form is testimony to the esteem it was accorded despite this fact (perhaps even because of it). Perhaps its critique of a too rigid version of Levite theodicy was thought to have merit, even among those who were certain of God's righteous rule of the universe. At the same time, it declares unequivocally that this critique must itself be critiqued and tempered by a humility that recognizes that as mere mortals our wisdom is limited.

4. Proverbs

The identity of the final editors of this huge compendium of wisdom literature (the largest of any known to us from the world of its time) may be hinted at in the short collection of teachings near its end attributed to "Agur" (Prov. 30:1–9). Agur (meaning "compiler") frankly admits to being an ignoramus when it comes to metaphysical issues such as the "name" of the deity who created the universe (30:2–4; cp. Deut. 30:12–14; Job 38). On matters such as this, he (faithful Yahwist that he was) is quite content to be guided by "God's every word" (Prov. 30:5; cp. Deut. 30:14). To this word *no* additions should be made, he says (Prov. 30:6), repeating what is stated in Deut. 4:2. In other words, the wisdom assembled here is in no sense to be understood as a replacement or addition to the teachings enshrined in the Torah of Yahweh given to Moses. God grant, he prays in the only prayer of its kind in the book, that neither poverty nor wealth should ever cause him to fall away and say "Yahweh—who is Yahweh?" (30:7–9; cp. Deut. 6:12). It was to strengthen and enrich the hearts and minds of devout covenant-loyal Israelites such as this that this compilation was made in the form it now has. In other words, just as in the Psalter older collections of hymns and prayers of David and others were arranged, supplemented and edited to serve as a resource for Torah-faithful individuals in the period after the Ezra-Nehemiah reforms, so also, it appears, in the book of Proverbs a similar thing was done with an older tradition of wisdom associated with Solomon and others among the ruling elite of Jerusalem.

More specifically, as now edited, to a major collection of Solomonic "proverbs" (10:1–22:16) have been added a compendium of introductory teachings (chs. 1–9) and a series of appendices bearing an array of titles: "Sayings of the sages" (22:17–24:22), "also from the sages" (24:23–34), "more of Solomon's proverbs, transcribed at the court of Hezekiah king of Judah" (25:1–29:27), "sayings of Agur" (30:1–33), "sayings of Lemuel" (31:1–9; 31:10–31). Precisely when and how this large "collection of collections" was assembled and arrived at its final form is still a matter of some considerable debate and uncertainty, as is the issue of the place of wisdom teachings generally within Jewish theology.[19] That the book's final editors had some exceedingly pressing and important pedagogical goals in mind is nevertheless apparent. Thus, the sentence which they carefully placed at its forefront in Prov. 1:7 (and which is repeated in one form or another throughout the corpus) declares categorically that "the fear of Yahweh" is the essential starting point for the acquisition of the kind of wisdom represented by the compilation as it now exists (one notable text calls "the fear of Yahweh" a "school of wisdom").[20] In other words, those who engage in the type of wisdom study for which *this* compilation is designed are never to forget that respect for the ways of Yahweh as set forth in his Torah and delight in his commandments (which is what "fear of Yahweh" means according to Psalms 128; 11:19; 112:1) is an absolute essential if one is to make any progress in becoming wise.[21] At the same time, one is a "fool" to "spurn wisdom and discipline" and not build on this foundation and learn "yet more" (1:5, 7b; 9:4). This is why the older teachings of the collection which reflect the court traditions and professional needs of the Jerusalem royal establishment as taught by professional sages (Prov. 22:17) are regarded as still valid and valuable. However, before turning to these collections, it is important (they seem to be saying by the way they have organized the collection) that one begin by first paying attention to the instructions of covenant-loyal *fathers and mothers* (1:8f.; cp. 6:20–23 and Deut. 6:6–9; 11:18–21), and that one learn how to avoid sinners (1:10–19) and affairs with foreign women (2:16–19; 5:1–23; 6:20–35; 7:6–27), and how to be a person of character who trusts Yahweh rather than "your own perception" (3:1–8). In other words, the primary purpose of the volume (as presently edited) was to help young people and parents who "fear Yahweh" to learn what it means to be wise, so that they can be even better members of Yahweh's covenant-faithful people (become even more respectful of Yahweh and even more knowledgeable of God) and thereby be among the "good people" for whom the land is "their home" (Prov. 1:33; 2:1–6, 20–22; cp. Deut. 32:47).

But what, more specifically, *is* the "wisdom" they are referring to here, and how *will* it serve the ends and goals alluded to in these opening teachings of the book? The cluster of definitions placed before the reader in the book's very first words (1:2–6) suggests that they had in mind very broadly, *all* that pertains to human thoughtfulness, the use of one's mind for study and reflection. Elsewhere, those who lack wisdom are characterized as gullible and naive, ready to believe anything, as being hotheaded and reckless (14:15f.). The wise, on the other hand, "give thought to their ways" (14:8, 15), "fear and shun evil" (14:16), look ahead, "see danger and take refuge" (22:3). What is especially valued here is the ability to track consequences and see connections (what forms of behavior result in what kinds of outcomes). The devout in Israel believed that studying Yahweh's Torah can by itself make one wise in this sense (see Psalm 19:7; 119:97–104; cp. Deut. 4:6). In addition, the editors of Proverbs seem to have believed that studying wisdom can in turn enhance one's understanding of Yahweh's Torah. In other words, while becoming wise may be a fruit *of* Torah study, it is also essential *for* studying the Torah.[22]

It was only a small step from this perception to the far-reaching epistemological conclusions drawn in the poem that stands at the climax of the prefatory teachings of Proverbs, in 8:1–31. Here wisdom, in an address presented to the whole of humanity, declares that she alone is the source of *all* truth, knowledge, fairness, and all right laws made by kings and rulers on earth (8:1–16). She is this, the poem goes on to state, by virtue of the fact that she alone was with Yahweh prior to and during the creation of the universe, hence is cognizant of everything he did and does (8:22–31; cp. 3:19–20). Long before Abraham or Moses or any other form of law or knowledge on earth, there was wisdom, the poem declares; wisdom is thus anterior to everything except God himself. It was this perspective that made it possible for those who compiled and edited "the Law and the Prophets" to both design and see meaning in the total world-story recited there. The book of Proverbs is at the same time the most practical and the most philosophical of all the books added to the Law and the Prophets. Like the Psalter it served both to undergird the fidelity of covenant-faithful individuals, and also to enlarge their minds and hearts so that life in all its complexity throughout the universe could be seen as the domain of one universally ruling and caring deity (16:4).[23]

5. Ecclesiastes

This too is a wisdom booklet, but with a quite different purpose than the book of Proverbs. More like Job, it seems to reflect ongoing debates among the compilers and editors of the Hebrew scriptures over the place and importance of wisdom per se in the instructional enterprise to which they were devoted, for in its opening discourses its author adopts the persona of a youthful Solomon who wants to understand "everything that happens under heaven" (1:12). "I have acquired a greater stock of wisdom than anyone before me in Jerusalem," Solomon declares. "I myself have mastered every kind of wisdom and science" (1:16). Yet it availed him little or nothing, the author states. Such a pretentious approach to life by means of wisdom alone is branded "futile," "chasing after the wind" (1:14). Later on he states in his own voice that after "having applied myself to acquiring wisdom and to observing the activity taking place in the world," he was forced to conclude that

> you cannot get to the bottom of everything taking place under the sun; you may wear yourself out in the search, but

you will never find it. Not even a sage can get to the bottom of it, even if he says that he has done so (8:17).

The protest here is thus not against the pursuit of wisdom as such. Qoheleth "weighed, studied and emended many proverbs," we are told in the epilogue to his book (12:9), and there is proof of this in his small collection of wry sayings in chapter 10. "Wisdom is worth more than weapons of war," he writes (9:18a). The protest of this book is against Solomonic pretensions that by wisdom *alone* life can be mastered. It is a protest against overestimating wisdom's power either to understand or to master human existence. Yes, "wisdom is worth more than weapons of war," but "a single sin [or sinner] undoes a great deal of good" (9:18b). Like Job and Proverbs, Qoheleth counsels humility as the "beginning" of wisdom. "I know that whatever God does shall be forever—to this there is nothing to add, from this there is nothing to subtract, and the way God acts inspires fear" (3:14). "Therefore, fear God" (5:6). "God will call you to account for everything" (11:9). "Remember your Creator while you are still young ..." (12:1). "To sum up the whole matter: fear God and keep his commandments, for that is the duty of everyone. For God will call all our deeds to judgment, all that is hidden, be it good or bad" (12:13f.).[24] Solomonic wisdom untempered and unrelated to the wisdom of Yahweh's Torah revealed to Moses is an inadequate resource or foundation for arriving at a meaningful understanding or approach to life—this seems to be the overall message of this book. It is one the Levites earlier sought to convey through their historical overview of the Solomonic reign in Kings where it is subtly implied that, after Solomon's dismissal of them from the priesthood, his great wisdom did not save him from apostasy. Only wisdom linked to Yahweh's Torah is true wisdom (again, see 1 Chron. 22:12f.).

6. Song of Songs

The Song of Songs, with its celebration of the delights of nuptial love, may have been added to fill a gap in the canonical library. There is evidence for believing that high among the objectives of the groups responsible for compiling this library was the renewal and preservation of Israelite family values in the face of trends toward infidelity, divorce and intermarriage.[25] To meet this crisis renewed emphasis was placed on fidelity and love and the sacredness of vows made before God at the time of the wedding (Mal. 2:13–16; Prov. 2:16–19). However, there is an obvious deficiency right at this point in the literature thus far assembled: poetry and songs celebrating the erotic love of those being married is in very short supply (the only other example being Psalm 45). In the cycle of poems in Song 3:6–5:1 the poetic dialogue between the male groom, personified as King Solomon on his wedding day (3:7, 9, 11), and his "promised bride" (4:10–12; 5:1), unfolds without a trace of prudery toward the ecstasy of their first full sexual embrace (4:16–5:1). In an especially beautiful concluding poem the bride exclaims that her love for her betrothed "is as a flash of fire, a flame of Yahweh himself" (8:6; cp. Deut. 4:24); she wants her husband to "seal her" indelibly on his heart, tattoo her on his arm (8:6; cp. Prov. 3:3; Deut. 6:6; 11:18; Jer. 31:33). The betrothed says in response that his love for her "no flood can quench, no torrents drown. Were a man to offer all his family wealth to buy love, contempt is all that he would gain" (8:7). Their dialogue reads like a dramatization of the creation account in Gen. 2:22-24, where the man upon first beholding the woman Yahweh created as his companion cried out: "This ... at last is bone of my bones and flesh of my flesh" (Gen. 2:23)—and the narrator explains: "This is why a man leaves his father and mother and becomes attached to his wife, and they become one flesh" (2:24). "In the rest of the Bible marriage is usually viewed from a social point of view, the union of families and property, and the importance of descendants," comments Roland Murphy. "In the Song sexual love is treated as a value in and for itself."[26]

7. Lamentations

The focus of every one of the five chapters of this book is the catastrophe that occurred at the apex of the history recounted in "the Law and the Prophets": the destruction of Jerusalem and the deportation of the surviving citizens of Judah in 586 (2 Kings 25). Commonly referred to as laments, these carefully constructed acrostic poems are more appropriately called "meditations," for their acrostic format was seemingly designed to help their devout readers come to terms with this pivotal event of Israelite history through a process of prayerful reflection.[27] The focus of the first two poems is on the tragic aspects of the event itself as an act of Yahweh in fulfillment of a threat made long ago through prophets (2:17). Especially emphasized is the horrific irony that "the greatest of nations" (1:1) is now "living among the nations" (1:3) and "heathens enter her sanctuary whom you had forbidden to enter your Assembly" (1:10). "Look, Yahweh, and consider: whom have you ever treated like this?" (2:20).

In the prayers of ch. 3 the focus shifts to the struggles of those living in the aftermath of this catastrophe and, looking back, wondering what to expect next and what to do. Here a variety of spiritual strategies are advocated as a means for coming to terms with these astonishing developments: contemplation of Yahweh's inexhaustible mercies and goodness which are new every morning (3:22–23); readiness to trust and hope in the midst of irrational adversity (3:24–33); willingness to place one's confidence in Yahweh's just rule of the universe despite evidence to the contrary (3:37–39); reflection over the lessons of the past and a resolve in repentance to return to Yahweh (3:37–41). This is quintessential Levite theology and piety as it took shape among those of the Second Temple who were striving to be faithful to Yahweh in the wake of the Ezra-Nehemiah reforms.

The fourth meditation picks up themes introduced earlier in the first and second meditations, such as the note of astonishment that "kings of the earth" were able to penetrate the gates of Jerusalem (something no "inhabitants of the world" ever thought would be possible, 4:12). But a new theme is introduced when *Jerusalem* prophets and priests are singled out as chiefly responsible for this catastrophe (4:13–16). Here too the fate of the Davidic king ("Yahweh's anointed") is mentioned for the first and only time, and what is emphasized is that even he of whom it was said, "In his shadow we shall live among the nations," was "caught in their traps" (4:20). One suspects that, as in the Psalter, the allusion to dashed monarchic hopes was meant to serve as a foil for the meditation that follows in ch. 5, where the certainty of *Yahweh's* enduring rule from age to age is strongly asserted (5:19), this as a counterpoint to the desolations Zion has experienced because of the sins of the ancestors (5:5–18).[28] In the concluding prayer that Yahweh would "make us come back ... and we will come back" and be restored, "unless you have utterly rejected us, in an anger which knows no limit" (5:21), we encounter once again the

ideas, aspirations and fears that were at the heart of the renewal movement launched among the covenant-faithful during the Ezra-Nehemiah
reforms (cp. Ezra 9:10–15; Neh. 9:32–37; Dan. 9:14–19). Norman
Gottwald has suggested that in its final form Lamentations "exhibits a
striking and innovative amalgam of prophetic, Deuteronomistic, and
wisdom notions that subordinates and neutralizes Davidic-Zion traditions without rejecting them outright."[29] This is correct, but this "amalgam" was hardly innovative. Rather, Lamentations is a carefully crafted confessional deposit of the core convictions of those who compiled
the Hebrew scriptures.

8. Daniel

The addition of Daniel to the corpus of Law, Prophets and
Writings must have occurred soon after the second century BCE hellenistic persecutions alluded to at the end of the four visions that make
up the book's final chapters (see Daniel 7:19–22; 8:9–12, 23–25;
9:26–27; 11:21–32). Sabbath observance and circumcision, temple services and sacrifice were banned during this ordeal; also, "books of the
Law that came to light were torn up and burned" (1 Macc. 1:57), and
those were executed who were "discovered possessing a copy of the
covenant or practicing the Law" (1 Macc. 1:57). According to 2 Macc.
2:14, it was at about this time (c. 168 BCE) that the "collection of
books" in Nehemiah's library was removed and "dispersed" for safekeeping. The very existence of Daniel in this library suggests that its
authors may have been among those active in protecting and preserving this invaluable legacy during this dangerous period.[30] They too,
then, would be the ones referred to in Daniel 11:31–35 as the "wise
among the people who instruct many" (11:32)—and also, as those who
"stand firm and take action" (Dan. 11:33; cp. 1 Macc. 1:62). Of them it
was also said that they "knew their God" (11:32), with the consequence that some were slain by "sword and flame, captivity and pil-
lage" (11:33) and were thereby "purged, purified and made clean"
(11:35).

How devoted they were in the study of the very scriptures that
marked them for such a martyrdom is confirmed by what the book of
Daniel has to say about its fictive heroes, Daniel and his friends. These
are described as young men schooled "in every branch of wisdom"

(1:3) who were fiercely "determined not to incur pollution by food and wine from the royal table" (Dan. 1:8; cp. 1 Macc. 1:62f.) and not to worship other gods no matter what the cost (Dan. 3:18). In other words, Daniel and his companions personify the highest ideals of the Torah-faithful of this testing, terrible period.[31] And yet, even wisdom such as theirs had its limits, it seems, for in Daniel 9 he is described as being greatly troubled and perplexed by Jeremiah's prophecy that Jerusalem would be restored in seventy years (Dan. 9:2). This informs us of an ongoing quest among the "wise" of this community over how to understand the fulfillment or non-fulfillment of certain prophecies, focused here on a text in Jeremiah, that looms large not only in "the Law and the Prophets," but in "the Writings" collection which is now nearing completion. The text in question is Jeremiah's prediction in Jer. 29:10 that "when the seventy years granted to Babylon are over," Yahweh will intervene to bring his people back to their homeland and and there give them a future and a hope. Both at the beginning of Ezra (Ezra 1:1) and the end of Chronicles (2 Chron. 36:22) it is announced that "to fulfill the word of Yahweh through Jeremiah, Yahweh roused the spirit of Cyrus king of Persia" to issue a proclamation that would in effect begin the process of realizing these hopes.

What in this light is especially astonishing is that Daniel's prayer of confession on this occasion (Dan. 9:4–19) voices virtually the same sentiments that Ezra and the Levites had expressed some two centuries earlier (Ezra 9:6–15; Neh. 9:5–37): the same sense of shame over the collective history of disobedience that had resulted in the destruction of the first temple; the same reverence for the Torah of Moses; the same prayer for God's power to be manifested in some greater manner so that his name might be glorified in the sight of the nations. What this suggests is that the covenant-faithful of this period were for all intents and purposes still living within a time-frame and theology determined by the Ezra-Nehemiah reforms. In other words, centuries may have passed, empires may have come and gone, but from their point of view the world was essentially the same and had not changed. For all practical purposes they were still in Babylon, still waiting for the fulfillment of Jeremiah's restoration prophecies. Nothing had happened that had moved the Israelite story beyond the very partial and limited restoration and reforms announced and implemented by Ezra and Nehemiah.[32]

At the same time they were also still fully convinced that this was *not* their story's end, the end-point of their history. Daniel's visions may be read as a resounding response to the doubt expressed at the conclusion of Lamentations. There a prayer had been uttered that Yahweh would yet "restore us as we were before unless you have utterly rejected us, in an anger which knows no limit" (Lam. 5:21f.). To that dark doubt ("unless you have utterly rejected us... ") Daniel's visions say "no"—Yahweh has not rejected Israel. God's plan is still intact. There is something yet to happen: a manifestation of God's power so great that it "will shatter and absorb all the previous kingdoms and itself last for ever" (2:44). Jeremiah's seventy-year prophecy remains valid even though seventy *weeks* of years have almost passed. And when the day of its fulfillment comes, those "who are wise" and "have instructed many in uprightness," even though "sleeping in the Land of the Dust," will experience it too, for they will "awaken to everlasting life ... as bright as the stars for all eternity" (Dan. 12:3). What is so impressive about these visions is the degree to which the cosmic and international perspectives of "the Law and the Prophets" are still being fully embraced despite the rather bleak exigencies and experiences of the subsequent Israelite history. The covenant-faithful of Israel are still sustained by a world vision. They still believe that their God is governing and guiding the whole universe with a redemptive goal in mind (2:44f.; 9:24). In that plan "the *people* of the holy ones of the Most High" (Dan. 7:13f.) are still envisioned as playing the decisive role. Through this book, one last time, Israel's unique world-transforming faith in itself and its God has found climactic expression.

9. Esther

Like the scroll of Daniel, Esther appears to have been fashioned in its final form during or immediately after the hellenistic persecutions of the second century BCE. Both use fictive heroes from an era prior to the Ezra-Nehemiah reforms to speak to the issues of their time.[33] In both instances these heroes are examples of courage in the face of religious persecution. Each book in its own way seeks to fortify a covenant-faithful people against apostasy in the face of such attacks on their faith. It should be noted, however, that the assault against Israel described in Esther is of an even more pernicious and dangerous type than the one alluded to in Daniel. In Daniel the opposition mounts a challenge to the people's beliefs; in Esther an evil-minded vice-regent of an all-powerful Persian king was determined to annihilate the Jewish *people* per se, just because they were Jews (Esther 3:13). Through the providence of God the plot failed and those attacked were permitted to defend themselves, which they did with great success (Esther 8:7–12). The outcome was that "light and gladness, joy and honor ... prevailed in every province and in every city ..." and respect for the Jews was so greatly restored that many of their Gentile neighbors converted and became Jews themselves (8:16f.).

To commemorate this miraculous reversal of fortunes, the festival of Purim was authorized (9:30–32). During this festival presents were to be exchanged and gifts made to the poor, and pure joy was to prevail (9:22). There appears to be a connection between this story of astonishing deliverance for the Jews during the reign of a Persian king and the equally astonshing success of the Maccabean revolt and self-defense during the hellenist persecutions of the Jews by Antiochus Epiphanes, as described in 1 Maccabees. The nature of this connection can be seen in the equally evident relationship between the festival of Purim authorized by Esther and the festival authorized by the Maccabeans to commemorate their victory during a climactic assault against Jerusalem mounted by a Syrian general named Nicanor (1 Macc. 7; cp. 2 Macc. 15). The goal of this assault, we are told, was not simply to take back Jerusalem (now in Maccabean hands), but "to exterminate the people" (1 Macc. 7:26). It is understandable, therefore, that Nicanor's defeat by the Maccabean-led forces on the *thirteenth* of Adar (the twelfth month of the Jewish calendar, or February-March) was regarded as such a notable "manifestation of God" (2 Macc. 15:27) that it merited being commemorated annually on the day of Nicanor's downfall (1 Macc. 7:48). Significantly, this day, it turns out, was the eve of yet another important festival that had come to be observed among the Jews of that period: "the Day of Mordecai," which was celebrated on the *fourteenth* of Adar (2 Macc. 15:36).

It is hardly coincidental that the story of the highly successful self-defense of the Jews against their enemies recounted by the book of Esther is described as having occurred on precisely these same days, the thirteenth and fourteenth of Adar (9:15, 17), nor that the festival of Purim which Mordecai's letters enjoin the Jews to commemorate

(Esther 9:20–22) was to be celebrated on the immediately following days, the fourteenth and fifteenth of Adar (9:20f.). Those who fashioned the book of Esther and through it authorized the annual celebration of the festival of Purim must have done so with the conscious intention of endorsing the decision of the Maccabeans to make the Day of Nicanor's defeat (on the eve of the Day of Mordecai) a festival which would *forever* commemorate the "joy" of the deliverance experienced at that time (see Esther 9:28). However, by using the story of Esther instead of the account of Nicanor's defeat as the rationale for this festival, they broadened its relevance: this day would henceforth be a celebration not just of *that* deliverance only, but of all the times when "sorrow had been turned into gladness" through God's providential deliverance of his people Israel from their enemies (Esther 9:22).

Only someone in a position of authority close to these events would or could have authorized an innovation in the calendar of Jewish festivals of this scope and magnitude—perhaps it was Judas Maccabeus himself or one of the brothers who succeeded him to leadership in Jerusalem.[34] In any case, around this time (c. 164 BCE), the library of "the Law, the Prophets and the Writings" was completed in the form it would henceforth have for Jews and Christians.[35] Nicanor's vicious attack on Jerusalem, and his defeat, may thus be identified as the culminating event in the formation of the Hebrew scriptures as we now have them.

C. RETROSPECT AND CONCLUSION

Each of the nine volumes reviewed in this chapter adds its own special accent to the older library of "the Law and the Prophets." Those at the forefront, Ruth, Psalms and Proverbs, evoke faith and optimism and intimate how, despite the loss of kingdom and power, Israel might yet remain faithful to its covenant with Yahweh and fulfill its divine mission as light to the nations. A more somber, struggling aspect of faith is sounded in the next two books: Job and Ecclesiastes. Here Israel's doubts about itself in the midst of an ongoing history that showed too few signs of Yahweh's providence or plan are allowed to surface and express themselves. The Song of Songs is unique in its affirmation of the delights of nuptial love. Lamentation's cathartic rendering of the essentials of biblical faith is also quite special. In the final two scrolls, Daniel, and Esther, we are confronted by the ordeal of religious persecution on a massive scale. It is indeed a miracle that Israel's vision of its God, of its calling and of world redemption remained intact in such a dark hour.

The texts looked at in this chapter serve to confirm the impression that during the two centuries following the Ezra–Nehemiah reforms a remarkable thing happened: the spiritual wealth of rival priesthoods at war with one another for centuries was at last appropriated and combined in a manner that left the most essential legacies, traditions and truths of each intact for the enrichment of the other. We have characterized the end product as "renewal literature," for it was aimed at helping this community to take stock of itself and survive as a Torah-obedient people in the midst of forces that would surely have destroyed it were nothing done. In the resulting library delight in God's grace, wisdom and power so magnificently expressed in Zadokite theology and liturgy was combined with Levite earnestness for right living, covenant loyalty and good teachings.

Chapter Ten

THE CHRISTIAN BIBLE IN ITS FINAL FORM: CONCLUDING REFLECTIONS

*By appending the Gospels and Acts to the Hebrew scrip-
tures, the early Christians reoriented in a dramatic way
the world-story related in their canonical history.*

In this final chapter I want to reflect on what we might have
learned in the preceding chapters that could help us better understand
the Christian Bible as a whole. How the Hebrew scriptures were
received, retained and supplemented to become the Bible of the
Christian church was noted in Chapter 1, but at that point of our study
it had not been ascertained what precisely these scriptures were, nor
how and why they had been initially assembled, nor, overall, what
their contents and basic themes were. Now that these matters have
been looked at, I want to ask what light this might shed on the nature,
purpose and message of the Christian Bible as a whole.

A. THE CHRISTIAN BIBLE AS A WHOLE

At the point when Christianity was born, the Hebrew scriptures
were already a defined and established compendium that was widely
known, studied and accepted as an authoritative literature by Jews
everywhere, and hence by Christians as well. Not only the *number* of
books in this collection was by then firmly fixed but also their chronological sequence and arrangement, so that, taken as a whole, it can be
said that "the Law, the Prophets and the Writings" convey a story that
begins with creation and culminates in the Ezra-Nehemiah reforms.
However, these reforms were understood not just as an ending but as a

new beginning guided and inspired by words of hope for a transformed Israel and world, words that seemed still far from being realized "seven times seventy" years after the anticipated time of their fulfillment (Daniel 9).

To be more specific, the contents of this corpus may be roughly outlined as follows:

Genesis 1–11	Genesis 12–Kings	Prophets-Nehemiah	The Writings
It opens with stories of God's creation of the universe, the origins of the human family, the rise, corruption and dispersal of the nations.	This is followed by a long account of Israel's origins, enslavement, exodus, and covenant with God (Exodus to Deuteronomy), prefaced by the promise that this people will bring blessings to the nations—to which is attached an even longer record of Israel's entry into Canaan, rise to nationhood and subsequent decline and destruction because of sin (Joshua to Kings).	However, with this the story is not ended, for attached to this history of the world from creation to Israel's judgment for sin are the four scrolls of the prophets (Jeremiah, Ezekiel, Isaiah, and the Twelve), plus Ezra-Nehemiah, which, in addition to relating why this tragedy had occurred, speak eloquently of a new beginning for Israel, and of the coming transformation of both Israel and the world.	Much that was anticipated of this new beginning was unrealized. Yet "other books" were added –which testify to the determination of those who lived by "the Law and the Prophets" that these hopes for Israel and the world might yet be activated through witness (Ruth), worship (Psalms), wisdom (Proverbs), and enduring faith and devotion (Job, Ecclesiastes, Song of Songs, Lamentations, Daniel, Esther).

Thus, from the prophets onward Israel looked back to creation and the Torah of Moses, and took stock of its history of sin and judgment, while facing forward toward a future tenaciously believed to be bright with the promise of a universe that would one day be transformed. However, as this library of Hebrew scriptures was being completed, during the hellenistic persecutions and Maccabean wars, there were mounting perplexities as well. The path to renewal and world redemption seemed blocked and opaque: just when and how would God's plans for Israel and the world witnessed to in "the Law and the Prophets" ever be realized? Intensifying Israel's quandary were unan-

ticipated institutional and theological developments that led to its frag-
menting into competing parties (Pharisees, Sadducees, Essenes) in a
manner reminiscent of the period prior to the Ezra-Nehemiah reforms.[1]
It was in the midst of this rising tide of fragmentation, conflict and
despair that Jesus of Nazareth appeared with his unique message and
vision. Seen in this light the New Testament apostolic writings which
reflect the events resulting from his mission may be viewed as a dramatic new development and chapter in the age-old story of creation,
fall and redemption recorded in the Hebrew scriptures. The thematic
bridge from the one to the other was *eschatology,* the filling in of
"gaps" regarding how God's age-old plan for Israel and the world
would eventually be fulfilled.[2]

This apostolic literature was eventually added to the Hebrew
scriptures *after* Ezra-Nehemiah and Chronicles, with the consequence
that this older collection has now been given a wholly new terminus or
ending. Heretofore, great care had been taken by the custodians of this
library to make sure that in the arrangement of its books the accounts
in Ezra-Nehemiah and Chronicles of the reforms initiated at that time
would always remain at its *end* or apex. Thus, even though Daniel and
Esther were fashioned as responses to developments occurring long
after these reforms, they were crafted, dated and arranged so that they
would precede Ezra-Nehemiah and Chronicles and not dislodge them
from their position of honor as the chronological climax of the collection as a whole. When adding the Gospels and Acts in their proper
chronological sequence *after* the Ezra-Nehemiah reforms, the
Christians of the first three centuries CE disregarded this tradition and
reoriented the canonical story and library in a dramatic way. The history recounted in "the Law, the Prophets and the Writings" was now
openly and explicitly carried forward into a new time period and given
a new chronological focus and thrust. Its framework is thereby
changed from being one that encompasses the time from creation to the
Ezra-Nehemiah reforms (Genesis to Chronicles), to one extending
from creation to the advent of Jesus and the mission of his church to
the nations (as recounted in the Gospels and Acts). As a consequence
the Ezra-Nehemiah reforms have a diminished (although still important) role to play in this canon as a way-station in an expanded drama
of redemption that extends to a new point of fulfillment in the mission
of Jesus and his church.[3]

However, even with this expansion, the Christian canon also ends rather abruptly and inconclusively at the end of Acts, with a future-oriented, open-ended horizon that seems also to have "gaps" that need filling out. To be sure, the Christian additions to the Hebrew scriptures bring a fresh certainty regarding "the way" to prepare for the future now dawning, and also powerful reassurance of the reality of an eternal realm beyond death. Christians are certain now as well about *who* it is who will preside at the world's consummation, and hence have a greater confidence regarding how the temporal age will *ultimately* end. But still, precisely what can be hoped for in the temporal realm *between* the present and that ultimate consummation remains clouded and subject to debate even among Christians who cherish this newly fashioned Bible. This poses a challenge for a Christianity that seeks to be guided by scriptures that are as strongly oriented as these are toward the salvation of both Israel and the world. A canonically based Christianity that lacks either the capacity or the courage to speak authoritatively in the light of these scriptures to this issue in particular would appear to be flawed at its core.[4] I do not presume to be able to deal adequately with this matter here at the conclusion of this study, but I do wish to underline several features of the Christian Bible that this study has brought to our attention that do appear to be relevant to a recovery of some greater certainty in this regard.

B. THE CHRISTIAN CANONICAL WITNESS TO THE FUTURE OF THE WORLD

Our study of how the Hebrew scriptures were compiled, taken up and supplemented by the Christian movement to become the Bible of the church has served to highlight the revolutionary way in which the biblical story begun in Genesis was thereby brought to a new apex of fulfillment with the story recounted in the Gospels and Acts. What I now wish to emphasize is that it is in truth this new pentateuch of books at the *opening* of the Apostolic scriptures (Matthew, Mark, Luke, John, Acts) which do in fact bring the biblical story recounted in the Hebrew scriptures to their climax and close, and *not* the *final* volume of these scriptures, Revelation, for this end-book of the Christian canon does not purport to be a history of the same genre as Acts. Rather, it offers the reader a symbolically complex, visionary sketch of history's ultimate future like that of its canonical counterpart Daniel.

Put another way, Revelation suggests (but only suggests) what Christians hope for in the *ultimate* sense, but does not displace the Gospels or Acts as the *historical* terminus to their canon. It is these latter volumes, therefore, that supersede and replace Ezra-Nehemiah and Chronicles as the new chronological end-point of the canon for Christians. Thus, these are the scriptures we look to as Christians with that special care and attention with which Jewish believers look to the events culminating in the Ezra-Nehemiah reforms. It is here that *our* history and *our* future as Christians is related and configured.[5]

What then is it that we are told about what Christians can hope for, and how does this relate to the expectations for Israel and the world earlier enunciated in the Hebrew scriptures? These are the kinds of questions Christians ought to be asking when searching for light regarding their future and the future of the world—and the question that should be *first* addressed is the one regarding the expectations engendered by the older Hebrew scriptures, for it is in them that the hopes for Israel and the world were originally expressed that form the vocabulary and reference point for the reconfiguration of those hopes in the Gospels and Acts.[6] On the basis of our prior survey of prophetic expectations as these are set forth in the Hebrew scriptures (see Ch. 5) I wager the proposal that two somewhat differing scenarios present themselves there: in the one, Israel is envisioned as being reconstituted and renewed as the people of God in such a spectacular manner that the nations of the world either stand in awe, convert and are saved, or, if rebellious, are judged and destroyed (Ezek. 36–39); in the other, Israel is renewed and reconstituted as a missionary community that witnesses to the world in the less spectacular (less militant) manner of the prophets—that is, through upright living and by the "sword of the mouth" and martyrdom (Isa. 42:1–9; 45:14–25; 49:1–7; 53; Jonah).[7]

The history related in the Gospels and Acts does not even try to hide the fact that a similar conflict of visions flared up between Jesus and his own innermost circle of disciples over precisely these issues— that is, over who *he* thought himself to be and what *he* expected would happen, versus *their* expectations. Certain that Jesus was the long awaited Messiah, sure that this could only mean that Israel was now about to have its kingdom restored in some spectacular manner that would also involve a simultaneous judgment and redemption of the nations, Jesus' disciples are said to have been devastated when instead he was arrested, tried and crucified.[8] And their perplexity persisted into the post-resurrection period, when to their question as to whether it was at this time that God would restore the kingdom to Israel, Jesus is depicted as answering that it was not for them to know "times or dates that the Father has decided by his own authority," but that they were to return to Jerusalem and await the promised Holy Spirit, at which point they would be empowered to be his witnesses "not only in Jerusalem but throughout Judea and Samaria, and indeed to earth's remotest end" (Acts 1:6–8). These words which echo those at the conclusion of Matthew's Gospel (where Jesus is also said to have commissioned his apostles to begin a mission that would be directed toward making "disciples of all nations") stand at the heart of the story which Christians appended to "the Law, the Prophets and the Writings" to complete their canon of scriptures.

What follows in Acts is the account of how *this* end-time scenario *began* to unfold: how as the apostolic community waited in Jerusalem, the promised Holy Spirit was given, the church of the now crucified and resurrected Messiah was born, and, as foretold, these disciples were in fact empowered to go forth witnessing from Jerusalem to Judea and Samaria and outward to the world of nations of that time.[9] How this finale to the biblical story relates, more concretely, to the expectations alluded to above (those set forth in the Hebrew scriptures) is open to diverse interpretations. My own belief is that the way to proceed is by determining what in the older prophecies was thereby corrected or superseded by this new and fuller eschatological perspective; what can still rightly be hoped for that is envisioned or alluded to there; and what of that which can be hoped for lies on the temporal horizon of our existence, or belongs, rather, to the realm of the eternal beyond time and history as we know it. Clearly, everything pertaining to life after death and Christ's return (when time will flow into eternity) has to do with our ultimate or eternal hopes. But what are we to make of those prophecies that envision *within time* a reconstituted Davidic commonwealth and temple, for example, or an international judgment and destruction of nations—and where are we to locate that new world order so prominent in prophetic expectations, especially that vision twice repeated of ambassadors of the world's nations meeting to have their disputes adjudicated in the light of God's word and law and, as a consequence, beginning to disarm (Isa. 2; Micah 6; Jer. 3:17)?

I will suggest here no more than this: that the message conveyed by the Gospels and Acts that the crucified and resurrected Jesus of Nazareth truly is the long-awaited Messiah and that with his appearance the consummation of the world's history has begun, but that before its completion his followers are to be engaged in a mission aimed at bearing witness to the nations of what he had done and taught—this message has reconfigured Israel's legacy of prophetic hopes *by opening up an extended time period for missionary outreach, repentance and change* within the older eschatological scenarios. That is, between the Messiah's first coming in humble service and love and his second coming to usher in the final consummation, it is now understood that there is going to be ample time for change and discovery and for God's kingdom to dawn more gradually upon the life of the world's many peoples, for God is now clearly understood to be far more patient, loving and ready to forgive than had heretofore been thought, "wanting nobody to be lost and everybody to be brought to repentance" (2 Peter 3:9; James 5:7–11; Rom. 2:4–11). The canonical story, as Christians are privileged to understand it from the perspective of the Gospels and Acts, thus leaves us extremely hopeful that over time, through the Spirit-energized mission of the church of Jesus Christ to the world, much can be accomplished in bringing this world forward toward the goal set for it by God at creation.[10]

APPENDIX

THE HEBREW SCRIPTURES

As listed in *The Babylonian Talmud*, Baba Bathra 14b, Soncino Press translation	As listed in the *The Standard Jewish Bible* of the Jewish Publication Society
"Our Rabbis taught:	TORAH The five books of Moses
	Genesis
	Exodus
	Leviticus
	Numbers
	Deuteronomy
"The order of the Prophets is	NEVI'IM The Prophets
Joshua,	Joshua
Judges,	Judges
Samuel,	I Samuel
	II Samuel
Kings,	I Kings
	II Kings
Jeremiah,	Isaiah
Ezekiel,	Jeremiah
Isaiah, and	Ezekiel
the Twelve Minor Prophets ...	The Twelve Minor Prophets
"The order of the Hagiographa is	KETHUVIM The Writings
Ruth,	Psalms
the Book of Psalms,	Proverbs
Job,	Job
Proverbs,	The Song of Songs
Ecclesiastes,	Ruth
Song of Songs,	Lamentations
Lamentations,	Ecclesiastes
Daniel	Esther
and the Scroll of Esther,	Daniel
Ezra	Ezra
	Nehemiah
and Chronicles."	I Chronicles
	II Chronicles

JEWISH, CATHOLIC AND PROTESTANT BIBLES COMPARED

THE JEWISH BIBLE		THE CHRISTIAN OLD TESTAMENT *	
TORAH	Genesis	TORAH	Genesis
	Exodus		Exodus
	Leviticus		Leviticus
	Numbers		Numbers
	Deuteronomy		Deuteronomy
		HISTORICAL	
PROPHETS	Joshua	BOOKS	Joshua
	Judges		Judges
			Ruth
	1 & 2 Samuel		1 & 2 Samuel
	1 & 2 Kings		1 & 2 Kings
			1 & 2 Chronicles
	Isaiah		Ezra
	Jeremiah		Nehemiah
	Ezekiel		Esther
	The Twelve		**Judith**
			Tobit
			1 & 2 Maccabees
		WISDOM	
WRITINGS	Psalms	BOOKS	Job
	Proverbs		Psalms
	Job		Proverbs
	The Song of Songs		Ecclesiastes
	Ruth		Song of Songs
	Lamentations		**Ecclesiasticus**
	Ecclesiastes		**Wisdom of Solomon**
	Esther		
	Daniel	PROPHETS	Isaiah
	Ezra		Jeremiah
	Nehemiah		Lamentations
	1 & 2 Chronicles		**Baruch**
			Ezekiel
			Daniel
			The Twelve

* The seven books in bold letters are found only in Catholic Bibles. They are commonly referred to as the Apocrypha, or the "deutero-canonical" books.

WHY JEWISH, CATHOLIC AND PROTESTANT BIBLES DIFFER (A SYNOPSIS)

1.	2.	3.	4.
The first point to understand is that the Jewish list is the earlier one; these were the scriptures of the early Christians, the ones referred to in the New Testament writings. Also keep in mind that these early scriptures were not bound together in a book as we have them today. They existed as a collection of separate scrolls; these scrolls were shelved and arranged in a certain sequence. Remember too that many Jews could no longer read or understand Hebrew, so that during **the third century BCE** a Greek translation of the Hebrew scriptures known as the Septuagint was made. When Christianity spread westward, the Septuagint was virtually the only Bible known to Greek speaking Christians.	At the beginning of **the third century CE** books began being used instead of scrolls and Christians gradually began publishing their sacred writings in large codexes. This forced them to decide which books to include and in what order. At the time these volumes were being published the churches of the west had lost touch with what books in what order were in the Hebrew scriptures of the first Christian Bible. As a consequence other Jewish writings which they valued were also included. Likewise the original arrangement was forgotten, so they bound the books together according to their own preferences. When Latin translations were created, the practice of entitling the two parts as "Old Testament" and "New Testament" was begun.	Now something else rather significant happened. About **400 CE** the Pope commissioned St. Jerome to prepare a new Latin translation of the Bible. While doing so, he became aware of the differences that existed between the translated Old Testament scriptures in use in the churches of the west and the older Hebrew scriptures. Although he believed the books (and parts of books) that had been added to this collection by western Christians were edifying, he used the term "Apocrypha" to identify them and recommended that only the Jewish Hebrew scriptures be regarded as authoritative ("Apocrypha" was a term earlier used by Christians for rejected Gnostic writings; it means "hidden" or "secret").	The latest chapter in this ongoing story is this: while St. Jerome's Latin translation became the common Bible of the western church ("the Vulgate"), the distinction he had drawn between the Hebrew scriptures and the Apocrypha was largely ignored until the sixteenth century Protestant reformation, which more or less adopted it. However, **in 1546** at the Council of Trent the Roman Catholic Church responded by declaring that the apocryphal writings were as inspired as the others. In Bible publishing generally the practice was continued of arranging the biblical books in the manner that had become traditional in the Greek and Latin codexes of the western churches.

A NOTE TO BIBLE PUBLISHERS

In the course of this study I have often wished that those for whom I was writing had the Hebrew scriptures before them in the three-part format referred to in the Bible's apostolic scriptures. While I can understand and appreciate the reasons for the rearrangement of these scriptures in the later Greek and Latin versions that came to be used by the churches of the west, it still seems preferable that the respective books should appear in the arrangement they had when the Bible was first formed. For one thing, Christians would then recognize the relevance of New Testament references to "the Law and the Prophets." More importantly, the chronological profile, structural components and overall design of these scriptures would be more readily apparent and it would be easier to see how the specifically Christian scriptures relate to the older compilation. Were this done, I would also urge that the specific list and sequence of Hebrew scriptures specified in Baba Bathra 14b be seriously considered for adoption. I believe that many issues related to the form, content and messages of the four scrolls of the Prophets and eleven scrolls of the Writings will be better understood when they are read and studied in that arrangement (see Chs. 7 and 9).

I might add that the arrangement of the apostolic letters that was traditional in the churches of the fourth century also seems preferable to me over later arrangements that continue to be followed today. In the older sequence the seven General Epistles (James, 1 and 2 Peter, 1, 2, 3 John and Jude) come right after Acts and thus precede rather than follow the letters of Paul (see Ch. 1, fn. 25). This sequence is more natural in that it builds on and reflects church history as recounted in Acts where James is recognized as the first head of the church, and Peter (as first missioner to the Gentiles) and other "pillar apostles" (John and Jude) are shown to be antecedent to Paul.[1] The contents of these letters (regardless of questions that might be raised regarding their origins or authorship) are also functionally more relevant as an *introduction* to the Pauline corpus than as an epilogue, since they provide the kind of theological "frame" and advice needed for the proper reading and interpretation of the Pauline writings. This is especially true of 2 Peter with its matured Christian eschatology (3:1–10) and explicit warning of the dangers of misinterpreting Paul's letters (3:11–18). Were list and order of books in both Hebrew and apostolic scriptures restored in this manner, we would again have a Bible with the chronological and theological coherence it once had.

A new name is also needed for this total collection, one that both distinguishes and holds its several parts together as an organic whole. The term "Bible" under which these scriptures are currently published is unfortunately not strong enough to bind them together when the books within it named "the Old Testament" are separated off as they invariably are from scriptures called "the New Testament." Especially regrettable is the practice of publishing the New Testament scriptures by themselves, apart from the Hebrew scriptures. Serious consideration should be given to restoring the designation "Prophets and Apostles" commonly used for these scriptures among Christians of the first two centuries—and indeed, within the apostolic scriptures themselves (2 Peter 3:2).[2] I would also recommend the retention of the traditional nomenclature for the divisions of the *Hebrew* scriptures. Were this done, what we would have is a three-part Bible made up of "the Law and the Prophets" (Part One), "the Writings" (Part Two) and "the Apostolic Scriptures" (Part Three), bound together in one volume and known collectively as "Prophets and Apostles."

It is not my intention, in making these proposals, to overlook or diminish the inherent importance of the seven deuteronomical books of the Catholic Bible. These too merit being made easily accessible to Christians in some form or arrangement. However, it disrupts the flow of books in the "the Law and the Prophets" and "the Writings" when these volumes are included *within* these older collections (as they frequently are in Roman Catholic Bibles), and it is equally confusing to encounter them *between* the two Testaments (as they frequently are in Protestant Bibles). In both instances, books of the Bible that belong together are disconnected and displaced in a manner that can threaten their coherence. In my opinion the proper place for the deuterocanonical or apocryphal books is in an appendix, with introductory comments that would inform the reader of their status and relationship to the preceding corpus.

So far as I know, a Bible along the lines being suggested does not yet exist in English translation, but there is a French version somewhat like the one I am proposing in that it preserves the older tripartite arrangement of the Hebrew scriptures, and locates the deuterocanonical books in a separate section. Entitled, *Traduction Oecumenique de la Bible* (Le Cerf: Alliance Biblique Universelle), it was first published in 1970 and has found a remarkably wide acceptance among French speaking people (according to information received from Catherine Eyer, a graduate student from France to whom I am indebted for calling this version to my attention).

NOTES

PREFACE

[1]For synopses of some of the more important recent books on this subject, see the Annotated Bibliography of Recent Canonical Studies in the Appendix. By "canon" or "canonical" in the following study I refer to an identifiable collection with a continuing, normative authority that sets it apart from other religious writings.

1. HOW THE HEBREW SCRIPTURES BECAME
PART OF THE CHRISTIAN BIBLE

[1]See especially the works of Campenhausen, Beckwith, Ellis, Farmer, Kugel and Greer, and Metzger synopsized in the Annotated Bibliography at the end of this volume.

[2]The closest parallel to "Old Testament" in New Testament writings is the use of the term "old covenant" for the Torah or Pentateuch in 2 Cor. 3:14.

[3]For a listing of these titles as they appear in the Jewish sources of the period, see Roger Beckwith, *The Old Testament Canon of the New Testament Church* (Grand Rapids: Eerdmans, 1985), Ch. 3.

[4]*Against Apion,* I. 38–42; quotations are from the translation by Thackeray, in the Loeb Classical Library.

[5]The text in question opens with the expression, "the Rabbis taught," signifying that the list of books that follows is a "baraita" or teaching of the religious leaders of the Mishnaic period (c. 200 CE).

[6]For a comparison of the format of this list with the one found in Jewish Bibles today, see "The Hebrew Scriptures" in the Appendix. That Josephus numbers and lists the books somewhat differently seems to be due to the fact that his purpose in *Against Apion* was to explain the Jewish scriptures to Gentiles who knew nothing about them, in defense of his credibility as a historian. Thus, he cites the books in their chronological (rather than their traditional) arrangement.

It appears that he arrived at the number twenty-two (the number of letters in the Hebrew alphabet) by grouping Ruth with Judges and Lamentations with Jeremiah. Both 2 Esdras 14:45 (first century CE) and Jerome (fourth century CE), the latter in the prefaces to his Vulgate translation of the books of the Old Testament, confirm that twenty-four was the older Jewish way of numbering these books (2 Esdras 14:45 refers to "twenty-four books" which were published "for the worthy and unworthy to read"). That uncertainty existed during the first century CE over what books were part of this collection is unlikely in the light of the unequivocal declaration of Josephus that there were in his time a precise and "justly accredited" number of books which Jews *everywhere* regarded as so sacrosanct that they would neither "add," "remove" or "alter a syllable" and were prepared to die for them.

[7]The great esteem accorded this library during this period can also be sensed from a first century CE legendary account of its miraculous origins, 2 Esdras 14, and in the innumerable ways it is repeatedly cited and referred to in the writings of Philo, 1 and 2 Maccabees and other literature of the time (regarding these, see again Beckwith, *Old Testament Canon,* pp. 71–80).

[8]Marcion's own writings (*Gospel of Marcion, Apostles, Antitheses*) are known only through quotations in the works of his opponents. For an overview of what can be known about his *Gospel* (which was an edited version of Luke), see Robert Grant, "Marcion, Gospel of," *Anchor Bible Dictionary IV* (New York: Doubleday, 1992), pp. 516–520.

[9]Hans von Campenhausen, *The Formation of the Christian Bible* (Philadelphia: Fortress, 1972), pp. 149–50. On Marcion's theological outlook, see also Stephen G. Wilson, "Marcion and the Jews," in *Anti-Judaism in Early Christianity,* Studies in Christianity and Judaism, 2, Stephen G. Wilson, ed. (Waterloo: Wilfred Laurier University, 1986), pp. 45–58.

[10]*Ibid.,* p. 150.

[11]Henry Chadwick, *The Early Church* (Baltimore: Penguin Books, 1967), p. 39.

[12]*Ibid.*

[13]Campenhausen, *Formation,* p. 151.

[14]*Ibid.,* p. 152.

[15]*Ibid.,* pp. 152–53.

[16]*Ibid.,* p. 154.

[17]*Ibid.,* pp. 154–55.

[18]*Ibid.* p. 150.

[19]According to J. Clabeaux, "Marcion," *Anchor Bible Dictionary, IV* (New York: Doubleday, 1992), p. 515, scholars conjecture "that in numbers alone the Marcionites may have nearly surpassed non–Marcionites in the decades of the 160s and 170s." "While not all-scholars agree that Marcion forced the creation of the Christian canon," he states, "we cannot deny that his was the first. His influence in this matter is manifest in the composition of the NT canon that was later to emerge." Bruce Metzger, *The Canon of the New Testament, Its Origin, Development, and Significance* (Oxford: Clarendon Press, 1987), p. 99, puts the matter this way: "it was in opposition to Marcion's criticism that the Church first became fully conscious of its inheritance of apostolic writings."

[20]Rowan A. Greer, "The Christian Bible and Its Interpretation," in James L. Kugel and Rowan A. Greer, *Early Biblical Interpretation,* Wayne A. Meeks, ed. (Philadelphia: Westminster, 1986), p. 155.

[21]*Ibid.* The New Testament itself does mention Christian scriptures being read and used in the churches along side of the Jewish scriptures, as in 2 Peter, where both "prophets" *and* "apostles" are referred to as authorities (3:2); reference is also made in this same writing to a collection of Paul's letters which were being read in the churches alongside "the rest of scripture" (3:16). However, 2 Peter is poorly attested as a canonical writing among the Church Fathers and goes unmentioned in the Muratorian Canon (Campenhausen, *Formation,* p. 255, fn. 245). Evidence is therefore lacking that anything like the present canon of Christian scriptures was in place prior to the end of the second century.

[22]Irenaeus, "Against Heresies," Book 3,1, *Early Christian Fathers,* The Library of Christian Classics, Vol. I, translated and edited by Cyril C. Richardson (Philadelphia: Westminster, 1953), p. 370.

[23]*Ibid.,* pp. 367-68 (Book 1, 27).

[24]*Ibid.,* p. 181. According to Hans-Joachim Schoeps, *Jewish Christianity, Factional Disputes in the Early Church* (Philadelphia: Fortress, 1969), pp. 126-130, Jewish Christianity played an important role in this struggle. "It is important to make clear," he writes, "that

according to all indications the fight against the Simonians, the Marcionites and so forth, at least on Syrian soil, was led not by orthodoxy but by Ebionitism" (p. 129).

[25]*Jesus and the Gospels* (Philadelphia: Fortress, 1982), p. 226. The precise list that Irenaeus wished to instate as an alternative to that of Marcion's is a bit uncertain, but Farmer (p. 203) suggests it included the following twenty-two books in no particular arrangement: Matthew, Mark, Luke, John, Acts, Romans, Corinthians (1, 2), Galatians, Ephesians, Philippians, Colossians, Thessalonians (1, 2), Timothy (1, 2), Titus, Philemon, Peter (1), John (1, 2?), Hermas (?). On this development, see also Kenneth L. Carrol, "Toward a Commonly Received New Testament," *Bulletin of the John Rylands Library* 44 (1962), pp. 335f., who writes that "the earliest New Testaments, no matter how much they varied, were bound to possess three groups or types of books": four Gospels and the book of Acts; Paul's letters in the expanded form of thirteen letters with the Pastorals; plus a final section containing a number of general epistles and/or apocalypses. The twenty-seven New Testament books of our present Bible are listed for the first time in a Festal Letter written by Bishop Athanasius of Alexandria in 367, but they appear there in a different order than the one currently in use in most churches: the "Catholic" Letters of James, 1 and 2 Peter, 1, 2 and 3 John and Jude come right after Acts (thus before the Letters of Paul which now include Hebrews). For comments in defense of this older arrangement and the possibility of adopting it in Bible publishing today, see the "Note to Bible Publishers" in the Appendix.

[26]Campenhausen, *Formation,* p. 188.

[27]Greer, "Christian Bible," pp. 166–67.

[28]*Ibid.,* p. 167.

[29]*Ibid.*

[30]Lloyd Gaston, "Sola Scriptura," *Bulletin of the Canadian Society of Biblical Studies* 47 (1987), p. 15.

[31]For a similar assessment, see John Clabeaux, "Marcion," p. 516, who writes: "The vociferous insistence of anti–Marcionite Christianity on the validity of the OT within the canon is a point which should not be missed in our time. Since rejection of the OT was an essential feature of Marcionism, it is straining the point only a little to say that among Christians today there are many virtual Marcionites."

[32]Gaston, "Sola Scriptura," p. 15. For the small steps that culminated in the use of the Greek term *diatheke* (covenant) for the two parts of the Christian Bible, and then in the translation of that term as *testamentum* in the Latin Bible, see Campenhausen, *Formation,* pp. 264-268. His judgment on this development is even harsher. "In eccesiastical usage," he writes, "*testamentum* is a typical example of Christian translator's jargon; and by applying it, on the Greek model, to the parts of the holy Scripture the Church deprived it of all flexibility, and merely made its meaning totally obscure" (p. 267). Indeed, it is Campenhausen's belief that the names Old and New Testament by themselves are not adequate to open up the meaning of that which they denote or protect or make them a living reality (p. 268). For the suggestion that we consider returning to the once widely used name "Prophets and Apostles" for the two parts of the Christian Bible, see my comments in "A Note to Bible Publishers" in the Appendix.

[33]See the Appendix for charts showing the differences between early (Jewish) Christian and later Catholic and Protestant Bibles, and a synopsis of how and why these differences arose and were perpetuated. E. Earle Ellis, "The Old Testament Canon of the Early Church," *Mikra, Text, Translation, Reading and Interpretation of the Hebrew Bible in Ancient Judaism and Early Christianity,* Jan Martin Mulder, ed. (Assen: Van Gorcum; Philadelphia: Fortress, 1988), suggests that since no two Septuagint codexes are alike in either the list or arrangement of the books they contain, and since "no uniform Septuagint 'Bible' was ever the subject of discussion in the patristic church … the Septuagint codexes appear to have been originally intended more as service books than as a defined and normative body of scripture" (p. 168).

[34]The outstanding exception to this is Codex Alexandrinus, where Ezra is still near the end and the prophetic books remain in close proximity to Kings.

[35]For a discussion of the way this rearrangement of books has contributed to the neglect of "the post-exilic portions of the Old Testament" among Christian Old Testament scholars and in Christian theology generally, see Rolf Rendtorff, *Canon and Theology, Overtures to an Old Testament Theology* (Minneapolis: Fortress, 1993), pp. 54-56.

[36]I will have more to say about these matters in Chs. 8, 9 and 10 especially.

2. A FIRST LOOK AT WHEN AND WHY
THEY WERE COMPILED

[1]For this insight and the interpretation that follows I am indebted to Roger Beckwith, "Formation of the Hebrew Bible," *Mikra, Text, Translation, Reading and Interpretation of the Hebrew Bible in Ancient Judaism and Early Christianity,* Jan Martin Mulder, ed. (Assen: Van Gorcum; Philadelphia: Fortress, 1988), p. 52.

[2]I might add that this conclusion replaces a long held scholarly assumption that the canon of Hebrew scriptures was in some considerable flux prior to actions taken at a Rabbinic assembly meeting at Jamnia in 90 CE. For a review of the rise and fall of this oft repeated "Council of Jamnia theory" and the recommendation that it "be relegated to the limbo of unestablished hypotheses," see Jack P. Lewis, "Jamnia (Jabneh), Council of, *Anchor Bible Dictionary"* III, pp. 634-637.

[3]Evidence will be cited in Chs. 8 and 9 for believing this library was deliberately arranged so that nothing in it would postdate or follow the accounts of the Ezra-Nehemiah reforms. For a somewhat more complete synopsis of the story told in these scriptures, see Ch. 10.

[4]For a similar conclusion, based on the fact "that a given work cannot be earlier than the latest specific historical reference found in it" or later than "the next significant historical event known from other sources which, so far as we can determine, would have figured in the historical account had the author or editor known of it," see David Noel Freedman, "The Law and the Prophets, *Supplements to Vetus Testamentum* IX, Congress Volume, Bonn, 1962 (Leiden: E. J. Brill, 1963), pp. 250–265. Also Bleddyn J. Robarts, "The Old Testament Canon: A Suggestion," *Bulletin John Rylands Library* 46 (1963), pp. 164-178, singles out the period of Ezra as affording the conditions "for a suitable background to the general study" of canon formation (p. 165) and argues that "from the side of Rabbinic tradition and from that of apocalyptic interpretation it would appear that long before the

Mishnaic and Christian disputations on canonicity the Hebrew Old Testament was regarded as a corpus of Scriptures" (p. 178).

⁵For evidence supportive of the historical authenticity of this letter, see Ben Zion Wacholder, "The Letter from Judas Maccabee to Aristobulus, Is 2 Maccabees 1:10b—2:18 Authentic?" *Hebrew Union College Annual,* XLIX (1978), pp. 89-133.

⁶Since a clear distinction is drawn in the citation in 2 Macc. 2:13 between the library originally assembled by Nehemiah and the "complete collection" assembled by Judas Maccabaeus, it does not follow that "the materials listed in 2 Macc. 2:13 as the library of Nehemiah must, in fact, have been the contents of the protocanon reassembled by Judah," as Lawrence Schiffman, "2 Maccabees," *Harper's Bible Commentary* (San Francisco: Harper & Row, 1988), p. 901, suggests. The canon Judas assembled was obviously further along in its development than that earlier one, as has already been noted in our discussion above of the Foreword to Sirach (and as will be shown in greater detail in our discussion of Daniel and Esther in Ch. 11).

⁷For a similar opinion, see Rendtorff, *Canon and Theology,* pp. 53f., who believes that "lack of knowedge about this period is largely due to the lack of interest which it has hitherto evoked among scholars," and states that "if research into this era were to be pursued with the same intensity once devoted—and devoted still—to Israel's early period, I am sure that we could expect results which would provide a firmer basis for a reconstruction of the historical, social, and religious warp and weft of the time." My own examination and assessment of what can be known from these sources will emerge as our discussion unfolds; for my examination of those sources that bear most directly on the Ezra-Nehemiah reforms themselves, see the discussion in Ch. 7.

⁸Paul Hanson, "Israelite Religion in the Early Postexilic Period," *Ancient Israelite Religion,* Essays in Honor of Frank Moore Cross, Patrick D. Miller, Jr., Paul D. Hanson, S. Dean McBride, eds. (Philadelphia: Fortress, 1987), p. 487.

⁹For the evidence supportive of this traditional dating, see Joseph Blenkinsopp, *Ezra-Nehemiah, A Commentary* (Philadelphia: Westminster, 1988), pp. 139–144.

¹⁰For the evidence for dating Malachi before Ezra's reforms against marriages with foreign women, but after the rebuilding of the Second Temple, most likely during "the poor economic circumstances" of the

early years of the reign of Artaxerxes I (465–425), see Beth Glazier-McDonald, *Malachi, The Divine Messenger,* Society of Biblical Literature Dissertation Series 98 (Atlanta: Scholars Press, 1987), p. 17.

[11]This is the opinion of Julia M. O'Brien, *Priest and Levite in Malachi,* SBL Dissertation Series 121 (Atlanta: Scholars Press, 1990), although she believes Malachi was also aware of the tradition recorded in Num. 25:11–13, where Phineas, grandson of Aaron, is rewarded with a "covenant of peace" guaranteeing him the right "forever ... to perform the ritual of expiation for the Israelites." "Malachi's description of a 'covenant with Levi,' " she writes, "appears to integrate these [two] passages into a distinctive portrait of the ideal priest. As in Deut. 33, the eponymous ancestor Levi is lauded for his faithfulness, and the priesthood is described as involving both teaching and sacrifice. As in Num. 25, the faithful priest is the recipient of a covenant of perpetual priesthood—a gift described in the characteristic language of the grant" (p. 106).

[12]"Messenger of Yahweh" is terminology used elsewhere in our sources for prophets (as in Hag. 1:13; Isa. 44:26; 2 Chr. 36:15–16).

[13]O'Brien, *Ibid.,* p. 147.

[14]The background of the issues surrounding Malachi's designation of this priesthood as "sons of Levi" and his appeal to a "covenant with Levi" are subjects that will be addressed in the following three chapters.

[15]For our further discussion of this important development, see Ch. 8.

[16]Paul Hanson, "Israelite Religion in the Early Postexilic Period," p. 503, places Malachi "among dissident Levites who formulated their own position with the aid of an old tradition concerning God's covenant with Levi...." See Ch. 5 for our further comments on Malachi's possible social location.

[17]Morton Smith, *Palestinian Parties and Politics that Shaped the Old Testament,* second edition (London: SCM Press, 1987), p. 99, characterizes the "lenders" mentioned here as "landed gentry" and "leaders of the assimilationist party."

[18]Ezra's remarkable prayer in response to this problem, in Ezra 9:6–15, affords an especially vivid sense of the motivational dynamics behind his reform efforts; further to this issue, see Beth Glazier-McDonald, "Intermarriage, Divorce, and the *bat-'el nēkār:* Insights

into Mal. 2:10–16," *Journal of Biblical Literature,* 106/4 (1987), pp. 603–611, and our discussion of these texts in Ch. 6.

3. THE WIDER BACKGROUND: ISRAEL'S RIVAL PRIESTLY HOUSES

[1]For a list of the citations, see Jacob M. Myers, *I Chronicles, Anchor Bible* (Garden City: Doubleday, 1965), pp. XLIX–LXII; Myers believes that the Chronicles' author "had at his disposal" the tetrateuch "and the great history of the Deuteronomist, which included the books of Deuteronomy, Joshua, Judges, Samuel, and Kings" (p. LXII).

[2]Further regarding this research and the role of 1 and 2 Chronicles within the canon of Hebrew scriptures, see Chs. 7 and 8. The above comments are not meant to imply that the books of Chronicles are of no help at all in tracing the preexilic history of Israel's priestly houses, but only that priority for such a reconstruction belongs to the older sources.

[3]The coherence of the Deuteronomistic History (as first demonstrated by Martin Noth's *Überlieferungsgeschichtliche Studien,* original edition 1943) has been substantiated by the work of Richard Elliott Friedman, *The Exile and Biblical Narrative, The Formation of the Deuteronomistic and Priestly Works,* Harvard Semitic Monographs 22 (Chico: Scholars Press, 1981), pp. 1–43. Wellhausen's earlier demonstration of the chronological priority of Deuteronomy to the Priestly traditions of the Tetrateuch and the superficial manner in which Tetrateuch and Deuteronomistic History have been spliced together is helpfully reviewed by Joseph Blenkinsopp, *Prophecy and Canon, A Contribution to the Study of Jewish Origins* (University of Notre Dame Press, 1977), pp. 54–59, 80–95. On the manner in which the two complexes were edited to form one larger compilation, see Ch. 7.

[4]Only once in Deuteronomy is the Aaronite priesthood mentioned (Deut. 10:6).

[5]See especially Neh. 13:10–13. Neh. 13:30 states that it was Nehemiah who first "drew up regulations" to deal with this problem (further to this issue, see Ch. 8).

[6]This is the conclusion of Baruch Halpern's erudite study, *The First*

Historians, The Bible and History (San Francisco: Harper & Row, 1988), where he characterizes the Deuteronomistic History as an account of Israel's sojourn in Canaan from the point of view of a "cultic interpretation of it" (p. 235); see also John van Seters, *In Search of History, Historiography in the Ancient World and the Origins of Biblical History* (New Haven and London: Yale University Press, 1983), who characterizes the Deuteronomist author as "the first Israelite historian, and the first known historian in Western civilization truly to deserve this designation ..." (p. 362).

[7]The appointment of the Levites to priestly duties is portrayed somewhat differently in Exod. 32:25–29. There their special status is viewed as a reward for their having taken Moses' side in the controversy over the golden calf. The still earlier references to Levi in Gen. 34:25–31 and 49:5 suggest that this group was once a secular tribe. Regarding this, see Aelred Cody, *A History of Old Testament Priesthood* (Rome: Pontifical Biblical Institute, 1969), pp. 29–38, 50–52, who proposes that since the sources inform us that Moses too was from this tribe (Exod. 2:1f.) and "his sons after him were priests" (Judges 18:30), the tradition may be correct when it portrays him as having chosen Levite kinsmen to serve as priests at the desert sanctuary and when it implies that this was how the transition was made from being a secular tribe to being a tribe of priests.

[8]In Deut. 9:20 we are told that because of Aaron's apostasy with the golden calf, Yahweh was "so enraged" with him that he wanted to destroy him, but only refrained from doing so because of Moses' intercession. The one reference in the book of Deuteronomy to the Aaronite priesthood (Deut. 10:6) looks like an editorial "patch" to help harmonize Deuteronomy with the preceding tetrateuchal library. For details on how and why the two complexes were editorially combined, and by whom, see Chs. 7 and 8.

[9]Judges 20:28, which locates the ark at Bethel under the Aaronite priesthood, appears to be another editorial patch (similar to the one in Deut. 10:6) aimed at mitigating the tensions between the Levite history of the priesthood and the prior tetrateuchal sources.

[10]Although 1 Sam. 2:27–36 is generally thought to be a late insertion that renders the briefer warning to Samuel in 1 Sam. 3:11–14 superfluous, it is nevertheless of the utmost importance for reconstructing the history of Israel's priestly houses, for here is an explicit acknowledg-

ment that the Levites were in fact the original priestly house in Israel (cf. 1 Sam. 2:27–29; cp. Deut. 33:8–11); here too it is clearly specified precisely how it came about that it lost that status and was replaced by another priesthood (1 Sam. 2:35–36). While the replacement priesthood is not named, its characterization as "an enduring House" which will walk in the presence of Yahweh's "Anointed forever" (2:35) leaves no doubt that the Zadokites of Jerusalem, the only priesthood remaining after Abiathar's dismissal (see below), were the intended reference. In fact, the sharp polemical tenor of this text suggests it may have been incorporated at Zadokite insistence in the final editing of these volumes. Note too what 1 Sam. 2:36 has to say about the way Levites were demeaned by these developments.

[11]It should be observed that the Hebrew of this verse does not list Abiathar, but "Ahimelech *son* of Abiathar" as the priest in question. This appears to be a scribal error, since elsewhere Abiathar is identified as the appointee (1 Kings 2:26–27; 4:4) and Ahimelech is identified as his father, not his son (1 Sam. 22:20).

[12]The reference in 2 Kings 23:9 to "brother-priests" whom Josiah brought to Jerusalem from "the towns of Judah" and supported there *may* be a reference to Levites, even though this is not explicitly stated. If Levites are the intended reference, then Josiah's action in bringing them back to Jerusalem at this juncture might be regarded as a first step in their return to active temple duty. However, the text specifies that they were not allowed to officiate at the altar. The question is thereby posed as to what they were permitted or mandated to do? Ezekiel's recommendation a half century later was that they were to function strictly as temple "servants" and nothing more (see Ezek. 44:10–14). For our further discussion of how these contentious issues were subsequently resolved, see Chs. 6, 7 and 8.

[13]Several kings, Asa (1 Kings 15:9–15), Jehoash (2 Kings 12:1–4), Amaziah (14:1–4) and Uzziah (2 Kings 15:1–4), are commended for having done right up to a point. However, they too did not abolish the "high places"—the meaning seems to be that while ridding *Jerusalem* of alien gods, they still permitted other gods to be worshiped "on the high places, in the towns of Judah and the neighborhood of Jerusalem" (2 Kings 23:5), nor did they bring the "brother priests" (Levites) to Jerusalem from the high places where they offered sacrifice (2 Kings 23:8).

[14]The Levite historians do report a protest against these developments in the north by King Jehu (2 Kings 9–10), who was assisted by the prophets Elijah and Elisha (1 Kings 17–19; 21; 2 Kings 1–8), but not even he, they report, abandoned "the sins into which Jeroboam son of Nebat had led Israel, the golden calves of Bethel and Dan" (2 Kings 10:28–33).

[15]The origins of this book will be discussed in Ch. 4.

[16]This is the opinion of Frank Moore Cross, *Canaanite Myth and Hebrew Epic, Essays in the History of the Religion of Israel* (Cambridge: Harvard University Press, 1973), p. 212, fn. 62.

[17]The arguments for and against this proposal are summarized by Cody, *Old Testament Priesthood,* pp. 91–93.

[18]Cross, *Canaanite Myth,* p. 210.

[19]This hypothesis, first put forward by Cross, *Ibid.,* pp. 195–215, is defended by Merlin D. Rehm, "Levites and Priests," *Anchor Bible Dictionary, IV* (New York: Doubleday, 1992), pp. 306–309. Similar conclusions have been drawn by Saul Olyan, "Zadok's Origins and the Tribal Politics of David," *Journal of Biblical Literature* 101/2 (1982), pp. 177–193, who argues that Hebron was "a major Kenite shrine city."

[20]Cross' summary of these developments, *Canaanite Myth.,* p. 215, is as follows: "David's unusual choice of two chief priests, like many of his decisions in relation to Israel's new central sanctuary in Jerusalem, was based on sure diplomatic grounds; he chose a priest from each of the great, rival priestly families: Abiathar of the Shilonite house of Eli which claimed descent from Moses, Zadok from the Hebronite clan which traced its line to Aaron."

[21]This is the conclusion of Merlin Rehm, "Levites and Priests," p. 309, who points out that the priests of this tradition are referred to in our sources as "the sons of Aaron" when referring to them in the period prior to Solomon, and as Zadokites (or sons of Zadok) from Solomon onward (as in Ezek. 44:15).

[22]This possibility was suggested by a student, Andrew Fry, in a graduate seminar where these traditions were under discussion.

[23]That Aaron's name had to be written on the branch of Levi (as Num. 17:3 presents it) implies that before this it was not there. The need to do this would first have arisen in the wake of the Josiah reforms when the scroll of Deuteronomy began to be viewed as author-

ative literature within Jerusalem Zadokite tradition (see above, and our further discussion of these issues in Chs. 4 and 7).

[24]As to when and why this legislation was later added to the Tetrateuch, see the discussion of these texts in Ch. 7.

[25]Exod. 18:1–12 may be characterized a cult legend tracing the origins of the Aaronite-Zadokites to the Yahweh traditions of Moses' father-in-law. The wisdom of this father-in-law is further accented in the follow-up account of his sage advice to his son-in-law Moses regarding how to handle the judicial affairs of the community (Exod. 18:13–27); note how in the retelling of this episode in the Levite source (Deut. 1:9–18), *Moses,* not the father-in-law, is credited with having initiated these judicial reforms. Aaronite and Levite traditions obviously viewed the Yahwism of Moses' Kenite father-in-law differently. For the view "that Exodus 18 has transmitted an alternative version of the origins of the legal tradition ..." see also Blenkinsopp, *Pentateuch,* p. 138 (and the further discussion of this matter below).

[26]For an analysis of these differing land-entry traditions and their implications for cult history, see especially Ronald Clements, *Abraham and David, Genesis 15 and its Meaning for Israelite Tradition,* Studies in Biblical Theology, Second Series 5 (Naperville: Alec R. Allenson, Inc., 1967), pp. 35–46.

[27]For the view that Judah was not originally a member of the older pre-monarchic Israelite federation of the north, see Clements, *Abraham and David,* p. 44, who notes the lack of any reference to Judah or Simeon in the pre-monarchic Song of Deborah (Judges 5). M. Weinfeld, "The Emergence of the Deuteronomic Movement, The Historical Antecedents," in *Das Deuteronomium, Entstehung, Gestalt und Botschaft,* Bibliotheca Ephemeridum Theologicarum Lovaniensium LXVIII, ed. Norbert Lohfink (Leuven University Press, 1985), p. 94, suggests that Judges 1:1–2:5 may be a late Judahite document containing "ancient material which was added as an appendix [to the Levite history] in later times."

[28]Actually, the evidence indicating close links between the clans of Judah and the Kenites, and especially Hebron and the Kenites, is far more substantial than is generally recognized, as Olyan, "Zadok's Origins" (see fn. 20), has shown.

[29]On this fusion of Yahwist and pre-Yahwist traditions at Hebron, see Clements, *Abraham and David,* pp. 44–46.

[30]For a review of the El epithets in the patriarchal narratives of Genesis, see Cross, *Canaanite Myth,* pp. 46–60, and the further discussion of this tradition in Ch. 4.

[31]*Ibid.,* p. 71.

[32]Cross, *Canaanite Myth,* pp. 198f., conjectures that because the bull-icon at Bethel obviously "had connections with the house of Aaron," the priests there must have claimed Aaronic descent as well. To support this thesis, he refers to "an archaic tradition (in Judges 20:26–28) placing Phinehas the son of Eleazar the son of Aaron at the sanctuary of Bethel." Based on Judges 18:30 he also speculates that a Mushite (Levite) priesthood was put in place at Dan, and concludes "that Jeroboam carefully appointed two priesthoods for his two national shrines [Dan and Bethel], one of Mushite stock, one of Aaronite ancestry" (p. 199). However, if it is true that calf-icons were placed at both shrines (see 1 Kings 12:28–30), this would mean that a Levite priesthood was put in charge of a calf-shrine, something not very likely in the light of the harsh criticism levied against these shrines in Levite writings. The impression conveyed by the Levite historians that Jeroboam was both following traditions, but also innovating, when he set up this priesthood and the cult of these shrines, seems credible (see 1 Kings 12:32f.).

[33]Evidence that Levite communities, even so, remained intact and continued to perpetuate their own unique traditions in both northern kingdom Israel and Judah during this period, and, moreover, made their point of view known at these national shrines, will be the focus of our discussion in Ch. 5.

4. DIFFERING THEOLOGIES AMONG THE PRIESTLY HOUSES

[1]Cross, *Canaanite Myth,* p. 47, notes that many of the attributes and epithets attributed to El in Canaanite texts are reproduced in our biblical sources: *'El elyon,* El Most High, "Creator of heaven and earth" (Gen. 14:18); *'El shaddai,* "El of the mountain" (Gen. 17:1; Exod. 6:2f.); *'El 'olam,* "El of eternity" (Gen. 14:18f.); *'El elohe yisrael,* "El, god of [the patriarch] Israel" (Gen. 33:20); *'El Bethel,* "El Bethel" (Gen. 35:7); most of these epithets are associated with one or another of the patriarchal sanctuaries: "El the eternal" (Beersheba); "El Most

High" (Jerusalem); "El god of Israel" (Shechem); "El Bethel" (Bethel). On the basis of Gen. 17:1 it is has been conjectured that "El Shaddai" was the name associated with the altar at Hebron, although it is also associated with Bethel (Gen. 48:3) and seems to have had a more generalized usage. Cross observes that "unlike the great gods who represent the powers behind the phenomena of nature, 'El is in the first instance a social god. He is the primordial father of gods and men, sometimes stern, often compassionate, always wise in judgment" (p. 42).

[2]For an interpretation of these texts as cult legends preserved and transmitted at the Hebron shrine and revelatory of the theological and territorial self-understanding of the groups that worshiped there, see Ronald Clements, *Abraham and David, Genesis 15 and its Meaning for Israelite Tradition,* Studies in Biblical Theology, Second Series (Naperville: Alec R. Allenson, Inc., 1967).

[3]Cross, *Canaanite Myth,* p. 71.

[4]Cross, *Canaanite Myth,* p. 72. Examples cited are: Yahweh's role as judge in the court of El (Psalm 82; Psalm 89:6–8) and the general picture of Yahweh as the head of the Divine council; Yahweh's kingship (Exodus 15:18; Deuteronomy 33:15; Numbers 24:21); Yahweh's wisdom, age, and compassion ... and above all, Yahweh as creator and father (Genesis 49:25; Deuteronomy 32:6). For a review of the evidence suggesting that "the original god of Israel was El," see also Mark Smith, *The Early History of God, Yahweh and the Other Deities in Ancient Israel* (San Francisco: Harper & Row, 1990), pp. 7–12.

[5]*Canaanite Myth,* p. 72.

[6]The Canaanite origin of these calf-icons was already noted and discussed in Ch. 3.

[7]It should be observed, however, that the Holiness Code has Moses-only sections spliced in as well. Regarding these "Deuteronomic" supplements, see Joseph Blenkinsopp, *The Pentateuch, An Introduction to the First Five Books of the Bible* (Doubleday: New York, 1992), pp. 223–225. Also, the "cultic decalogue" in Exod. 34:17–27 should possibly be added to the list of the Pentateuch's Kenite-Aaronite sources (see H. H. Rowley, "Moses and the Decalogue," *Bulletin of the John Ryland's Library* XXXIV [1951–52], pp. 81–118).

[8]The opinion of Cross, *Canaanite Myth,* p. 73, and Friedman, *Who Wrote the Bible?,* p. 186, that the Tent of Meeting which Josh. 18:1

reports was set up at Shiloh was the *Aaronite* Tent of Meeting is questionable in the light of the fact that only Joshua is reported to have
been present at this shrine (Joshua 18:3; cp. Exod. 33:11) and the later
traditions about Shiloh report nothing about the existence or survival
of such an elaborate structure at that place, but only of the presence
there of the ark of God within a modest house of Yahweh, cared for by
a single priest and his two sons (1 Sam. 1:3, 9; 3:3). Yet, our sources
report there *was* a Tent of Meeting in Jerusalem prior to the building of
the temple (see 1 Kings 8:4), although Chronicles states that it was
located not where the ark was, but "on the high place at Gibeon" and
that it was cared for by the Zadokites (1 Chron. 16:37–42); from there
it was taken, with the ark, into the completed temple (2 Chron. 1:3;
5:5). For the hypothesis (first suggested by Gerhard von Rad) that *this*
Tent of Meeting was initially located at Hebron before being trans-
ferred to Jerusalem, see Murray Lee Newman, Jr., *The People of the
Covenant, A Study of Israel from Moses to the Monarchy* (New York,
Nashville: Abingdon Press, 1962), p. 6.

[9]The way this Psalter was supplemented and edited for use in the
Second Temple period is discussed in Ch. 9.

[10]Regarding the date and theology of this Psalm, see Leslie C. Allen,
Psalms 101–150, Word Biblical Commentary 21 (Waco: Word Books,
1983), pp. 207–209, who rejects the notion that it is post-exilic, on the
basis that "there is no hint that Jerusalem has suffered the exile" and it
so clearly "presupposes the Davidic monarchy as a contemporary institution" (p. 207). In Deut. 10:1–5 the ark serves primarily as a reposito-
ry for the Decalogue. On the transfer of the ark to Jerusalem, see also
Psalm 78 (a Levite Asaph Psalm), which portrays this happening as a
consequence of actions taken by Yahweh in the wake of northern
Israel's apostasy (78:59–72).

[11]Clements, *Abraham and David,* p. 63, suggests that "by its application to the royal covenant of the Davidic house it [Yahweh's
covenant with Abraham] came to be subsumed within it."

[12]For evidence suggesting that not just the ark, but the Tabernacle,
formerly at Hebron (see above, fn. 8), actually was incorporated into
the "holy of holies" at this same time (as 2 Chron. 1:3–6; 5:2–5 suggest), see Friedman, *Who Wrote the Bible?,* pp. 174–187.

[13]For the primacy of this theme within the Jerusalem Zion tradition
in the pre-exilic period, see Bernhard W. Anderson, "Introduction:

Mythopoeic and Theological Dimensions of Biblical Creation Faith," in *Creation in the Old Testament,* ed. Bernhard W. Anderson, Issues in Religion and Theology, 6 (Philadelphia: Fortress, 1984), pp. 1–24; Ben C. Ollenburger, *Zion the City of the Great King, A Theological Symbol of the Jerusalem Cult* (Sheffield: Academic Press, 1987); John J. Schmitt, "Pre-Israelite Jerusalem," *Scripture in Context, Essays on the Comparative Method,* Pittsburgh Theological Monograph Series 34, Earl D. Evans, William W. Hallo, John B. White, eds. (Pittsburgh: The Pickwick Press, 1980), pp. 101–121.

[14]The Deuteronomistic History identifies Solomon as having taken the initiative in this important new development, a point confirmed by three headings of the book of Proverbs (Prov. 1:1; 10:1; 25:1). Regarding the plausibility and significance of this *novum* in Israelite tradition, see Walter Brueggemann, "The Social Significance of Solomon as Patron of Wisdom," in *The Sage in Israel and the Ancient Near East,* John Gammie, Leo Perdue, eds. (Winowa Lake: Eisenbrauns, 1990), pp. 117–132, and our further discussion of this issue in Ch. 9, fn. 19.

[15]The unity of Israel's two priestly houses in the praise of Yahweh near the Psalm's end (135:19–20) is likely redactional, reflecting the ecumenical ideals and goals of those who edited the Psalter in its final form (further to this point, see the discussion of the Psalter's final redaction in Ch. 9).

[16]The first to notice the absence of references to Moses in his role as covenant mediator in Psalms of this type was Gerhard von Rad, *The Problem of the Hexateuch, and other essays* (London: SCM Press, 1966), pp. 1–78; however, he thought Psalm 106 was an exception, since only here and in Neh. 9, he wrote, "does the Sinai episode appear as an event of the redemption story" (p. 53). However, the Sinai episode "as an event of the redemption story" is also missing from Psalm 106 (the only thing mentioned is the sins committed there). This leaves Neh. 9 as the sole example of a recitative hymn in which these diverse traditions (creation, promise to the patriarchs, land entry *and* Sinai covenant) are brought together. On the importance of Neh. 9 as a climactic chapter of the Hebrew scriptures and a key to its theological and editorial intentions, see Ch. 7.

[17]Both the cultic decalogue (Exod. 34:17–26) and the Holiness Code prohibit metal "godlets" (Exod. 34:17–26; Lev. 19:4), but it is not

clear that this was meant as a ban against worshiping all other gods. In any case, from Solomon onward other gods were worshiped at Jerusalem (1 Kings 11:5–8) and the priesthood there does not seem to have objected so long as Yahweh was honored as "Most High over all the earth, far transcending all gods" (Psalm 97:9; Exod. 17:11). For a similar conclusion, see R. H. Lowery, *The Reforming Kings, Cults and Society in First Temple Judah,* Journal for the Study of the Old Testament, Supplement Series 120 (Sheffield: Academic Press, 1991), whose "study of the pre-Assyrian period ... shows that syncretism was the norm in the First Temple cult from the very beginning" (p. 139). Further to this issue, see below.

[18]The eradication of Bethel and the other shrines of this region by the Judean reformer, Josiah, is noted in 2 Kings 23:15–20.

[19]The references to Joshua personally studying and teaching "everything written in the Book of the Law of Moses" in the earlier parts of Joshua (1:6–9; 8:32–35; 23:1–16) are not carried over to Joshua 24, nor are any subsequent leaders so characterized until Josiah, (2 Kings 23:25), although David (1 Kings 2:1–4), Solomon (1 Kings 3:14; 8:57) and Hezekiah (2 Kings 18:6) are said to have followed the commandments and teachings of Moses, and in one instance King Joash is said to have followed a specific commandment which was "in accordance with what is written in the Book of Moses" (2 Kings 14:6).

[20]Regarding this, see Dale Patrick, *Old Testament Law* (London: SCM Press, 1986), pp. 64f., who dates both the Book of the Covenant and its narrative framework, consisting of the initial negotiation of the covenant (19:3–8) and the ceremonial ratification of this code (24:3–8), to the period of the judges (1200–1000 BCE).

[21]Of Hezekiah it is reported that no king after him "could be compared with him—nor any of those before him" (2 Kings 18:5). In other words, not even David was regarded as being as faithful to the "commandments of Moses" as was Hezekiah.

[22]It is generally agreed that Deut. 4:44–28:68 was the original book; for a review and analysis of its origins during the cataclysmic events leading up to the Assyrian invasions and the destruction of the northern kingdom Israel, see M. Weinfeld, "The Emergence of the Deuteronomic Movement, The Historical Antecedents," *Das Deuteronomium, Entstehung, Gestalt und Botschaft,* Bibliotheca Ephemeridum Theologicarum Lovaniensium LXVII (Leuven:

University Press, 1985), pp. 76–98; also Moshe Weinfeld, *Deuteronomy 1–11, A New Translation with Introduction and Commentary, Anchor Bible*, (Doubleday: New York, 1991), pp. 44–53.

[23]For a review of the evidence supportive of a possible connection between Deuteronomy and the levitical priests of Anathoth, see Friedman, *Who Wrote the Bible?*, pp. 119–135. This suggestion is not meant to preclude the thesis of Moshe Weinfeld (*Deuteronomy 1–11*, pp. 55–57), that a "school of scribes" closely associated with Hezekiah was responsible for creating this book, since it seems quite possible that the Levites of this period forged the kind of links between their teachings and the wisdom-traditions of Jerusalem that are reflected in the wise sayings attributed to "the men of Hezekiah" (Levites?) in Prov. 25–29. Further to the way these traditions are interrelated in the final redaction of Proverbs, see Ch. 9.

[24]Weinfeld, *Deuteronomy,* pp. 47f., dates the beginning of this reform movement to the exile of the Israelite population, which started in 732 with the invasion of Tiglath Pileser III into Galilee (2 Kings 15:29), and conjectures that this event "deeply shocked the nation of Israel" and prompted "the faithful of the nation ... to ponder Israel's destiny." Also worth noting are the references in Kings to "the people of the land" who were active in reforms of this type from the mid-ninth century BCE onward (2 Kings 11:13–20; 14:21; 21:24). Blenkinsopp, *Pentateuch,* p. 217, in agreement with von Rad, suggests that "the religious and political views of these people" were shared by the country priests referred to in Deuteronomy and that "it was this constituency that found a voice, the voice of Moses, in the political, social, and religious program of Deuteronomy."

[25]Weinfeld, *Deuteronomy* pp. 4f., believes the book's genre is modeled either on Egyptian antecedents ("wisdom instructions ... dressed in the form of testaments of kings and viziers to their successors"), or on a ceremony of succession attested in the neo-Assyrian Empire in the vassal treaties of Esarhaddon ("Deuteronomy, Book of," *Anchor Bible Dictionary* II, p. 169). The Code of Hammurabi also affords illuminating parallels: with its central section itemizing certain laws, just as in Deut. 12–26, introduced and concluded by personal speeches of Hammurabi himself in which the source, wisdom and authority of the law being set forth is explained and advocated, as in Deut. 1–11;

27–28. This was the way in which national covenants or constitutions were drafted and promulgated in the world of that time.

[26]I am indebted to Ronald Clements, *God's Chosen People, A Theological Interpretation of the Book of Deuteronomuy* (London: SCM Press, 1968), for this and several other insights in this section of my study. He writes that "Deuteronomy represents a very early, and a remarkably comprehensive, attempt at reforming religion by a programme of religious education in which every person was to be included, from the king as the head of the nation to every child in every home" (p. 13). Weinfeld, *Deuteronomy,* p. 55, characterizes the book similarly as "a manual for the king and the people," one whose "main interest is the education of the king and his people"; its contents "revolutionized all aspects of Israelite religion" (p. 37).

[27]Weinfeld, *Ibid.,* p. 10.

[28]The way Deuteronomy upgrades and replaces older laws, especially those of the Book of the Covenant, is helpfully surveyed by Weinfeld, *Ibid.,* pp. 19–24.

[29]Clements, *Abraham and David,* pp. 66f.

[30]*Ibid.,* p. 67. Clements puts the matter also as follows: the "two covenants were not unrelated in the Deuteronomic view, for the oath given to Abraham served as a kind of prophetic anticipation of the Horeb covenant, since it was through the latter that the promise of the land was brought to fulfilment. In Deuteronomy it is the Horeb covenant, rather than the Davidic, which forms the fulfillment of the promise to the patriarchs" (p. 66).

[31]The point of ambiguity in Exod. 34 lies in the fact that in 34:27 Moses is told to put the cultic laws just cited in Exod. 34:10–26 into writing, and it is these which are then specifically identified as "the covenant which I [Yahweh] made with you and with Israel," whereas in the very next verse (34:28), yet another list is referred to: the "Ten Words" which God had written on stone tablets (Exod. 32:16), but which were broken (32:19), and had to be rewritten by God (34:1, 28). One has the impression that the redactors of Exod. 34 wanted to forge a compromise by ascribing a status of some sort to *both* lists of laws. For further analysis of the redactional complexities of this section of the Tetrateuch, see Ch. 7.

[32]For a review of the wealth of evidence indicative of the syncretis-

tic practices in vogue at Israel's national shrines during this period, see Mark S. Smith, *The Early History of God*, pp. 145–152.

[33]It is not clear to me why modern researchers such as Bernhard Lang, *Monotheism and the Prophetic Minority, An Essay in Biblical History and Sociology* (Sheffield: The Almond Press, 1983), reject out of hand what the Levites themselves imply regarding the origins of this conviction, namely, that it was at Horeb in the time of Moses that the monotheistic foundations of Israelite faith were established.

[34]Weinfeld, "The Deuteronomic Movement, "p. 91, states that "such a rigorous policy, obliging the extermination of the whole population of the land whether fighting or passive is utopian and is indeed unheard of in the historical accounts of Israel." He conjectures that it "reflects the bitter struggle with the Canaanite religion and culture ongoing from the time of Elijah until the time of Josiah. Indeed the reason for the annihilation of the Canaanites in Deut. 20:18 is one of *Kulturkampf* ....It seems that Deuteronomy adopted the ancient doctrine of Herem from the North (cf. also 1 Kgs 20:42) and applied it theoretically towards the seven nations of the land of Canaan" (p. 92).

[35]Weinfeld, *Ibid.,* p. 86, suggests that the novel proposal that worship be centralized in Jerusalem was assisted by the de facto destruction of outlying worship centers by the Assyrian invasions.

[36]Weinfeld, "Deuteronomy, Book of," pp. 175–178, states that "there is not one example in the Deuteronomic literature of God's *dwelling in the temple* or the building of a *house of God.* The Temple is always the *dwelling of his name* and the house is always built *for his name.*" This literature also downplays the importance of sacrifice "for its own sake," Weinfeld writes. For example, nowhere are sacrifices ever spoken of as the "food of God" (as frequently in Leviticus), and there are also no references to sin-and-guilt offerings. Rather, as 1 Kings 8:27–28, 41–61 indicates, the sanctuary is "conceived as a house of prayer, and not as a cultic center" (p. 176). In his opinion, innovations such as these represent "a turning point in the evolution of the faith of Israel" (p. 175).

[37]Weinfeld, *Deuteronomy,* p. 24, points out that in contrast to the older sources where instruction of children is connected with certain ceremonies, the instructional approach advocated here "is divorced from all ceremony" and carried out in the midst of daily life.

[38]The importance of this Psalm within the Psalter's final redaction will be noted in our discussion of this issue in Ch. 9.

[39]For a description and interpretation of these two theologies, see Jon D. Levenson, *Sinai and Zion, An Entry into the Jewish Bible* (San Francisco: Harper & Row, 1985); like others, Levenson is puzzled over Zion's "deafness to the voice of Sinai" and why this was so (p. 216).

5. HEIGHTENED TENSIONS DUE TO THE "BATTLE OF THE PROPHETS"

[1]The pioneering work in viewing the prophets within their diverse theological traditions was that of Gerhard von Rad, *The Message of the Prophets* (New York: Harper & Row, 1967); however, it was Robert R. Wilson's seminal study, *Prophecy and Society in Ancient Israel* (Philadelphia: Fortress Press, 1980) that called attention to the differing social locations of these diverse traditions and the implications this had for their interpretation.

[2]For details, see Trent C. Butler, *Joshua,* Word Biblical Commentary. 7 (Waco: Word Books, 1983), p. 226.

[3]John Gray, *Joshua, Judges and Ruth,* New Century Bible (Greenwood: Attic Press, 1967), p. 133.

[4]Norman Gottwald, *The Tribes of Yahweh, A Sociology of the Religion of Liberated Israel, 1250–1050 B.C.E.* (Maryknoll: Orbis Books, 1979), p. 372.

[5]In making this point I have in mind Wilson's too sharp distinction (in his *Prophecy and Society,* Chs. 4 and 5) between prophets of the northern Ephraimite and southern Judean traditions.

[6]Although unspecified in his book, most commentators agree that Hosea was a resident of the northern kingdom, since most of the place names mentioned are in that region. His home might have been at Shechem, a city venerable to the Levites (Deut. 11:29; 27:11–14; 1 Kings 12:1) and one of the few place names mentioned in his book without criticism (see Hos. 6:9).

[7]Our discussion concerns only chs. 1–3 of his book; the oracles of hope in Micah 4–7 are generally thought to be not from Micah but

from the compilers of the book's final edition (see Ch. 7 for further comments on why these books were edited as they now are).

[8]This is the suggestion of Hans Walter Wolff, *Micah the Prophet* (Philadelphia: Fortress, 1978).

[9]See Ch. 4 for a discussion of other forces that may have converged to bring about the Levite reforms at this juncture. For a comparable perspective on the origins and appropriation of the writings of these prophets "by descendants of an ancient order of priests, known as Levites," see William Doorly, *Isaiah of Jerusalem. An Introduction* (New York: Paulist, 1992), p. xvii.

[10]The kind of renewal Isaiah anticipated is alluded to in Isa. 7:17. There he states it will be "times for you, your people and your ancestral House, such as have not been seen since Ephraim broke away from Judah" (in other words, unity, prosperity and honor such as Israel had not experienced since the reigns of David and Solomon before the kingdom was divided).

[11]Richard Elliott Friedman, *The Exile and Biblical Narrative,* Harvard Semitic Monographs 22 (Chico: Scholars Press, 1981), p. 74; Friedman believes that this was "an age in which two priestly houses were close to power ..." (pp. 75f.).

[12]*Ibid.,* p. 71.

[13]Whether from Jeremiah or others, these texts inform us of the kind of thinking about the future that was going on in Levite circles during the period following Jerusalem's destruction, just as a comparable set of teachings in Ezekiel 40–48 inform us of what Zadokite circles of the time were thinking (see below).

[14]Robert R. Wilson, *Prophecy and Society,* p. 284, is of the opinion that while influenced by the Deuteronomic reform movement, Ezekiel did not become "a total convert to the Deuteronomic position," but "seems to have attempted to make his own personal synthesis of the Zadokite and Deuteronomic positions." Gordon H. Matties, *Ezekiel 18 and the Rhetoric of Moral Discourse,* Society of Biblical Literature Dissertation Series 126 (Atlanta: Scholars Press, 1990), pp. 24f., may be closer to the truth when he proposes that while influenced by the Deuteronomistic School, Ezekiel "finds commonality with the Priestly tradition as it seeks to define itself over against the Deuteronomistic School," but "differs significantly enough" from even that (the Priestly tradition) to represent "an independent voice in the midst of competing

claims between 597 and 516." My own conclusion is that Ezekiel was deeply influenced by the Levite Moses-traditions, but the foundations and structural features of his thought remain fundamentally Zadokite.

[15]Chs. 38–39 of Ezekiel are generally recognized as a late insertion, disturbing somewhat the connections between the promise in Ezek. 37:28 and the description of that sanctuary in chs. 40–48. However, even with these chapters included the vision remains essentially the same in terms of the overall impact of the restoration temple on the world of the nations: "And the nations will know that I am Yahweh the sanctifier of Israel, when my sanctuary is with them for ever" (Ezek. 37:28).

[16]For the mythological roots of this vision and its importance for the total theological outlook of Ezekiel, see Jon Douglas Levenson, *Theology of the Program of Restoration of Ezekiel 40–48,* Harvard Semitic Monograph Series 10 (Missoula: Scholars Press, 1976).

[17]This legislation might therefore be characterized, not so much as a "replacement torah" for the Deuteronomic teachings (Levenson, *Ibid.,* p. 39), but as an interpretation (or midrash) aimed at reconciling the two priestly traditions. Some of the challenges to be faced in the decades ahead are thus clearly indicated for the first time (see our discussion in the following chapters for how this challenge was met).

[18]According to the census of the heads of families of those "who returned from the captivity of the Exile" in Ezra 2, the ratio of Levites to priests was roughly sixty to one (2:36–40).

[19]Joel also reflects Zadokite tradition but is generally dated to a period *after* the Ezra-Nehemiah reforms and is, therefore, not directly germane to the issues under investigation at this point in our study; further to how his and the visions of these prophets generally relate to biblical eschatology overall, see our comments in Ch. 10.

[20]Perhaps the gloss in the Hebrew text of Hag. 2:5 which states that "this is the covenant which I made with you when you came out of Egypt" (missing from the Greek Septuagint version) may be regarded as an early attempt at rectifying the one-sided theology of this book.

[21]How to date and interpret Zech. 9–14 continues to baffle scholars; most regard these chapters as addenda that were composed in the final decades of the fourth century BCE, after Alexander the Great's conquests of this region; thus, like Joel, they belong to a period *after* the

Ezra-Nehemiah reforms and are not immediately relevant to the purposes of this chapter.

[22]Further to this novel reinterpretation and its theological implications, see Mark S. Smith, "Běrît 'am/Běrît 'ōlām: A New Proposal for the Crux of Isa 42:6," *Journal of Biblical Literature,* 100/2 (1981), pp. 241–243.

[23]This analysis differs with that of Paul D. Hanson, *The People Called, The Growth of Community in the Bible* (San Francisco: Harper & Row, 1986), p. 267, when he characterizes the communal tensions of this period as the result "of party strife" among a number of nameless "little groups" each of which "derived its sense of direction and purpose from the mandates of its leaders, leaders intent on establishing their authority over all opposition, and not hesitating to call the judgment of God on the heads of their rivals." Closer to the truth is his perception that "a surge of chaos" welled forth "within a strife-ridden community" in "the oracles the Zadokites addressed against Levites, and the Levites addressed against Zadokites ..." (p. 267).

6. THE EZRA-NEHEMIAH REFORMS AS A RESPONSE

[1]That such rules were compiled right at this time is explicitly stated in Neh. 13:30; that it was one of the purposes of Chronicles to enshrine these rules in writing is the conclusion drawn by several recent studies which will be cited and examined more closely in Chs. 7 and 8.

[2]For a review of the scholarly debate over whether Nehemiah's mission preceded instead of followed Ezra's, and the arguments in support of the biblical chronology, see Blenkinsopp, *Ezra-Nehemiah A Commentary,* The Old Testament Library (Philadelphia: Westminster, 1988), pp. 139–144.

[3]Blenkinsopp, *Ezra-Nehemiah,* p. 45, puts the argument in support of this conclusion as follows: "To the extent that Neh. 8 records an actual event, which it clearly did in the intent of the author, it is also more likely that Ezra discharged his task with respect to the law shortly after his arrival rather than waiting twelve years to do so."

[4]Whether or not Hilkiah was in fact Ezra's grandfather, the report in 2 Kings 22:8–20 of Hilkiah's response to discovering the Book of the Law affords a striking point of comparison for the picture (in Ezra) of

Ezra's involvement with this same book. The Zadokite priest Hilkiah of 2 Kings 22 appears to be surprised and unfamiliar with the book he has discovered; on the other hand, Ezra is an avid student and exponent of its teachings.

⁵For details on Persian policy in this period, see Joseph Blenkinsopp, *The Pentateuch,* pp. 238f., who cites evidence indicating that the Persians seemingly "had no uniform legal code of their own," so as a consequence, respected and fostered "the very diverse political and social systems obtaining throughout their vast empire, granting semi-autonomous status as long as edicts were obeyed and tribute paid." Indeed, there is a document (the Demotic Chronicle) that reports of a very similar commission being set up by Darius I to codify the traditional Egyptian laws.

⁶On this point, see Blenkinsopp, *Ezra-Nehemiah,* p. 160.

⁷This separatist action is to be distinguished from the one described in Ezra 9–10, which had to do with the specific issue of what Israelite men should do who were *already* married to foreign wives. That action may have been a consequence of the more generalized "separation" from foreigners alluded to here.

⁸The proposals made in Ezek. 44:10–14 regarding what Levites may and may not do at the temple can serve as a kind of benchmark for measuring the progress that actually occurred under the leadership of Ezra and Nehemiah.

⁹On this point, see our previous discussion of this text (Neh. 9) in Ch. 4, and the survey of data pointing to the prominence of Deuteronomic tradition in "the Law" that Ezra promulgated, in Blenkinsopp, *Ezra-Nehemiah,* pp. 152–156.

¹⁰So Blenkinsopp *Ezra-Nehemiah,* p. 178, who describes them as a "prophetic-eschatological group" also known as "servants of Yahweh" in Isa. 65:8–16; regarding this same group, see also the comments of Paul Hanson, *The People Called,* pp. 284–285, who suggests that "fear of Yahweh" was their badge of distinction.

¹¹Blenkinsopp, *Ezra-Nehemiah,* p. 346, explains the inclusion of Ezra's name at the head of one of the two choirs involved in dedicating the walls Nehemiah had built (see Neh. 12:36) as "an editorial addition from the time when the activity of the two men had been amalgamated into one movement of reform." The same can be said of Nehemiah's name in Neh. 8:3, which is missing in the parallel version in 1 Esdras.

[12]See Ch. 2 (B, 2,d) for an earlier discussion of this incident.

[13]The interlude between that era and the age of Nehemiah is explicitly noted in Neh. 12:46f. For additional comments on the role of the Davidic era in providing the mandates and models for Levite participation in Second Temple affairs, see the discussion of Chronicles in Ch. 8.

[14]On the considerable significance of this intrusion on Nehemiah's part into the domain of the temple and his subsequent sweeping assertion of authority in the affairs of this community, see Michael Fishbane, *Biblical Interpretation in Ancient Israel* (Oxford: Clarendon Press, 1985), pp. 127–128.

[15]Further regarding their role in the formation of this library, see Ch. 8.

7. THE BIRTH OF A SCRIPTURE BASED COMMUNITY: THE LAW AND THE PROPHETS

[1]"The kings and prophets" might refer to the books of the Deuteronomistic History (Joshua, Judges, Samuel, Kings) and the prophetic books that introduce and follow them (the Pentateuch and four prophetic scrolls); by "the writings of David" the Psalms must be meant, and "the letters of the kings on the subject of offerings" could be a reference to Ezra-Nehemiah, where such letters are to be found.

[2]I will have more to say in Chs. 8 and 9 about the custodians of this collection and how it grew, was accessed and became authoritative in the wider community.

[3]It is generally thought that the many stylistic and theological features which Ezra-Nehemiah and Chronicles have in common mark them as the product of a single guild or school—for the evidence supportive of this conclusion, see Blenkinsopp, *Ezra-Nehemiah,* pp. 47–54.

[4]This is the conclusion of Myers, *Ezra-Nehemiah, Anchor Bible* (Garden City: Doubleday, 1965), p. LXX. Had its author compiled this work in a later period, he writes, "there would doubtless have been clear hints, if not overt reference, to some conspicuous events.... The reason the [genealogical] lists end where they do is that they represent the situation at the time of writing (ca. 400)."

[5]The following are examples: Neh. 8:1, 8; 9:13–14, 26, 29, 34; 12:44; Ezra 3:2; 7:6; 1 Chron. 6:49; 22:13; 28:7–8; 2 Chron. 25:4; 30:16; 33:8; 34:31–33.

[6]Examples would be: Deut. 7:3 in Neh. 13:25; Deut. 30:1–5 in Neh. 1:8–9; Deut. 24:16 in 2 Chron. 25:4; Lev. 23:42–43 in Neh. 8:14–15.

[7]Blenkinsopp, *Ezra-Nehemiah,* p. 157. This is also the conclusion of Judson R. Shaver, *Torah and the Chronicler's History Work,* Brown Judaic Studies 196 (Atlanta: Scholars Press, 1989, p. 128, and Michael Fishbane, *Biblical Interpretation in Ancient Israel* (Oxford: Clarendon Press, 1985). The latter states it as his impression, based on an examination of the exegetical techniques being used, that this community had "Torah and its exegesis at its living centre" (p. 114).

[8]For a comparison of these two literary complexes, see *A Synoptic Harmony of Samuel, Kings, and Chronicles, With Related Passages from Psalms, Isaiah, Jeremiah, and Ezra,* James D. Newsome, Jr., ed. (Grand Rapids: Baker Book House, 1986, and the listing of these parallels in Jacob M. Myers, *I Chronicles, Anchor Bible* (New York: Doubleday, 1965), pp. XLIX–LXII.

[9]Examples would be the characterization of Second Temple Israel as a "holy seed," in Ezra 9:2, in fulfillment of the "holy seed" prophecies of Isa. 6:13 and 61:9 (see Fishbane, *Biblical Interpretation,* p. 123); Ezra's patterning of his return from Babylon on the "second exodus" prophecies of Second Isaiah.

[10]For a similar conclusion, see Donn Morgan, *Between Test and Community, The "Writings" in Canonical Interpretation* (Minneapolis: Fortress, 1990), pp. 64–66.

[11]The "separation" spoken of here (which is to be distinguished from that referred to in Ezra 9–12, which had to do with the issue of foreign wives) is often misconstrued. It was not a physical separation, which under the circumstances would have been impossible, but the assumption of a new collective identity that would enable this community to live and survive as a self-conscious enclave within the ethnic and political multiculturalism of its surrounding world.

[12]For a similar observation, see Peter R. Ackroyd, "The Theology of the Chronicler," Ch. 11, *The Chronicler in His Age,* Journal for the Study of the Old Testament, Supplement Series 101 (Sheffield: JSOT Press, 1991), pp. 280–289, who characterizes the theology of both this and the Chronicler's writings as a whole as a "unification theology"

that seeks "the reconciliation in one body of literature" of both priestly and deuteronomic strands (p. 283).

[13]The only other recitation of this kind in the Hebrew scriptures that comes close to this one in theological and historical scope is Psalms 105–106, but even there (as noted earlier in Ch. 4) Aaronite-Zadokite perspectives predominate and themes vital to Levite tradition are still missing.

[14]Cross, *Canaanite Myth*, pp. 278–285; Friedman, *The Exile and Biblical Narrative*, pp. 1–25.

[15]The extraordinarily explicit reference in this prophecy to "Josiah" (1 Kings 13:2) as the one who will slaughter the priests of the high places is commonly regarded as a splice added when the account of his reforms was appended (see 2 Kings 23:20); otherwise, the prophecies of this chapter have to do with the destruction of the shrines of the northern kingdom and with the extinction of that kingdom (1 Kings 13:32–34), prophecies which the accounts in 2 Kings 17:5–41 of the Assyrian invasion view as having been fulfilled at that time (see 2 Kings 17:13–18, 21–23; 17:19–20 is another later splice merely stating, parenthetically, that "Judah did not keep the commandments of Yahweh their God either ..."). It may thus be argued that the reforms of Hezekiah and the fall of the northern kingdom were "the literary focus" of the original edition of the Deuteronomistic History, and not the reforms of Josiah (as Friedman proposes, *Ibid.,* p. 7).

[16]As will be noted in Ch. 9, there are also reasons for believing that early editions of the Psalter and the book of Proverbs were also produced at this time, with similar goals in view.

[17]Whether there is another "full stop" right after the report of the Josiah reforms, as Friedman suggests (*Ibid.,* p. 7), is thus unclear; rather the purpose of this final section (following the "stop" at 2 Kings 18:12) seems to be to report that after the destruction of the northern kingdom and the reforms of Hezekiah, developments occurred, including later mistakes by Hezekiah himself (see 2 Kings 20:12–19), which prompted Yahweh to decide that despite Josiah's sweeping reforms Judah too had to be destroyed, simply because in its case also the people failed to "listen" to "the whole Law which my servant Moses prescribed for them" (2 Kings 21:8–15).

[18]For the importance of the dynastic promises to David for Deuteronomistic theology, see Cross, *Canaanite Mythology,* pp. 281f.

[19]For a discussion of these superscriptions and their relevance for an understanding of how these volumes were assembled and edited, see Gene M. Tucker, "Prophetic Superscriptions and the Growth of the Canon," in *Canon and Authority, Essays in Old Testament Religion and Theology,* George Coats and Burke O. Long, eds. (Philadelphia: Fortress, 1977), pp. 56–70.

[20]For a more detailed discussion of this pattern, see Ronald E. Clements, "Patterns in the Prophetic Canon," *Canon and Authority,* pp. 42–55.

[21]The prologue in Exod 1:1–7, which emphasizes how few in number the Israelites were when they first migrated to Egypt, but then how numerous and powerful they became, is only loosely and somewhat awkwardly linked to the prior story about Joseph in Genesis. It seems apparent that it once functioned as the beginning of an independent account of Israel's formation as a people and its covenant with God. Blenkinsopp, *Pentateuch,* p. 135, points out that no similar break occurs in Exodus, Leviticus and Numbers. Rather what is notable here, he writes, is a structuring device that has a shorter book (Leviticus) between two longer books of roughly equal size (Exodus and Numbers), and these three books are in turn "enclosed by the much more distinctive and self-contained first and fifth books [Genesis and Deuteronomy]."

[22]For an account of some of the problems this entailed, see the prior discussion of these reforms in Chs. 2 and 6.

[23]For the following analysis of the redactional complexities of this section I am indebted to Brevard Childs, *The Book of Exodus,* The Old Testament Library (Philadelphia: Westminster, 1974), especially his comments on Exod. 34, pp. 604–610.

[24]It is important to note that the writing on stone "tablets" mentioned in Exod. 34:28 refers back to the writing *Yahweh* promised to do on the two stone tablets cut by Moses (see 34:1); this is *not* to be confused with the writing which Moses is commanded to do in 34:27. What is said in the latter verse (34:27) is that *Moses* was the one who wrote down "these words" (that is, the preceding cultic instructions), but *Yahweh* is the one who rewrote the decalogue of Exodus 20:1–17 (the Levite decalogue). Thus, it is this latter decalogue (the one in Exod. 20) that retains the position of preeminence it originally had for the Levites. Just so that there would be absolutely no question about this

matter, the text of this decalogue is repeated in Deut. 5, with a prologue and epilogue stressing that *this is it*—this and nothing else is what Yahweh wrote on the two stone tablets (see Deut. 5:22).

[25]For a comparable analysis, see Thomas Dozeman, *God on the Mountain, A Study of Redaction, Theology and Canon in Exodus 19–24,* SBL Monograph Series 37 (Atlanta: Scholars Press, 1989), who concludes that these chapters are a "canon-conscious" collation of deuteronomic and priestly legislation "as one literary Torah" (p. 199).

[26]John Van Seters, *Prologue to History, the Yahwist as Historian in Genesis* (Louisville: Westminster/John Knox, 1992).

[27]*Ibid.,* p. 331.

[28]*Ibid.,* p. 330.

[29]Especially to be observed is the extraordinarily detailed ethnographic map of the world's peoples in Gen. 10, which, along with the story depicting how Yahweh confused their languages and scattered them over the face of the earth because of their hubris (Gen. 11:1–9), forms the immediate backdrop for the story of Israel's origins and history which is begun in Gen. 11:10–32.

[30]I will be commenting further on this theme in the next two chapters. For a similar estimate of its centrality in the Hebrew scriptures, see Th. C. Vriezen, "Man and history. Israel and the world of nations. (Missionary activity)," in *An Outline of Old Testament Theology* (Oxford: Blackwood, 1960), pp. 227–231.

[31]My views as to who took the initiative in this enterprise and what they were essentially trying to do, are, I believe, not dissimilar from the conclusions of Joseph Blenkinsopp, *The Pentateuch,* p. 130, who conjectures that these volumes are fundamentally an amalgam of priestly and deuteronomic tradition and may be thought of either as "the D edition of the history up to the time of Moses" or as the opening part of a "continuous Deuteronomistic History extending from creation to the Babylonian exile." I believe it to be the latter, and that in its final redaction the four scrolls of the prophets were regarded as an integral and indispensable part of this collection as well.

[32]Dozeman, *God on the Mountain,* p. 200, observes that the pentateuchal compilers in Exodus went "out of their way not to harmonize the dissimilar traditions," with the result, he adds (tongue in cheek) that the "canonical Sinai complex" has truly become "Mosaic Legislation"!

8. CUSTODIANS AND TEACHERS OF THE
SECOND TEMPLE LIBRARY

[1]James A. Sanders, "Canon [Hebrew Bible]," *Anchor Bible Dictionary* (Doubleday: New York, 1992), I, p. 843, puts the matter as follows: "the canonical process was ... one of the bodies of literature passing the tests of time and space in terms of their value for many scattered believing communities." Donn Morgan, *Between Text & Community, The "Writings" in Canonical Interpretation* (Minneapolis: Fortress, 1990), believes this literature reflects "the agendas of many different communities in Israel and the Diaspora" (p. 53) and hypothesizes that individual "Writings" were first accepted in one of five communities of discourse (sages, liturgists, community builders, visionaries, and storytellers) before being accepted by the Jewish people as a whole (pp. 53–55).

[2]Morgan, *Ibid.,* p. 117.

[3]This is the point of view of Brevard Childs, *Introduction,* pp. 62–79. For a critique of Childs in this regard, see Mark G. Brett, *Biblical Criticism in Crisis? The Impact of the Canonical Approach on Old Testament Studies* (Cambridge University Press, 1991), pp. 150–153.

[4]The public accessibility of this library is also alluded to in II Esdras 14:45 when its "twenty–four books" are characterized as volumes which are available "for the worthy and unworthy to read" (Anchor Bible Translation). The role of temple officers in exercising oversight of these scriptures is reflected in the account given in the Letter of Aristeas of how their translation into Greek (the Septuagint) was carried out in Egypt by scholars commissioned and sent for that purpose by the High Priest at Jerusalem. For additional evidence of "The Temple as the shrine of the canon," see Beckwith, *Old Testament Canon,* pp. 80–86.

[5]On the origins, date and contents of this tractate, see Jacob Neusner, *Invitation to Midrash, A Teaching Book* (San Francisco: Harper & Row, 1989), pp. 8–17.

[6]Among books attributed to the "men of the Great Assembly" by the Babylonian Talmud are Ezekiel, the Scroll of the Twelve, Daniel, Esther, Ezra and Chronicles (Baba Bathra 15a).

[7]For a similar conclusion, see David Orton, *The Understanding*

Scribe, Matthew and the Apocalyptic Ideal, Journal for the Study of the New Testament, Supplement Series 25 (Sheffield, JSOT Press, 1988), p. 51, who proposes that since our sources speak of no other "men" in this period who would be more likely candidates, the Levites are in fact the persons Abot had in mind.

[8]According to André Lemaire, "Writing and Writing Materials," *Anchor Bible Dictionary,* VI, p. 1004, precisely how scrolls were housed in ancient libraries in order to keep them in their proper arrangement is not known, since "archaeological excavations have not yet discovered any ancient Egyptian library with scrolls still in situ."

[9]Beckwith, *Old Testament Canon,* pp. 181–234.

[10]The text in question opens with the expression, "the Rabbis taught," signifying that what follows is a "baraita" or an accepted teaching of the leaders of the Mishnaic period (second century CE).

[11]In arguing for its antiquity, Beckwith, *Ibid.,* pp. 211–22, notes that the saying of Jesus in the New Testament Gospels regarding the blood of martyrs from "the blood of Abel to the blood of Zachariah ..." (Luke 11:49–51/Matt. 23:34–36) presupposes the existence of a scriptural library like the one referred to in this text, one that began with Genesis and ended with Chronicles, since the murder of Abel is recorded in Genesis (4:1–8) and the murder of Zachariah in Chronicles (2 Chron. 24:19–22).

[12]It should be observed that while the four prophetic scrolls (Jeremiah, Ezekiel, Isaiah and the Book of the Twelve) overlap chronologically *at their beginnings,* in every case in *their final chapters* they end up at a point chronologically farther down the road than the previous volume. Thus, "the Law and the Prophets" may be viewed as a history of the world extending, stage by stage, from the beginning of time to a period just prior to the Ezra-Nehemiah reforms.

[13]*Ibid.,* p. 211.

[14]The evidence supportive of this conclusion is summarized by Blenkinsopp, *Ezra-Nehemiah,* pp. 47–54.

[15]In 2 Kings 23:8–9 reference is made to the coming to Jerusalem during the Josiah reforms of certain "priests of the high places ... to share unleavened bread with their "brother-priests" (2 Kings 23:8–9). As noted earlier, this may be a reference to Levites, but nothing is said here of their assuming a teaching role at Jerusalem at this time, but

only that despite being brother-priests to the Zadokites they were not permitted "to officiate at the altar ..." (23:9).

[16]A single pentateuchal text addresses this issue with a degree of specificity, and that is Num. 16:1–18:7, but even there the point clarified is more what Levites are *not* permitted to do vis-à-vis the priests than what their duties actually are. For a detailed analysis of what these chapters specify in this regard, see Ch. 7.

[17]Simon J. de Vries, "Moses and David as Cult Founders in Chronicles," *Journal of Biblical Literature,* 107/4 (1988), pp. 619–639 (p. 638).

[18]"The priests have Moses and Aaron," de Vries writes, "but who can substantiate levitical claims except David?—not his powerless descendants and not the authority figure in an eschatological program, but David and the preexilic Davidides whose deeds are narrated" (*Ibid.* p. 638).

[19]John W. Wright, "The Legacy of David in Chronicles: The Narrative Function of 1 Chronicles 23–27," *Journal of Biblical Literature* 110/2 (1991), pp. 229–242.

[20]*Ibid.,* p. 229.

[21]*Ibid.,* pp. 233f. Wright identifies seven instances in this corpus where the Davidic legislation cited in 1 Chron. 23–27 is alluded to as authorization for the duties of Levites and/or priests (1 Chron. 6:16–17; 9:22; 2 Chron. 8:14–15; 23:18–19; 29:25; 35:4, 15; Neh. 12:24, 45).

[22]In an essay entitled, "The Theology of the Chronicler," first published in 1973 (*Lexington Theological Quarterly* 8, pp. 101–116 and recently republished as Chapter 11 in *The Chronicler in His Age,* Journal for the Study of the Old Testament, Supplement Series 101 (Sheffield: JSOT Press, 1991), Peter R. Ackroyd develops the thesis that what we have in these volumes is the "reconciliation in one body of literature" of Priestly and Deuteronomic strands of thought which elsewhere in the Hebrew canon (the Law and the Prophets) are in a "somewhat incomplete union." This prompts him to ask: "Is the Chronicler thus perhaps the first theologian of the canon?" (p. 284). He believes that he was in that he "aimed at presenting a unifying concept of the nature of the Jewish religious community and hence of its theology and the meaning of its rich and varied traditions" (p. 280).

9. EDITING AND ADDING "THE OTHER BOOKS"

[1]See the chart in the Appendix for a comparison of this list and the list of books in modern Jewish Bibles. The list of these "Writings" in Baba Bathra 14b is chronologically arranged, whereas in later Jewish Bibles the smaller books were grouped together because of their association with certain Jewish festivals: the Song of Songs (Passover), Ruth (Pentecost), Lamentations (Ninth of Av), Ecclesiastes (Tabernacles), Esther (Purim). For our earlier comments on this talmudic text, Baba Bathra 14b, see Chs. 1 and 8.

[2]W. Zimmerli, *The Law and the Prophets, A Study of the Meaning of the Old Testament,* Harper Torchbooks (New York: Harper and Row, 1965), believes that only the two headings, "the Law and the Prophets," have what he terms "a particular theological signification" (p. 10); as a consequence he completely excludes "the Writings" from his otherwise insightful study of "the meaning of the Old Testament."

[3]The importance of Ezra-Nehemiah being at the temporal apex of this collection was noted in our prior discussion of this matter in Ch. 8.

[4]The degree to which Ezra-Nehemiah and Chronicles presuppose the existence and authority of "the Law and the Prophets" was already noted in Ch. 7; for a review of the evidence indicating that the other volumes of the "Writings" do so as well, see Donn Morgan, *Between Text & Community, The "Writings" in Canonical Interpretation* (Philadelphia: Fortress, 1990), who states that "when viewed as a whole," these books "clearly reflect the fact that the texts of Torah and Prophets were widely known and used" (p. 71).

[5]The Rabbis of the Talmud taught that Ruth comes first not just because the story it relates is chronologically first, but because, as they put it, "we do not begin with a record of suffering" but of "suffering with a sequel of [happiness], as R. Johanan said: Why was her name called Ruth?—Because there issued from her David who replenished the Holy One, blessed be He, with hymns and praises" (Baba Bathra 14b).

[6]For an analysis of the way this theme is reflected in the thematic design of "the Law and the Prophets" as a whole, see Ch. 8.

[7]I am indebted to André LaCocque, *The Feminine Unconventional, Four Subversive Figures in Israel's Tradition,* Overtures to Biblical Theology (Minneapolis: Fortress, 1990), p. 102, for this suggestion.

However, his characterization of the book's authors as "subversive" is not completely appropriate, in my opinion. They are actually quite conservative in their approach to scripture and tradition and seem to be working to humanize the attitudes of this community *from within* the framework of commonly accepted norms.

[8]Gerald Wilson, *The Editing of the Hebrew Psalter,* Society of Biblical Literature Dissertation Series 76 (Chico: Scholars Press, 1985), p. 207.

[9]Seventy-three psalms are assigned to David in the Massoretic Text; in thirteen of these notes are provided linking these psalms to specific incidents in David's life as these are described in Samuel (the specific Psalms are 3, 7, 18, 34, 51, 52, 54, 56, 57, 59, 60, 63, 92). According to Childs, *Introduction,* p. 521, in these prefatory notes "David is pictured simply as a man … who displays all the strengths and weaknesses of all human beings…." In this way "Psalms which once functioned within a cultic context were historicized by placing them within the history of David" and they were made immediately relevant for "the inner life of the psalmist."

[10]For the arguments supportive of the intentionality of this placement of royal Psalms as well as other features of this collection, see Gerald H. Wilson, "The Shape of the Book of Psalms," *Interpretation,* XLVI (1992), pp. 133f.; *The Editing of the Hebrew Psalter,* pp. 207–228.

[11]This is the opinion of of Harry P. Nasuti, *Tradition History and the Psalms of Asaph,* Society of Biblical Literature Dissertation Series, 88 (Atlanta: Scholars Press, 1988, pp. 188–191.

[12]For evidence of significant redactional activity at this time, see the discussion of this literature in Chs. 5 and 7, and our comments below (fn. 19) regarding the "men of Hezekiah" edition of Proverbs. Clinton McCann, Jr., "Books I–III and the Editorial Purpose of the Hebrew Psalter," in J. Clinton McCann, ed., *The Shape and Shaping of the Psalter,* JSOT, Supplement Series 159 (Sheffield: JSOT Press, 1993), pp. 105f., rightly notes that the placement of Levitical Korah and Asaph Psalms at the beginning of Book Two (42–49) and Three (73–83) points to the circles who compiled these books.

[13]Levitical hopes in this regard are also hinted at in the final verses of the Deuteronomistic History which report of the release from prison in Babylon of the heir to the Davidic throne, King Jehoiachin (2 Kings

25:27–30); hopes for a restoration of the Davidic kingdom are also expressed in several books of the prophets which were likely compiled and completed during this same period (see Hosea 3:4f.; Amos 9:11f.; Jer. 33:14–26; Ezek. 37:15–28). Thus, I cannot agree with McCann, *Ibid.,* p. 98, when he writes that the two rehearsals of Davidic/Zion theology in Book Three (Psalms 78:67–72; 89:1–38) and the two songs of Zion (Psalms 84 and 87), juxtaposed as they are with laments of the community, have the effect of making "the traditional hope ring hollow at best." I see no evidence in Book Three for thinking the hopes expressed were not authentic.

[14]Wilson, "Shape of the Book of Psalms," p. 141, suggests that Psalm 145, "draws the Psalter to an end and precipitates the concluding *hallel* of Psalms 146–150."

[15]See Ch. 7, section (d). For a useful summary of the data suggesting that (as in the case of "the Law and the Prophets") the Levites were again the guild chiefly responsible for this project, see Mark S. Smith, "The Levitical Compilation of the Psalter," *Zeitschrift für die alttestamentliche Wissenschaft* 103/2 (1991), pp. 258–263.

[16]Roland Murphy, *The Tree of Life, An Exploration of Biblical Wisdom Literature* (New York: Doubleday, 1990), p. 34. Some of the other places where such doubts are voiced are: by Abraham in Gen. 18:22–32, by Jeremiah in his "confessions" (Jer. 12:1–5), by the prophet Habakkuk (1:4, 13), and in several psalms (37, 49, 73).

[17]"With its central metaphor of conflict," summarizes Leo G. Perdue, *Wisdom in Revolt, Metaphorical Theology in the Book of Job,* Bible and Literature Series 29 (Sheffield: the Almond Press, 1991), p. 269, "the book of Job is a narrative journey of a character whose life is a quest for the knowledge of God and the why of human existence."

[18]"Canonization arbitrarily arrested the current shape of the Joban tradition … ," writes Leo Perdue, *Wisdom in Revolt,* p. 80, fn. 1. As a totality it is disjointed and confusing at points: the Elihu speeches in 32–37 seem tacked on; the relation of the prose narrative (1–2, 42:7–17) to the dialogues is ambiguous; the Yahweh speeches and Job's responses (38:1–42:6) seem intrusive; the arrangement of the Wisdom Hymn (28) and the speeches of the third cycle of dialogue (24–27) are confusing.

[19]For a review of these issues and some fresh proposals, see R. E. Clements, *Wisdom and Theology* (Grand Rapids: Eerdmans, 1992).

My own conclusions about the book's redactional history (which I hope to set forth in detail in a separate monograph) are that a first major edition of Proverbs was created by "the men of Hezekiah" mentioned in Prov. 25:1 and that this refers to the guild of Levites who supported the Hezekiah reforms by producing first editions of Deuteronomy and the Deuteronomistic History, and the first two books of the Psalter (see above, and our discussion of these matters in Ch. 7). This "men of Hezekiah" edition extended from Prov. 10:1 to 29:27 (note that the reference to "more of Solomon's Proverbs" in Prov. 25:1 refers back to the title in Prov. 10:1), and its aim appears to have been to link the "wisdom of Solomon" tradition (which prior to the Hezekiah reforms had been the chief source of social guidance in Jerusalem) to the religious and social ideals of the Deuteronomic "Torah of Moses" tradition. The theological compatibility of these two traditions, as the Levites viewed it, was already set forth in the Deuteronomistic History, in their account there of how Yahweh was pleased with Solomon's prayer for wisdom (1 Kings 3:4–15). From their point of view Solomon should have adhered to the Torah of Moses as his father David had recommended (1 Kings 2:1–4) and *also* to the wisdom given him by Yahweh (1 Kings 3:11–15). His failure was that he was less than "wholehearted" about the "Torah of Moses" tradition (see 1 Kings 11:4–8). In their reforms the "men of Hezekiah" set about reuniting the two traditions by adding sentences pertaining to the character of Yahweh and his ways (and about the fate of those who do or do not live according to his ways) throughout the initial Solomonic collection in 10:1–22:17 (but especially at its center in 14:26–15:33), and also by crafting addenda to the supplementary collections which forcefully advocated trust and respect for Yahweh (22:18; 23:17; 24:21) and his Torah (28:4, 5, 7, 9; 29:18). The teachings of the prologue (chs. 1–9) and epilogue (chs. 30–31) were added in the period after the Ezra-Nehemiah reforms. As Claudia V. Camp has put it, *Wisdom and the Feminine in the Book of Proverbs,* Bible and Literature 11 (Decatur: Almond, 1985), p. 253, the themes discussed here "reflect the renewed recognition accorded to the importance of the family in the kingless sociological configuration of the exilic and post-exilic period."

[20]See Prov. 15:33, which heads a poem right at the center of the collection. The term, "fear of Yahweh," appears not only at the opening

(1:7) and end (9:7) of the introductory teachings (chs. 1–9), thus framing them, but at regular points in between (1:29; 2:5; 3:7; 8:13), and then again at regular intervals throughout the central collection of Solomonic proverbs (10:27; 14:2, 16, 26, 27; 15:16, 33; 16:6; 22:4), as well as in the shorter collections that follow (23:17; 30:8–9; 31:30).

[21]According to Gerald Wilson, 'The Words of the Wise,' The Intent and Significance of Qohelet 12:9–14," *Journal of Biblical Literature* 103/2 (1984), pp. 175–192, the last verses of Ecclesiastes (Eccl. 12:12–14) are an epilogue not just for Ecclesiastes, but for Proverbs as well, and were thus meant to provide the canonical key to the interpretation of both books. More specifically, the statement in Eccl. 12:13 that to "fear God and keep his commandments" is the "end" or "sum" forms an inclusio with the opening teaching of Proverbs that the "fear of Yahweh" is the "beginning" (Prov. 1:7).

[22]This is the point of view expressed in 1 Chron. 22:12f. where the purpose of Solomonic wisdom is no longer thought of as an autonomous wisdom for governing, as in 1 Kings 3:9, but as a resource for strengthening one's Torah-obedience. The same relation between wisdom and Torah is also presupposed by several strategically placed texts in Deuteronomy: in Deut. 1:12–15 being wise is identified as the chief requirement of those appointed by Moses to assist him in administrating the law, and in Deut. 34:9 Moses himself is said to have had a "spirit of wisdom" which he passed on to Joshua, implying that it was his wisdom that made him the great lawgiver he was.

[23]Prov. 16:4, at the exact midpoint of the 375 proverbs that make up the central collection of this book, states that "Yahweh made *everything* for its own purpose, yes, even the wicked for the day of disaster." For evidence that it was within this field of discourse and thought that the Hebrew scriptures were edited and studied in the Second Temple period, see Gerald T. Sheppard, *Wisdom as a Hermeneutical Construct, A Study in the Sapientializing of the Old Testament* (Berlin, New York: Walter de Gruyter, 1980).

[24]On the redactional importance of these final verses (Eccl. 12:13f.) for the canonical interpretation of both Ecclesiastes and Proverbs, see fn. 21 above,

[25]These themes are prominent not only in the accounts of the Ezra-Nehemiah reforms (Ezra 9–10; Neh. 13:23–27), but also in Malachi's

teachings (Mal. 2:13–16), and in the introductory instructions to the book of Proverbs (2:16–19; 5:1–23; 6:20–35; 7:1–27).

[26]Roland Murphy, "Song of Songs, Book of," *Anchor Bible Dictionary,* VI, p. 153.

[27]Norman K. Gottwald, "Lamentations," *Harper's Bible Commentary* (San Francisco: Harper & Row, 1988), p. 647, states that this device was meant "to foster a comprehensive catharsis of grief and confession linked to an inculcation of faith and hope, to be accomplished literally by covering the subject 'from A to Z'." In this way, he adds, the "impulse to explore the trauma until the topic is 'exhausted' is both realized and held in check...."

[28]It is the opinion of Samuel T. Lachs, "The Date of Lamentations V," *Jewish Quarterly Review* 57 (1), 1966, pp. 46–66, that the "desolations" alluded to in ch. 5 correspond better to what happened to Jerusalem during the Hellenistic persecutions of the second century BCE than to what occurred during the Babylonian destruction of the city in 586 BCE.

[29]Norman Gottwald, "Lamentations," pp. 648f.

[30]That the book of Daniel was compiled and added to this library at about this time is also indicated by Daniel's absence from the list of "illustrious men" in Sira's survey of biblical history in Sirach 44–49, something hard to imagine were Daniel part of this library then already (c. 180 BCE).

[31]Their historical counterparts are likely to be found among "the Hasidaeans," referred to in 1 Macc. 7:12–18 as "scribes" and in 1 Macc. 2:42 as the party that devoted itself to the Law. Regarding this group and associated developments, see John Kampen, *The Hasideans and the Origin of Pharisaism, A Study in 1 and 2 Maccabees,* SBL Septuagint and Cognate Studies Series 24 (Atlanta: Scholars Press, 1988), and our comments below and in Ch. 10.

[32]According to Ben Zion Wacholder, *Messianism and Mishnah, Time and Place in the Early Halakhah,* The Louis Caplan Lecture on Jewish Law (Hebrew Union College Press, 1979), this remained the temporal perspective of the Rabbis of the early Mishnah; their concern was predominantly with the scriptural past up to the time of Ezra, and with the messianic world of the future, not with the present (p. 40).

[33]The Persian king in whose reign the story of Esther unfolds is referred to as Ahasuerus in Esther 1:1. Ahasuerus is a Latin-English

transcription of the Hebrew form of the Persian name Xerxes; this is the Xerxes of Ezra 4:6 who reigned from 486-465 BCE.

³⁴We are told that Judas was active in reassembling "a complete collection of the books dispersed in the late war" (2 Macc. 2:18) and that his brothers, despite their lack of Aaronite credentials, took charge of the High Priesthood (see 1 Macc. 10:18–21; 13:40). They were thus well placed to do this.

³⁵This is the opinion of Beckwith, *Old Testament Canon,* pp. 262, 316, who explains the absence of Esther at Qumran as probably due to the fact that the fourteenth day of the twelfth month (one of the days specified for celebrating Purim) was an Essene Sabbath, and for them holy days were not permitted to fall on Sabbath days, lest unnecessary work would be required (see pp. 291–294).

10. THE CHIRSTIAN BIBLE IN ITS FINAL FORM: CONCLUDING REFLECTIONS

¹When faced with an Aaronite priesthood ready to hellenize Jerusalem and persecute its own Torah-loyal people (1 Macc. 7; 2 Macc. 14–15), the Maccabean leaders themselves took over the high priestly duties, "pending the advent of a genuine prophet" (1 Macc. 14:40; cp. 12:6). It seems that it was in this period that Pharisaism was born, based on the concept of authority stated in Abot 1:1, where it is said that Moses passed his authority to Joshua (not to Aaron), who passed it to the prophets and "the men of the great assembly" (not to the Zadokites). It was from such "a great assembly" that the teachers of Pharisaism emerged; it was such an "assembly" that also authorized the Maccabean take-over of the high priesthood (1 Macc. 14:28). Irving M. Zeitlin, *Jesus and the Judaism of His Time* (Cambridge: Polity Press, 1988), p. 19, believes that the point of view expressed in Abot 1:1 was tantamount to canonizing the books of the Prophets and the Writings ("thus constituting those writings together with the Pentateuch as the Holy Scriptures ..."), and that it was this that precipitated the split between parties, since neither the Essenes of Qumran nor the Zadokites (Sadducees) were prepared to accept these new interpretations which subverted what the Law itself had to say about who should serve as high priest. For an overview and analysis of these

complex developments, see Ellis Rivkin, *A Hidden Revolution: The Pharisees' Search for the Kingdom Within* (Nashville: Abingdon, 1978), and John Kampen, *The Hasideans and the Origins of Pharisaism.*

[2]Regarding the importance of this "bridge" for understanding the essence of Christianity and its scriptures, see I. Howard Marshall, "Is Apocalyptic the Mother of Christian Theology?" *Tradition and Interpretation in the New Testament,* Essays in Honor of E. Earle Ellis, Gerald F. Hawthorne with Otto Betz, eds. (Grand Rapids: Eerdmans, 1987), pp. 33–42; also Klaus Koch, *The Rediscovery of Apocalyptic,* Studies in Biblical Theology, Second Series 22 (London: SCM Press, 1972), who characterizes "the apocalyptic world of ideas" as representing "the change-over between the Testaments" and that "which, under the impression of the person of Jesus and his destiny, permitted a part of late Israel to merge into early Christianity?" (p. 129).

[3]Northrop Frye, *The Great Code, The Bible and Literature* (Toronto: Academic Press Canada, 1983), p. 76, aptly characterizes the total biblical story "as a vision of upward metamorphosis." On its significance as "world-story," see also the lucid comments of Amos Wilder, "The World-Story: The Biblical Version," in *Jesus' Parables and the War of Myths, Essays on Imagination in the Scripture* (Philadelphia: Fortress, 1982), pp. 43–70.

[4]For a similar assessment of the importance (yet neglect) of this theme, see Hendrikus Berkhof, *Christ the Meaning of History* (Richmond: John Knox Press, 1962); Arend Theodoor van Leeuwen, *Christianity in World History, The Meeting of the Faiths of East and West* (New York: Charles Scribner's Sons, 1964); Klaus Koch, *The Rediscovery of Apocalyptic.*

[5]One way of thinking of those apostolic writings which were added to the four Gospels and Acts would be as teachings for a people caught up in the ongoing drama of a history whose beginnings and character are traced in these opening volumes. In this sense, the New Testament letters (including John's Apocalypse) would have a similar relationship to Matthew through Acts as do "the Writings" to "the Law and the Prophets" (plus Ezra-Nehemiah). However, it must never be forgotten that the Gospels and Acts continue the story begun in "the Law and the Prophets" (plus Ezra-Nehemiah), so it is the total history (Genesis

through Acts) that forms the background to the apostolic letters and the Apocalypse.

⁶This point is similarly emphasized by Berkhof, *Christ the Meaning of History,* p. 55, who writes that we simply cannot understand what the New Testament has to say about the world's future, if we do not first listen intently to the Old Testament witnesses on this subject.

⁷For a similar analysis, see Joseph Jensen, "Mount Zion and Armageddon," in *Sin, Salvation, and the Spirit,* ed. Daniel Durken, O.S.B. (Collegeville: The Liturgical Press, 1979), pp. 134–145, who suggests that the conversion of the nations in some prophetic scenarios "is possibly compatible with a judgment that is corrective in nature, which it would follow … but it is not compatible with a destructive judgment that is conceived [as it sometimes is] as the final act in the eschatological drama, to be succeeded only by the full establishment of God's kingdom" (p. 139). I might add that it was in support of Israel's identity as a light to the nations (or "witness") that most of the writings were fashioned: Ruth, Psalms, Proverbs, even, I think, Daniel and Esther (see our discussion of these volumes in Ch. 9).

⁸What in general the disciples' expectations actually were (and hence why the crucifixion was such a devastating experience for them initially) may be inferred from Josephus' allusion to the belief of many Jews of his time that "a man from their country would become ruler of the world" (*Jewish War* 6.312). A fuller description of end-time events as commonly anticipated at that time is to be found in Psalms of Solomon 17:23-51 where the coming world-ruler is depicted as one who will purge Jerusalem from unrighteous nations, while gathering a holy people, all this as a prelude to nations coming from the ends of the earth to witness his glory.

⁹For a credible account of how this early Christian vision of world mission emerged and became central to the eschatological perspectives of early Christianity, see Charles H. H. Scobie, "Jesus or Paul? The Origin of the Universal Mission of the Christian Church," in *From Jesus to Paul, Studies in Honour of Francis Wright Beare,* Peter Richardson and John C. Hurd, eds. (Waterloo: Wilfrid Laurier University Press, 1984), pp. 47–60.

¹⁰Further to what Christians might legitimately hope for in the temporal realm, see A. T. van Leeuwen, *Christianity in World History,* pp. 431–437; J. W. Miller, "Envisioning the World's Future: Neglected

Prophetic Insights," *The Conrad Grebel Review* (Winter 1986), pp. 1–21; "Can We Hope for a New World Order?" *The Conrad Grebel Review* (Fall 1991), pp. 309–314; for the relevance of the canonical story for the identity and mission of the church, see the collected essays in *The Transfiguration of Mission, Biblical, Theological & Historical Foundations,* Wilbert R. Shenk, ed. (Scottdale: Herald Press, 1993).

A NOTE TO BIBLE PUBLISHERS

[1]The substantial Uncial manuscript support for this older arrangement is summarized by William Farmer, *Jesus and the Gospel* (Philadelphia: Fortress, 1982), p. 274, fn. 145. Ernest L. Martin, *The Original Bible Restored* (Portland: Ask Publications, 1991), p. 8, hypothesizes that the chief reason the order of books was changed in the western church and Paul's epistles were put before the others "was to exalt Paul (the Gentile apostle) over the Jewish apostles."

[2]Regarding this early Christian usage, see Campenhausen, *Formation,* pp. 257, 263.

ANNOTATED BIBLIOGRAPHY OF RECENT CANONICAL STUDIES

The following book-length studies are illustrative of the methods and opinions of those currently working in this field. In the annotations I have tried to capture the heart of each book as much as possible in the author's own words. Three distinct approaches to the study of the canon may be identified, although there may be some overlap within a given book. These are: the "literary," the "theological" and the "historical" perspective. The books by Frye and Wilder, with their attention to the Bible's unique qualities as "a world story" unified by a body of recurring imagery, illustrate the "literary" perspective. The "theological" approach is exemplified in the books by Barr, Bartlett, Barton, Brueggemann, Childs, Coats, Fishbane, Gnuse, Jadock, Hanson, Levenson, Mckim, Neuhaus, Rendtorff, van Ruler and Zimmerli. Here the primary focus is on the message or messages of the final form of individual books or larger sections, or the canon as a whole. The books by Beckwith, Blenkinsopp, Bruce, Campenhausen, Coote, Freedman, Friedman, Kugel, Leiman Lightstone, McDonald, Martin, Mellor, Metzger, Morgan, Mulder, Peckham, Sanders, Smith and Sundberg take up the "historical" approach. Here the primary concentration is on when, why and how these writings were formed in the first place.

Although many of these volumes have been my companions throughout this study, for reasons of focus and space I have not been able to interact with them as much as I would have liked. I might add that David Noel Friedman's provocative new study arrived on the very day I was completing this project, in time to be included in its bibliography, but that is all.

*　*　*

Barr, James, *Holy Scripture, Canon, Authority, Criticism* (Philadelphia: Westminster, 1983)

Argues that "within Judaism, if the idea of the Jamnia council must be abandoned, we really have no information about meetings or councils of authorities which established these matters, and it is not clear indeed that there were institutions with the power or the means to do so. More probably ... canons, in so far as such things existed, existed in the form of the different opinions of different groups; and a settlement was eventually reached not through a 'decision' but through the fact that one group became dominant, its opinion became more powerful and important, and other views simply faded away with the fading of the groups which had maintained them" (pp. 57f.). Believes that these and other considerations are "fatal to the notion that the idea of the canon is of first-rate importance for biblical Christianity. Scripture is essential, but canon is not. Canon is a derivative, a secondary or tertiary, concept, of great interest but not of the highest theological importance. It is unlikely in the face of the biblical evidence that it can be made into the cornerstone of any convincing biblical theology" (pp. 63f.).

Bartlett, David L., *The Shape of Scriptural Authority* (Philadelphia: Fortress, 1983)

Emphasizes the differing forms of scripture (word, narrative, wisdom, witness) and the differing ways each exercises authority in the church; also surveys the search for a unifying theological "center" in scripture, and how different traditions interpret scripture differently; concludes that "the search for a canon within the canon is a necessary part of the task of scriptural interpretation, a task which canonical interpretation needs to take into account" (p. 142). In that search a first guideline for Christians will be, he suggests, that "any appropriate canon within the canon will center in the good news of God's activity in Jesus Christ." In support of this he states that in the early church "the Old Testament from the start was seen as a source of reflection on what God had done in Jesus Christ. Books were chosen for the New Testament canon on the assumption that they faithfully witnessed to him" (p. 142).

Barton, John, *People of the Book? The Authority of the Bible in Christianity* (Louisville: Westminster/John Knox, 1988)

Argues that the Church in the first centuries spoke more of the "canon of truth" or the "rule of faith" than of the canon of Scripture. "This rather than Scripture itself," he states, "was the ultimate 'canon' according to which all teaching had to be assessed." Thus, "the books that are reckoned as holy Scripture [by the Church] are intimately related to the faith, indispensable for it, yet not coterminous with it" (p. 30).

Beckwith, Roger, *The Old Testament Canon of the New Testament Church and Its Background in Early Judaism* (Grand Rapids: William B. Eerdmans, 1985)

An erudite work that seeks to disprove the commonly held idea that "although Judaism possessed a canon of books which it held to be divinely inspired, the limits of that canon were not settled until about AD 90, well after it had been taken over by the Christian Church" (p. 12); rather, he argues, the closing of the canon took place "not less than 250 years earlier ..." and that this "is implied in the language of the prologue to Ecclesiasticus, and ... confirmed by the elaborate and logical structure which the canon displays" (p. 165). A major contribution to the field, with significant implications for how the canon is approached and studied.

Blenkinsopp, Joseph, *The Pentateuch, An Introduction to the First Five Books of the Bible* (Doubleday: New York, 1992)

Comes to the startling conclusion that the two most clearly identifiable constructs of the Pentateuch "are those traditionally designated Priestly (P) and Deuteronomistic (D) ..." and that as a consequence we may need to think of a "D edition of the history up to the time of Moses as a long preface to Dtr or of one continuous Deuteronomistic History extending from creation to the Babylonian exile" (p. 130). The final stage of the redaction, he believes, "represents a compromise between different interest groups with their own legal traditions worked out in several stages during the two centuries of Persian rule. As such, it was authorized by the imperial authorities as the law and constitution of the Jewish ethnos, and its implementation was backed by the same authorities" (p. 241).

Blenkinsopp, Joseph, *Prophecy and Canon, A Contribution to the Study of Jewish Origins* (University of Notre Dame Press, 1977)

Proposes that "if biblical theology means a theology of the Bible it must take account of the Bible in its final form and what that form means for theology" (p. 137). Argues that in its final form the Hebrew canon displays a tension between the final words of the "Law" which ascribe incomparable authority to the prophet Moses (34:10–12) and the final words of the "Prophets" (Mal. 3:22–24) which reflect "a progressive transformation of the prophets into heralds of a new age, a transformation which laid the groundwork for apocalyptic" (p. 120). As heirs of the prophets the sages continued to try to come to terms with this "central issue in the long process which eventuated in a tripartite canon ..." (p. 127). This was accomplished by means of "a shift from direct revelation through the person of the prophet to revelation accruing from the inspired interpretation of biblical texts" with the help of "wisdom theology" (p. 129). Second Temple Levites, he writes, were especially important to this latter development "since it seems that they stood at the confluence of priestly, scribal and prophetic movements" during this period (p. 135). One conclusion drawn from all this is that "the presence of prophecy as an essential part of the canon means that it will always be possible and necessary to remold the tradition as a source of life-giving power" (p. 152).

Bruce, F. F., The *Canon of Scripture* (Downers Grove: InterVarsity Press, 1988)

A factual, objective authoritative account of the formation of the Old and New Testament canons, recounted with special attention to the formation of the Christian canon of the bi-partite Bible. Bruce concludes his survey with an essay on "Canon, Criticism, and Interpretation," in which he states that "Canonical exegesis does not absolve the reader from the duty of understanding the scriptures in their historical setting.... Each part of the canon makes its contribution to the whole, but that contribution cannot be properly appreciated unless attention is paid to the historical setting of each part in relation to the whole" (p. 296).

Brueggemann, Walter, *The Creative Word, Canon as a Model for Biblical Education* (Philadelphia: Fortress Press, 1982)

The author contends that "the awareness of *how* the biblical material reaches its present form (canonical *process*) and the present form that it has reached (canonical *shape*) are important theological matters that tell us about the intent of the biblical community" (p. 3). Stimulated by the work of Sanders (see below), he regards the tripartite order of the Old Testament (Law, Prophets, Writings) as reflective of "different degrees and kinds of authority," each with "a distinct role to play" in the educational life of an enduring community. "It is important," he writes, "that Israel formed and valued all three parts of the canon, kept them in relation to each other, was relatively clear about the function and place of each, and never tried to make one of them substitute for another" (p. 5).

Campenhausen, Hans von, *The Formation of the Christian Bible* (Philadelphia: Fortress, Eng. Translation, 1972)

One of the definitive histories of how the canon of Christian scriptures was formed. Emphasizes that "the Old Testament had come with the Church at her birth" (p. 331) and that "the New Testament (considered as a 'canonical' collection) may ... properly be described as a creation of the post-Marcionite church" (p. 331, fn. 13). Believes that "the historical presentation of the circumstances and motives which brought it [the Christian canon] into being is itself of theological importance. For it would certainly not be 'legitimate' to support the traditional Canon with arguments which played no part in its formation" (p. 333).

Childs, Brevard S., *Biblical Theology in Crisis* (Philadelphia: Westminster, 1970)

Develops the thesis that "one of the persistently weak points of the Biblical Theology Movement was its failure to take the Biblical text seriously in its canonical form" (p. 102), nor did it "come to grips with the inspiration of Scripture" (p. 103). It is Childs' opinion that "the claim for the inspiration of Scripture is the claim for the uniqueness of the canonical context of the church through which the Holy Spirit works" (p. 104). "The formation of a canon of Scriptures is a recognition of the need for a context ... in which the Christian church continues to wrestle in every new age with the living God who continues to confront his people through the ancient testimony of the prophets and apostles" (p. 113).

Childs, Brevard S., *Introduction to the Old Testament as Scripture* (Philadelphia: Fortress, 1979)

Argues (against Sanders) that even though "there was a genuine historical development involved in the formation of the canon ... one searches largely in vain for solid biblical or extra-biblical evidence by which to trace the real causes and motivations behind many of the crucial decisions" (p. 67); but also argues (against Sundberg) that the tripartite canon was essentially in place well before 90 A.D., so that "the New Testament writers received the Hebrew tradition in its canonical form and did not stand outside the Jewish community in a new tradition-building process" (p. 669). Offers a book by book survey in which the "canonical intentionality" of each writing is ascertained, the goal being to actualize the "enormous richness of theological interpretation" which is "built into the structure of the text itself," and in this manner "render the text religiously accessible" to each generation.

Childs, Brevard S., *The New Testament as Canon: An Introduction* (London: SCM Press, 1984)

Argues that "the canonical editors [of the New Testament] tended to hide their own footprints, largely concealing their own historical identity"; thus, "the function of canonical shaping was often precisely to loosen the text from any one given historical setting, and to transcend the original addressee" (p. 23). A chief motivation behind this canonical process was to render the tradition in such a way that its message would be "accessible to every succeeding generation of Christians" (p. 40). Hence, "the effect of the canonical process finally was to assign a dynamic for its interpretation which was often quite different from its original historical role" (p. 24). In addition to a book by book interpretation, looks at the canonical significance of the four Gospels, the Pauline corpus, and the Catholic epistles.

Childs, Brevard S., *Old Testament Theology in a Canonical Context* (Philadelphia: Fortress, 1985)

Sees "the final canonical literature" as reflecting "a long history of development in which the received tradition was selected, transmitted and shaped by hundreds of decisions," a process which involved "a continual critical evaluation of historical options which were available to Israel and a transformation of its received tradition toward certain theological goals." In this way "divine truth acquired its authoritative form as it was received and transmitted by a community of faith" (p. 14). The Old Testament theologian "shares in that hermeneutical process of which the canon is a testimony, as the people of God struggled to discern the will of God in all its historical particularity" (p. 15). "The discipline of Old Testament theology derives from theological reflection on a received body of scripture ... " (p. 6). Acknowledges that the "canonical process involved the shaping of the tradition not only into independent books, but also into larger canonical units, such as the Torah, Prophets and Writings" (p. 13), but sees this as a built-in "dimension of flexibility which encourages constantly fresh ways of actualizing the material" (p. 13). Believes that "the issue of organization is sharply relativized" by these assumptions (p. 15); as his discussion of various themes and topics illustrates, there are innumerable "options within the theological activity of interpreting scripture which are available for grappling with the material" (pp. 15f.).

Childs, Brevard S., *Biblical Theology of the Old and New Testaments, Theological Reflection on the Christian Bible* (Minneapolis: Fortress, 1993)

Believes that "the Christian understanding of canon functions theologically in a very different way from Judaism. Although the church adopted from the synagogue a concept of scripture as an authoritative collection of sacred writings, its basic stance toward its canon was shaped by its christology.... The scriptures of the Old and the New Testament were authoritative in so far as they pointed to God's redemptive intervention for the world in Jesus Christ" (p. 64). Thus, "the juxtaposition of the two testaments to form the Christian Bible arose, not simply to establish a historical continuity between Israel and the church, but above all as an affirmation of a theological continuity. The church not only joined its new writings to the Jewish scriptures, but laid claim on the Old Testament as a witness to Jesus Christ" (pp. 73f.). In the process it "disregarded" the tripartite division of the massoretic text (Torah, Prophets, Writings) in favor of a new arrangement (and list) that "reflected its new, evangelical understanding of the Hebrew scriptures" (p. 75). Thus, "the collection of Jewish scriptures was envisioned as closed and a new and different collection began which in time evolved into the New Testament" (p. 75). "Both testaments make a discrete witness to Jesus Christ which must be heard, both separately and in concert." However, "the New Testament is not just an extension of the Old, nor a last chapter in an epic tale. Something totally new has entered in the gospel. Yet the complexity of the problem arises because the New Testament bears its totally new witness in terms of the old, and thereby transforms the Old Testament." The Old Testament seen "from the perspective of the gospel ... freely renders the Old as a transparency of the New" (p. 78).

Coats, George W., and Long, Burke O., eds., *Canon and Authority, Essays in Old Testament Religion and Theology* (Philadelphia: Fortress Press, 1977)

Several essays in the first part of this collection ("Stages in the Formation of the Canon") are especially noteworthy: Ronald Clements, "Patterns in the Prophetic Canon," and Gene M. Tucker, "Prophetic Superscriptions and the Growth of a Canon." These highlight the fact that in the final "collection of collections" the prophetic corpus "formed a recognizable unity not entirely dissimilar from that of the Pentateuch," one centered on the death and rebirth of Israel, interpreted theologically as acts of divine judgment and salvation" (Clements, p. 53). The "salvation" pointed to was in part that of the actual restoration which was achieved under Persia, but also, beyond that, of a more remote and transcendent salvation.

Coote, Robert B. & Mary P. Coote, *Power, Politics, and the Making of the Bible: An Introduction* (Minneapolis: Fortress Press, 1990)

States that "the Hebrew scriptures consist mainly of the scriptures of the temple cult of the god Yahweh in Jerusalem. The purpose of this cult was to legitimate rulers in Jerusalem, and this is what the scriptures are mostly about. Indeed, the writers of the scriptures became particularly active when rule changed hands and a new version of legitimacy had to be devised"; goes on to argue, more specifically, that "the initial purpose of the temple and its scriptures was to legitimate the ruling house of David (1000–520 B.C.E.) and after that the ruling priests established in David's name under Persian, Hellenistic, and Roman rule (520 B.C.E.–70 C.E.)" (p. 3).

Fishbane, Michael, *The Garments of Torah, Essays in Biblical Hermeneutics* (Bloomington & Indianapolis: Indiana University Press, 1989)

In two seminal essays (Chs. 4 and 5) traces the primary and secondary "breakthroughs" in ancient Israelite religious history that were essential to the emergence of Judaism. The first of these ("Israel and the 'Mothers' ") traces the centuries-long struggle to break free of what he calls the "mythic plenum" of ancient Near Eastern culture; the second essay ("From Scribalism to Rabbinism, Perspectives on the Emergence of Classical Judaism") traces "the movement from a culture based on direct divine revelations to one based on their study and reinterpretation. The principal custodians of the former were the sage-scribes of ancient Israel; the purveyors of the latter, the sage-scholars of early Judaism" (p. 65). Ezra (aided "by Levitical instructors who bring Torah understanding [*mebinim*] to the people [Neh. 8:7, 9] and convey to them the sense [*sekel*] of the text being studied [v. 8; cf. v. 13, le-haskil]") was the decisive figure in the emergence of this latter "breakthrough" (p. 66).

Freedman, David Noel, *The Unity of the Hebrew Bible* (Ann Arbor: The University of Michigan Press, 1993)

Presents "a case for the unity of the Hebrew Bible—as a literary composite" (p. 98). He believes "we can speak about compilation and organization, what we mean by editing or redacting in the broad sense. From a study of the Bible's contents, style, language, and literary features," he writes, "I conclude that there is a pervasive unity, elements that tie individual components into a complex but unified structure. Thus we can divide the Hebrew Bible roughly in half, each half consisting of two major parts. The first half consists of the largest unit in the Hebrew Bible, the Primary History, extending over nine books and containing 150,000 words, almost half of the total of 305,500. This work is a product of the Babylonian period (mid-sixth century).... The remaining parts of the Hebrew Bible, the Latter Prophets and the Writings, are products of a later period. The Latter Prophets are from the Persian era, perhaps late sixth or early fifth century; the Writings come mostly (and in organized fashion) from the time and hands of that odd couple, Ezra and Nehemiah. In addition, there is the Book of Daniel, a product of the Greek period (about 165 B.C.E.)" (pp. 98f.).

Friedman, Richard Elliott, *Who Wrote the Bible?* Englewood Cliffs: Prentice-Hall, 1987)

Marshals evidence pointing to the Levites of Shiloh, descendants of Moses, as the authors of the Pentateuchal documents E and D (Deuteronomy), while J was Judean and reflective of Hebron traditions. The two were united when the northern kingdom fell. He conjectures that P was written as an alternative to JE (p. 215), and was supported by King Hezekiah, while Josiah was the "darling" of the Levites (p. 211). JED and P were collated and edited in Second Temple times by Ezra, despite their contradictory aspects, for by then they were all regarded as authoritative. "How could the redactor have left any of these out? ... Besides, there were groups who supported these various texts. The Shiloh Levite priests who had produced E and D may not have been in priestly power in the second Temple days, but that did not mean that they did not exist" (p. 225).

Frye, Northrop, *The Great Code, The Bible and Literature* (Toronto: Academic Press Canada, 1983)

Canada's leading literary critic asks, "Why does this huge, sprawling, tactless book [the Christian Bible] sit there inscrutably in the middle of our cultural heritage like the 'great Boyg' or sphinx in *Peer Gynt,* frustrating all our efforts to walk around it?" (xviii) His answer comes in the form of an insightful analysis of its compelling *mythos* (overarching story) and unique language. "The emphasis on narrative, and the fact that the entire Bible is enclosed in a narrative framework, distinguishes the Bible from a good many other sacred books" (p. 198). "Literally, the Bible is a gigantic myth, a narrative extending over the whole of time from creation to apocalypse, unified by a body of recurring imagery...." Also traces a sequence of stages, each one more explicit than its predecessor" (p. 224); there are seven of these (five in the Old Testament, two in the New): Creation, revolution or exodus, law, wisdom, prophecy, gospel, and apocalypse (pp. 106–138). "This sequence is connected with one of the most striking features of the Bible: its capacity for self-recreation" (p. 225). "... What the Bible gives us is not so much a cosmology as a vision of upward metamorphosis ... " (p. 76).

Gnuse, Robert, *The Authority of the Bible, Theories of Inspiration, Revelation and the Canon of Scripture* (New York/Mahwah: Paulist, 1965)

Traces the history of views regarding Scripture in the pre-modern and modern periods, and concludes with a chapter on the "historical emergence of the authoritative Bible" where he speaks of "this literature" as having been "created by the community of faith in order to preserve its self-understanding in the face of new social and religious problems. Scripture thus arises out of the need to address new problems by means of the old religious traditions. A canon or fixed corpus of literature takes shape because a question of identity or a challenge to authority has arisen, and only later does this literature become unchangeable once the question of identity has been settled" (p. 104).

Jodock, Darrell, *The Church's Bible, Its Contemporary Authority* (Minneapolis: Fortress, 1989)

Argues that our concept of the Bible's authority must be attuned to the needs of the "postmodern age": "Postmodern society is characterized by a loss of the sense of transcendence, by the absence of any overarching story and by the disappearance of the undergirding structure that supports humane values and knits together individuals" (p. 88). The Bible speaks to each of these needs but "the truth of the Bible can be established only by praxis, by living its insights in fellowship with others" (p. 108). Its authority is both "functional" and "material." People in the churches turn to the Bible because they find it useful to do so—it is "profitable" (2 Tim. 3:16); but they also turn there "because its writings have the capacity to mediate the identity-forming presence of God" (p. 114). "No particular theory is necessary in order for functional authority to develop. A recommendation to use the Scriptures is enough" (p. 114).

Hanson, Paul D., *The People Called, The Growth of Community in the Bible* (San Francisco: Harper & Row, 1986)

This is an attempt at finding a unifying thread running through the biblical story found in the Christian Bible (Hebrew scriptures and New Testament). This unifying thread is the central biblical confession "that God is present in all reality, as its Creator and Purposer" (p. 529). While this confession is elaborated in various ways, it comes to expression so vividly "in certain events that they become paradigms for the community of faith" (p. 529). The Passover and Lord's Supper are two such paradigms; both foster a vision of a God acting true to a plan of universal peace and justice and draw us toward forms of community which are servants of the broken, the oppressed and the despised. While emphasizing the pluralism of the biblical story of faith, in practice this approach involves him in affirming certain features of the biblical story and not others.

Kugel, James L. and Greer, Rowan A., *Early Biblical Interpretation* (Philadelphia: Westminster, 1986)

Excellent historical reviews of the formation of the Old and New Testament canons and the process by which they respectively came to be studied and interpreted as sacred scripture among Jews and Christians. Kugel traces the major impulses for scripture study to the period of the restoration of Israel to Judah after its captivity in Babylon and the intense desire at that time not to repeat the mistakes of the past. Greer presents a compelling account of the role of Irenaeus in the developments that led to the formation of the Christian Bible and its subsequent interpretations.

Leiman, Sid Z., *The Canonization of Hebrew Scripture: The Talmudic and Midrashic Evidence, Transactions,* The Connecticut Academy of Arts and Sciences 47 (Hamden: Archon Books, 1976)

Argues that "the closing of the biblical canon did not occur at Jamnia" but that Jewish and Christian sources reflecting Jewish practice "support the notion of a closed biblical canon in most Jewish circles throughout the first centuries before and after the Christian era. The only possible indications of a larger biblical canon come from the sectarian Jewish community at Qumran and from Christian sources of the fourth century or later. [But] it is highly questionable to what extent, if at all, they reflect the biblical canon which obtained in official Jewish circles in Palestine and Alexandria during the first century." He concludes that "the talmudic and midrashic evidence is entirely consistent with a second century B.C. dating for the closing of the biblical canon" (p. 135).

Levenson, Jon D., *Sinai & Zion, An Entry into the Jewish Bible* (San Francisco: Harper & Row, 1985)

This is not, strictly speaking, a canonical study. But it does seek to take a "synchronic" approach to "the Jewish Bible," with the emphasis falling "not on the minor permutations in time, but on the enduring continuities understood in the broad historical context" (p. 12). So, it might be called an approach to the theology of the canon, written in full awareness of the contributions of modern historical scholarship, but with a Jewish sensibility to where the central themes and emphases lie. What emerges is a full-scale exploration of the two major theological traditions of the Bible, the one emanating from Sinai, the other from Zion, with concluding reflections regarding their inner tensions and relationships. His conclusion is that the "Davidic [Zion] covenant never displaced the Sinaitic in the Hebrew Bible," although "it did, in a sense, in the New Testament" (p. 216).

Lightstone, Jack N., *Society, the Sacred, and Scripture in Ancient Judaism: A Sociology of Knowledge,* Studies in Christianity and Judaism/Études sur le christianisme et le judaisme 3 (Waterloo: Wilfrid Laurier University Press, 1988)

Argues that "Deuteronomy and later the Pentateuch close theological and related cultic doors left open in Ancient Israel" and that it was "the Deuteronomic Reformation associated with Ezra and Nehemiah" that defined "as outside of Israel all who do not comply with Deuteronomy's theological standards" (p. 24). It was, moreover, Deuteronomy alone that first functioned in this sense as the "Torah-of-Moses"; then, gradually, one or another of the longer versions of the Pentateuch assumed this title. Finally, "sometime during the course of the second century and the beginning of the third [CE] rabbinism decided which documents belonged among scripture and which did not. Not less important," he adds, "the rabbis appear to have declared the Hagiographa a closed canon and with it the canon as a whole" (p. 61). In doing so they "included only those documents that dated, in their view, from the period of Ezra and Nehemiah and earlier" (p. 62).

McDonald, Lee Martin, *The Formation of the Christian Biblical Canon* (Nashville: Abingdon, 1988)

Tries to show that the final fixing of the canon of scriptures in

Judaism was a late development (not before the second century
C.E.) and that the early Church was not completely of "one mind
in the matter of which writings should be accepted as sacred
scripture" (p. 166). He raises questions about the necessity "of
tying the Church of the twentieth century to a canon that
emerged out of the historical circumstances in the second to fifth
centuries C.E.," and especially so in the light of the Bible's support of slavery and the inferiority and subjugation of women.
"The documents we possess sufficiently inform the Church ...
that *Jesus Christ alone is the true and final canon* for the child
of God (Matt. 28:18)," he writes (p. 170).

McKim, Donald, editor, *The Authoritative Word, Essays on the Nature
of Scripture* (Grand Rapids: Eerdmans, 1983)

A first-class compendium divided into three sections: Authority:
Sources and Canon; Authority: Doctrine and its Development;
Authority: Current Views. Especially fine essays by Robert
Grant and C.K. Barrett on New Testament use of the Old
Testament, by F. F. Bruce on Canon, and by Avery Dulles on
recent Protestant and Catholic views of scripture. Dulles suggests that "the increasing agreements among exegetes of different confessional traditions may well be the harbingers of future
agreements among the churches themselves" (p. 261). The book
concludes with a helpful annotated bibliography.

Martin, Ernest L., *The Original Bible Restored* (Portland: ASK
Publications, 1991)

Believes that as a result of the death of James in 63 CE, the dis-
ruptions caused by the Jewish War against Rome and the non-
fulfillment of Apostolic teaching regarding the near return of
Christ in that generation, "tens of thousands of Jewish believers
in Christ ... renounced Christianity," and it was these developments that prompted Peter's journey to Rome to consult with
Paul regarding the promulgation of "a set of standard books (like
those of the Old Testament) which would have the authority of
the apostles behind them" (p. 165); Peter's second letter was
written at about this time to present the definitive understanding

of the Christian message of which he and John and Paul were the chief guardians and which was now to be accepted in all churches (see esp. 2 Peter 1:12–21; 3:1–10).

Mellor, Enid, Ed., *The Making of the Old Testament,* The Cambridge Bible Commentary (Cambridge University Press, 1972)

Informative, objective, well-written survey of how (against the background of ancient Near Eastern literature) the Old Testament was formed and became the Bible of both Jews and Christians, and how it was and is used and studied in both traditions. There is no evidence, he writes, that the Old Testament books were acclaimed as sacred scripture the minute they became known; on the contrary most of them seem to have been in circulation for some time before people finally made up their minds about them" (p. 108).

Metzger, Bruce, *The Canon of the New Testament, Its Origin, Development, and Significance* (Oxford: Clarendon Press, 1987)

Part One contains two unique and exhaustive surveys of the literature on the canon prior to and during the twentieth century. Characterizes New Testament canon formation as not "the result of a deliberate decree by an individual or council near the beginning of the Christian era," but instead "a long continuous process" (p. 7). Writes that "the canon of Marcion may have been the first that was publicly proposed," but that it only accelerated "a process that had already begun in the first half of the second century. It was in opposition to Marcion's criticism that the Church first became fully conscious of its inheritance of apostolic writings" (p. 99).

Milet, Jean, *God or Christ? The Excesses of Christocentricity* (New York: Crossroad, 1981)

Discusses an issue of importance for a truly Christian appropriation of the canon: the bi-polarity of the Christian faith. "By that I mean," he writes, "that all the elements of the religious life which inspire it are ordered around *two poles of attraction:* belief in God and belief in Christ" (p. 1). His analysis of trends within the Roman Catholic Church over the centuries in this respect "has arrived at the conclusion that after a long period of supremacy, theocentricity was countered by a resurgence of christocentricity from the seventeenth century on: then this christocentricity, after a slow development, arrived at its maximal form in the twentieth century, in the 1960s and 1970s" (p. 217). He foresees a possible renaissance of theocentricity in the near future—a development he regards as restorative of an "equilibrium" in Christian faith "willed for it by its founder" (p. 217).

Morgan, Donn F., *Between Text & Community, The "Writings" in Canonical Interpretation* (Minneapolis: Fortress Press, 1990)

The focus of this study is on the formation of the third part of the tripartite Hebrew canon. His central thesis is that this third section was "not the common property of all Jewish communities" nor is there "clear evidence that the canon of Hebrew scripture was organized and referred to as Torah, Prophets, and Writings until well into the Common Era" (p. 18). "Nevertheless, Torah and Prophets were authoritative post-exilic texts to which the Writings were related and to which they responded." As such, he maintains, the status of the Writings "was always secondary to that of Torah and Prophets, always in need of being related to these primary literary corpora for their authority and point of reference" (p. 19). He further argues that the pluralistic theologies and perspectives of these Writings reflect the diverse communites in which they emerged. These are Sages, liturgists, community builders, visionaries and storytellers (pp. 53–54). How these Writings and not others came to be included with the Torah and Prophets as part of the Hebrew canon may never be known, he writes (p. 117).

Mulder, Jan Martin, ed., *Mikra, Text, Translation, Reading and Interpretion of the Hebrew Bible in Ancient Judaism and Early Christianity* (Assen: Van Gorcum; Philadelphia: Fortress, 1988)

Definitive essays (with a wealth of information) on the origins, formation, transmission, recitation, translation and interpretation of the Hebrew Bible in Judaism, the early Church and the Church Fathers. Especially notable are the complementary essays by Roger Beckwith and E. Earle Ellis on the "Formation of the Hebrew Bible" and "The Old Testament Canon in the Early Church"; Ellis supports Beckwith's contention that "the evidence offered ... argues that in the first Christian century (Philo, Josephus) and even two centuries earlier (Ben Sira) Judaism possessed a defined and identifiable canon, twenty-two books arranged in three divisions and regarded as an inspired and normative authority for the community" (p. 679). This highly important conclusion comes on the wings of what Ellis terms "the failure of the three-stage canonization theory" which in spite of reservations and opposition rapidly gained acceptance in the nineteenth century and continues to have a widespread currency (p. 680). Regarding Beckwith, Ellis writes: "Beckwith's book offers the most comprehensive treatment of the subject in this generation and promises to become the standard work from which future discussions will proceed" (p. 690). This sets the stage, he writes, for a reopening of the question of the "origin and meaning of the tripartite division of the Hebrew Bible" (p. 685).

Neuhaus, Richard John, *Biblical Interpretation in Crisis, The Ratzinger Conference on Bible and Church* (Grand Rapids: Eerdmans, 1989)

Important essays by leading, influential theologians (including the Pope's designate for maintaining doctrinal fidelity) on the urgency of retrieving the Bible as authoritive scripture if the church is to survive the challenges of modernity. George Lindbeck's contribution ("Scripture, Consensus, and Community"), now regarded by many as the most promising proposal for such a retrieval, calls for a return to a pre-constantinian "classic" hermeneutical appropriation of the Bible as a "unified whole telling the story of the dealings of the Triune God with his people and world ... " (p. 88).

Peckham, Brian, *History and Prophecy, The Development of Late Judean Literary Traditions* (New York: Doubleday, 1993)

> Believes the Bible was produced by and for a literate society; that what was first composed became a source for the next writer; that what seemed right or evident to one writer was disputed, corrected and reinterpreted by another. "What remains in the Bible is the literature of Judah that was preserved in the libraries of Jerusalem and that survived the sack of the city and became the theoretical basis of its reconstruction" (p. 1). "Its golden age was the period of Assyrian domination, from Hezekiah to Josiah, when peace was established and the principalities and kingdoms of the West were still prosperous. It was still vigorous and original in the exile during the Babylonian renaissance. With the advent of the Persians Judah gradually settled into being a poor, petty, and provincial enclave with a meager and self-serving literature to match" (p. 816).

Rendtorff, Rolf, *Canon and Theology, Overtures to an Old Testament Theology,* Overtures to Biblical Theology (Minneapolis: Fortress, 1993)

> This collection of essays is a call to "view the Old Testament texts in their "canonical" context, that is to say as a component part of the pre-Christian Jewish biblical canon" and to "interpret them theologically in that context" (p. 15). Rendtorff states that this leads to "new hermeneutical tasks for which the previous history of Christian biblical interpretation offers no models and but few guidelines" (p. 15). This will mean, he states, that we must "take the self-understanding of the Old Testament in its canonical form quite seriously" and "recognize, theologically as well, the historical fact that its influence has two separate strands, one Jewish and one Christian" (p. 56). "The first and fundamental step," he writes, "is to realize that the Hebrew Bible is the Jewish Bible first of all—not only that it was the Jewish Bible before it became part of the Christian Bible, but that it still is. In order that this fact may penetrate our awareness as deeply as possible, we [Christians] should try to study the Hebrew

Bible, at least for a while, as if there were no other, and in particular no Christian interpretation" (p. 205).

Sanders, James A., *Canon and Community, A Guide to Canonical Criticism* (Philadelphia: Fortress, 1984)

A sequel to Sanders' *Torah & Canon* (see below) which emphasizes that "canonical criticism shifts the focus of attention on canonization away from councils to a historical process" and, more specifically, to "periods of *intense canonical process...*" (p. 30; these were the sixth century B.C.E. and the first C.E.); then too it "focuses on the *function* of authoritative traditions in the believing communities" (p. 24). Thus, "Canonical criticism is very interested in what a believing community had in mind at that passing moment when the final form was achieved ..." (p. 25), but also in its "unrecorded hermeneutics which lie between the lines of most of its literature" (p. 46). The search for this latter has yielded so far five salient observations: a monotheizing perspective, a theocentric hermeneutic, a recurrent stress on God's grace working in and through human sinfulness, a divine bias for the weak and dispossessed, and a hermeneutic by which it adapted international wisdom (p. 51).

Sanders, James A., *From Sacred Story to Sacred Text* (Philadelphia: Fortress Press, 1987)

A collection of previously published essays (with one exception), in which the theses set forth in his two books on the subject are further elaborated and defended. Two aspects of his approach become clearer in these essays: (1) his belief that, "aside from the Pentateuch, the period [of canonical formation] prior to the end of the first century was marked by textual fluidity" (p. 82); (2) and the related thesis that "in the Judaism that would close its canon by the end of the second period of text transmission" (at the time of the encounter with Hellenism) the Pentateuch itself came to be conceived not basically as a story (which it really is), but as a legal code. "It was now basically sacred text. The ontology of scripture had shifted" (p. 144), and each word was now viewed as an oracle, sign, and riddle. In these essays he continues to elaborate an alternative approach to the canonization process, one which hypothesizes the "existential needs" of believing communities "in the periods of intense canonical process" (p. 82), and emphasizes the pluralism of the responses.

Sanders, James A., *Torah & Canon* (Philadephia: Fortress, 1972)

A pioneering work calling for "canonical criticism," which, Sanders states, must begin with a historical account of "the function" Israelite tradition was called upon to play in forging a set of identity-forming writings in the midst of "the crucifixion-resurrection experience of the sixth and fifth centuries B.C. and which provided the vehicle for Judaism's birth out of the ashes of what had been" (p. xix). His own account of this development stresses the relevance of the canon that emerged for supporting the identity of Diaspora Judaism in particular. Thus, under the leadership of Ezra, a priestly canon (the Torah) was forged that stopped short of the land entry story (Joshua), since that had become irrelevant for Jews in the Diaspora. The "prophets" section was then added for clues it might afford Diaspora Jews in coming to terms with "the destitution of old nationalist Israel" and in better understanding their "essential nature and identity, no matter how dismantling the crises might be which they would from time to time have to face" (p. 96). The wisdom literature helps to bridge the gap between this national epic and the daily life and needs of individuals.

Smith, Morton, *Palestinian Parties and Politics That Shaped the Old Testament* (London: SCM Press, 1971, 1987)

Traces with erudition and regret the emergence of a "Yahweh alone" faction within Israelite tradition and shows how it became the major force in shaping the canonical traditions of the Old Testament. Argues that Old Testament material as a whole came down primarily from and through three leading social groups within the major religious parties of the Second Temple period: "the gentry, the levites, and the priests of the Jerusalem temple" (p. 120). The gentry were primarily responsible for shaping Proverbs, Job, Ecclesiastes, and several short stories (Ruth, Jonah, Esther, Judith, Tobit) and Song of Songs (all essentially belletristic material); the levites, who were the backbone of the separatist (anti-syncretist) party, were chiefly responsible for Chronicles-Ezra-Nehemiah and Psalms (all of which have close ties with Deuteronomy and the deuteronomistic history); the priests were responsible for the final editing of the Pentateuch. Both Chronicles and the Pentateuch, Smith writes, are "compromise" documents enabling levites and priests to live and work together in the temple.

Sundberg, Albert C., *The Old Testament of the Early Church,* Harvard Theological Studies XX (Cambridge: Harvard University Press, 1964)

Argues that closed collections of Law and Prophets existed in early Christian times, but that "other writings generally circulated in Judaism that were not yet gathered into a formulated collection." "This situation, then, of closed collections of Law and Prophets and a third group of religious writings of undetermined proportions, obtained throughout Judaism. About the close of the first century A.D. a definitive collection of 'Writings' was gathered out of this third group, and the canon of scripture was closed by Palestinian Jews.... However, it was before the decision closing the canon for Judaism that Christianity arose and became distinguished from Judaism. The Christians, therefore, received their collection of holy writings from Judaism before a restricted collection of Writings and a closed canon was formulated in Judaism. It is a consequence of this that early Christian writings made use of the Law, the Prophets, and of the larger group of sacred writings as well, since the larger, undefined group of writings constituted part of the Christian heritage of religious writings from Judaism. And it was out of this larger Jewish legacy that the Christians came to determine independently the extent of their Old Testament" (p. 82).

van Ruler, A.A., *The Christian Church and the Old Testament* (Grand Rapids: William B. Eerdmans, 1971; German edition, 1955)

Proposes that "the Old Testament is and remains the true Bible" for Christians; the New Testament is its "explanatory glossary."

The Old Testament, as such, is the "canonical Word of God" which "constantly confronts us with its own authority" (p. 72). This means, he writes, that "both exegetically and homiletically one must continually begin afresh and remain occupied with the text of the Old Testament itself." Thus, the Christian church cannot do without the Old Testament; six key concepts or words point to how it must use it: legitimation, foundation, interpretation, illustration, historicization, and eschatologization (p. 75).

Wilder, Amos, *Jesus' Parables and the War of Myths, Essays on Imagination in the Scripture,* edited with a Preface, by James Breech (Philadelphia: Fortress), 1982)

In a chapter of this volume entitled "The World Story: The Biblical Version" (pp. 43–70) Wilder presents his thesis that "the narrative of the Bible takes time and its events seriously and, above all, provides a world-plot, with a beginning, middle, and end" (p. 45). Here he argues that biblical theology too often "operates selectively in its appeal to Scripture," "abstracts from the wholeness of the canon," and thus "tends to shortcut the concrete human givens that are basic to doctrine, especially as they are manifested in the Old Testament storytelling." On the other hand, "The plain reader of the Bible, nourished on the stories of the Pentateuch and the books of Samuel and the episodes in the Gospels and the Book of Acts, is already initiated into an implicit theology all the more negotiable in his own setting for being a matter of vivid story and poetry, rather than of abstractions" (p. 47).

Zimmerli, Walther, *The Law and the Prophets, A Study of the Meaning of the Old Testament* (New York: Harper & Row, 1963)

"The goal of a theological study of the Old Testament must be to make clear to the New Testament scholar, and the systematic theologian, what its message is, so that its place in the total biblical, and systematic theological, account of revelation cannot be ignored" (p. 3). The key to such an understanding lies in a careful consideration of the arrangement of the Hebrew canon into "law" and "prophets" (the "writings" section has no "theological" significance, writes Zimmerli, p. 10). When this is done, it becomes clear that "with the preaching of the prophets, and the historical events which accompanied it, Israel's confidence in the firmness of their foundations was shaken, and the people were confronted with an unknown and uncertain future." More to the point, "The prophets proclaimed that a new act of God was necessary to show that the holy and zealous Lord would really uphold his people, since the law had revealed their complete inability to obey his will" (p. 93). Thus, "in the preaching of the prophets, Israel became a people of hope and anticipation," since "the early post-exilic prophets Haggai, Zechariah and Trito-Isaiah show that the return from exile was in no way to be understood as the real fulfilment of the prophetic promise" (p. 94).

INDEX

Aaron, 18, 34, 41–46 *passim*, 55; and Levites, 146; and Moses, 116, 120; plague, 119

Aaronites, 41–46, 55, 120-21, 122, 125-26; calf-icons, 120, 121; and Levites, 34; in Numbers, 117, 118–19; theology, 49-56

Abiathar, 35, 36, 37, 40

Abihu, 120

Abot, 128, 129

Abraham, 18, 61, 65, 66, 109, 123; God's covenants with, 53, 55, 61, 65, 66, 109, 123, 146; shrine at Bethel, 56; shrine at Hebron, 45, 50, 53; worship of El, 47

Acts of the Apostles, 8, 12, 163, 164, 165, 166, 167

Against Apion (Josephus), 6–7

Against Heresies (Irenaeus), 11, 14–15

Agur, 148

Ahaz, King, 37, 74, 114

Amos of Tekoa, 57, 70-71, 72, 73, 114

Anathoth, 60

Animal sacrifice, 59, 77, 85–86, 137

Antiochus Epiphanes, 21, 158

Antitheses (Marcion), 8

Apocalypse, 12

Apochryphal writings, 16

Ark of the covenant, 62, 64; at Jerusalem, 36, 54, 59, 60; Levites and, 34, 37, 47, 62; at Shiloh, 52, 54

Artaxerxes, 20, 23, 92, 93, 94

Beckwith, Roger, 131, 132

Bethel, 37, 39–40, 46, 47, 51, 71, 72; destruction of, 112; theology, 56-58

Bible: division into two parts, 15–16; Hebrew scriptures as part of, 5-16; *see also* specific topics, e.g.: New Testament; Numbers

"Book of the Covenant," 59

"Book of the Law," 59, 92, 107

Bull-shrines. *See* Calf-shrines

Caleb, 18

Calebites, 44

Calf-shrines, 47, 51, 119–20; theology, 56-58; *see also* Bethel; Dan

Campenhausen, Hans von, 8–9, 10, 12–13

Canaan, 44, 45, 50–61 *passim*, 79

Chadwick, Henry, 8

Child sacrifice, 74, 77

Christ, 165–67

245

"Chronicler's History," 106–07, 135

Chronicles, 106-07; arrangement of, 7, 16, 19, 130, 131–34, 139, 163, 165; priesthoods, 40–41, 69, 90, 134-38, 140; as work of history, 32-33

Cross, Frank Moore, 47, 51, 112

Cyrus, 22, 32, 94, 108

Dan, 37, 39–40, 46, 47, 51, 56–58; theology, 56–58

Daniel, 7, 79, 132, 139, 140, 155–57, 158, 160, 163, 164

David, 18, 54, 59, 69, 86, 113, 135, 143; crowned king, 41; God's covenant with, 65, 66, 146; priesthoods, 40, 46, 50, 60, 68, 90, 135, 137; shrine at Jerusalem, 32, 35-36, 37, 41, 47, 53, 59; tent shrine, 32

"Day of Mordecai," 158, 159

De Vries, Simon J., 135

Decalogue, 52

Deuterocanonical writings, 16

Deuteronomic Code, 52

Deuteronomistic History, 33-34, 58–59, 61, 112-13, 122, 133, 145; scrolls of the prophets and, 114, 115, 116; sin and judgment as uniting factor, 123

Deuteronomy, 7, 18, 63, 64, 65, 77, 97, 99, 111–12, 113–14, 115, 122, 123, 145; dating of, 58, 60, 61; discovery of, 90, 92; intermarriage, 142; priest-hoods, 34; scrolls of the prophets and, 114

Divorce, 29, 88, 153

Ecclesiastes, 7, 132, 139, 151-52, 159

El, 45–46, 47, 50, 51, 53, 54, 58

Eli, 35, 59

Elijah, 18

Elisha, 18

Enoch, 18

Essenes, 163

Esther, 7, 132, 139, 140, 157-59, 160, 163

Eusebius, 7

Exodus, 7, 18, 62, 111, 117, 120, 124; Sinai events, 119–22

Ezekiel of Jerusalem, 7, 16, 18, 32, 42–43, 57, 67, 78–81, 84, 114, 116, 147; child sacrifice, 77; vision of second temple, 83

Ezra, 19, 21, 23, 109–10, 118, 129-30, 132; arrangement of, 16, 130–34, 139; covenant renewal, 95–97; dismissal of foreign wives, 97–98; inter-marriage, 29, 109; and Levites, 26, 94; reforms, 28, 92-98; return to Jerusalem, 93–95; Second Exodus, 93–94

Ezra-Nehemiah, 7, 16, 115, 136, 165; intermarriage, 29; place-ment of 130-34; reforms, 20, 21, 22, 23, 30, 33, 49, 67, 82, 88, 89–103, 105, 110, 118,

129, 141, 142, 143, 145, 154, 155, 156, 157, 163

Farmer, William, 13
Friedman, Richard Elliott, 77, 112

Gaston, Lloyd, 15
Genesis, 7, 18, 19, 45, 47, 56, 117, 123-25, 164, 165, 167
Gnostics, 7, 9
Golden calf, 121
Gospels, 7, 11–12, 163, 165, 167
Gottwald, Norman, 69, 155
Gray, John, 69
Greer, Rowan, 10, 14–15
Guilds (temple guilds), 138

Habakkuk, 75
Haggai, 21, 28, 82, 83, 84, 85, 87, 114
Hagiographa, 7, 131, 132, 133, 139–40; order of, 131
Hanson, Paul, 22
Hashabiah, 94, 95
Hebrews, 12
Hebron, 41, 44, 45, 47, 50-56 *passim*; tabernacle, 54
Hezekiah, King, 18, 75, 92, 112, 114, 133; priesthoods, 37, 38, 48, 74, 90, 137, 145; restoration of Davidic kingdom, 71; Solomonic proverbs, 149; worship of Yahweh, 60, 63–64, 138
Hilkiah, 38, 65, 75, 92
"Holiness Code," 52

Holy Writings. *See* Hagiographa
Horeb, 55, 61, 62, 116
Hosea of Israel, 57, 60, 71–72, 79, 85, 114
Huldah, 38

Intermarriage, 29–30, 88, 100, 102, 109, 143, 153; dismissal of foreign wives, 97–98
Irenaeus, 10–11, 11–12, 13, 14
Isaac, 18, 55, 61
Isaiah of Jerusalem, 7, 16, 18, 21, 67, 73–75, 85, 114, 115, 116
Isaiah, Second, 73, 84, 86, 87, 93–94, 123
Isaiah, Third, 73, 84, 86

James, 12
Jacob, 18, 47, 55, 56, 61
Jehoiachin, King, 113
Jehoiakim, King, 76
Jehoshaphat, King, 137
Jereboam, 18, 32, 46, 47, 51, 57–58
Jeremiah of Anathoth, 7, 16, 18, 57, 60, 63, 67, 75–78, 79, 114; seventy-year prophecy, 156, 157
Jeshua, 19
Jesus Christ, 165–67
Joash, King, 114, 137
Job, 19, 79, 132, 139, 147–48, 151, 152, 159
John, Apocalypse of, 12
Joseph, 47
Josephus, 6–7
Joshua, 7, 18, 44, 45, 50, 52, 62,

83, 112, 120, 122, 124, 129, 131, 132; succession of, 44, 122

Josiah, King, 18, 137, 145; book of Deuteronomy, 65, 76, 90, 111–12, 113; reforms, 39, 48, 58, 64, 92, 95, 97, 133, 145

Jotham, King, 114

Judas Maccabaeus, 20-21, 128, 159

Judeans, 6, 45, 50, 51, 53, 68, 90, 99

Judges, 17, 18, 112, 124, 131, 132

Kenites, 45, 46, 50, 51, 52, 53

Kings, 7, 18, 19, 32, 114, 115, 124, 131, 132, 133, 152; calf-icons, 56–57

Lamentations, 7, 132, 139, 153–55, 157, 159–60

"Law and the Prophets," 6, 16, 18, 19, 105–26, 127, 131, 138, 141, 153; in "The Chronicler's History," 106-08; editorial features, 111–14; in Nehemiah and Ezra, 108–11

Levi, 24, 25, 30, 34, 88, 146

Levites, 24, 42–43, 47, 68–69, 77, 81, 84–88, 108, 116, 133–34, 160; "assemblies," 130; death of Moses, 122; dismissal from Jerusalem, 48; and Ezra-Nehemiah reforms, 90-105 passim, 130, 140, 160; intermarriage, 29; at

Jerusalem, 46, 50; in Numbers, 117–19; priests distinguished, 25–26, 27, 30; and prophets, 68, 70, 71, 76, 84–88; Reform Document, 61, 62, 63, 65, 90; rivalries between priests and, 23–27, 33–39; in Second Temple Judaism, 134–38; at Shiloh, 45; theology, 56, 57, 58–66, 71, 82, 147; Zadokites distinguished, 46

Leviticus, 7, 18, 111, 117, 124

Luke, Gospel of, 11, 112

Maccabees, 19, 20-21, 158

Malachi, 21, 23–26, 27–28, 30, 84-88 passim, 132, 142; intermarriage, 29, 88; prediction of "messenger," 116; temple priesthood, 84, 85

Manasseh, 38, 39, 64, 75, 113

Marcion, 8, 9–10, 11-13, 15

Marcionite Gospel, 10

Marriage, 91, 153; dismissal of foreign wives, 97-98; divorce, 29, 88, 153; intermarriage, 29–30, 88, 100, 102, 109, 143, 153

Matthew, Gospel of, 166

Melchizedek, 40

Memoirs of Nehemiah, 20, 106

Messiah, 165–67

Micah of Moresheth, 72–73, 74, 76, 114

Midianites, 45

Mishna, 139

Mordecai, 158–59

Moses, 18, 42–47 *passim*, 51–66 *passim*, 84, 95, 105, 108, 109, 112, 113, 116, 124, 135; ark of the covenant, 36; as compiler of Deuteronomy, 58; death, 122; Horeb covenant, 61, 62, 66, 119; as miracle worker, 58; oracle-tent, 52; priesthoods, 24, 34, 37, 42, 44, 47; rebellion of Reubenites against, 117; Sinai covenant, 38, 69, 120, 121-22, 129; Torah, 109, 111, 122, 129, 148–49, 152, 156, 162; Yahwism, 72

Murphy, Roland, 147, 153

Nadab, 120

Nahum, 75

Nathan, 18

Nebuchadnezzar, 77, 78

Nehemiah, 21, 26, 28-29, 109, 114; and Levites, 100–03, 134; library of Hebrew scriptures, 106, 128, 155; reforms, 98–103; restoration of Jerusalem, 19, 99-100; social reforms, 100; *see also* Ezra-Nehemiah

New Testament, 5, 6, 7, 13, 15, 16

Nicanor, 158, 159

Noah, 18, 79

Numbers, 7, 18, 111; Aaronites and Levites in, 117–19; succession from Moses to Joshua, 122–24

Obadiah, 75

O'Brien, Julia, 25

Passover, 39

Paul, 8, 9–10, 12, 13

Pentateuch, 38–39, 42, 51–52, 107, 131

Pharisees, 163

Philemon, 12

Philistines, 36

Phinehas, 18, 55

Polycarp, 12

Priesthoods, 140; Levites distinguished, 25–26, 27, 30; levitical priests, 34; rivalries among, 23–27, 31-48; temple tithes, 85; theologies of, 49-66; *see also* specific headings, e.g.: Levites; Zadokites

Prophets, 7, 16, 18, 24, 67–88; Book of the Twelve Minor Prophets, 7, 16, 18, 67, 114, 116, 132; order of, 131, 132; scrolls of the prophets, 19, 24, 67, 114–16, 141-60; *see also* specific Prophets, e.g., Ezekiel; Jeremiah

Proto-Zechariah, 84

Proverbs, 7, 19, 132, 139, 148–51, 152, 159

Psalms, 7, 19, 53-55, 132, 139, 143–47, 151, 154, 159

Purim, 158–59

Qoheleth, 152

"Regulation Formula," 135

Rehoboam, 18, 73
Reubenites, 117
Revelation, 164
Ruth, 7, 132, 139, 140, 141–43, 159

Sacrifice, 77; animal sacrifice, 59, 77, 85–86, 137; child sacrifice, 74, 77
Sadducees, 163
Samuel, 7, 18, 32, 124, 131, 132
Sanballat, 102
Septuagint, 16
Shealtiel, 83
Shelters, feast of, 96
Sherebiah, 94, 95
Sheshbazzar, 83
Shiloh, 41, 44, 45, 47, 52, 59, 76; ark of the covenant, 35, 36, 41, 46, 54; priesthood of, 60
Simeon the Righteous, 129
Sira, 17, 18, 19, 21
Sirach, 17, 19, 139
Solomon, 18, 59, 151–52, 153; and Abiathar, 36, 37, 40; dismissal of Levites from Jerusalem, 38, 47, 48, 59, 60, 69, 97; temple of Yahweh, 124
Song of Songs, 7, 132, 139, 152–53, 159
Sons of Aaron, 33, 34, 41, 42, 52; see also Aaronites

Tabernacle, 51, 54, 57
"Tent of Meeting," 52–53

Tetrateuch, 33, 34, 42, 43, 45, 47, 116
Timothy, 12
Tithes, 85
Titus, 12
Tobiah, 102
Torah, 109, 111, 122, 129, 130, 143, 144, 148–49, 156, 162; wisdom and, 150, 152
Trinity, 15

Uriah, 37, 74
Uzziah, King, 114

Van Seters, John, 123

Wilson, Gerald H., 143, 144–45
Wright, John W., 135
Writings. See Hagiographa

Zadok, 36, 40, 41, 49–50, 53
Zadokites, 36, 37, 39–46, 58–66 passim, 69, 74–98 passim, 108, 116, 118, 125, 147; intermarriage, 98; kingship, 64; Levites distinguished, 46; permissive policy toward other religions, 63; theology, 49–50, 53–56, 58, 59, 61, 65–66, 76–77, 160
Zechariah, King, 21, 85, 86, 87, 114
Zephaniah, 75, 114
Zerubbabel, 19, 83–84, 86
Zion, 53, 54, 65, 66, 75, 146, 154

THEOLOGICAL INQUIRIES:

Serious studies on contemporary questions of Scripture, Systematics and Moral Theology. Also in the series:

J. Louis Martyn, *The Gospel of John in Christian History: Essays for Interpreters*

Frans Jozef van Beeck, S.J., *Christ Proclaimed: Christology as Rhetoric*

John P. Meier, *The Vision of Matthew: Christ, Church and Morality in the First Gospel*

Pheme Perkins, *The Gnostic Dialogue: The Early Church and the Crisis of Gnosticism*

Michael L. Cook, S.J., *The Jesus of Faith: A Study in Christology*

Joseph F. Wimmer, *Fasting in the New Testament: A Study in Biblical Theology*

William R. Farmer and Denis M. Farkasfalvy, O.Cist., *The Formation of the New Testament Canon: An Ecumenical Approach*

Rosemary Rader, *Breaking Boundaries: Male/Female Friendship in Early Christian Communities*

Richard J. Clifford, *Fair Spoken and Persuading: An Interpretation of Second Isaiah*

Robert J. Karris, *Luke: Artist and Theologian: Luke's Passion Account as Literature*

Jerome Neyrey, S.J., *The Passion According to Luke: A Redaction Study of Luke's Soteriology*

Frank J. Matera, *Passion Narratives and Gospel Theologies: Interpreting the Synoptics through Their Passion Stories*

James P. Hanigan, *Homosexuality: The Test Case for Christian Sexual Ethics*

Robert A. Krieg, *Story-Shaped Christology: The Role of Narratives in Identifying Jesus Christ*

Brad H. Young, *Jesus and His Jewish Parables: Rediscovering the Roots of Jesus' Teaching*

Dimitri Z. Zaharopoulous, *Theodore of Mopsuestia on the Bible: A Study of His Old Testament Exegesis*

William R. Farmer and Roch Kereszty, *Peter and Paul in the Church of Rome: The Ecumenical Potential of a Forgotten Perspective*

Urban C. vonWahlde, *The Johannine Commandments: 1 John and the Struggle for the Johannine Tradition*

Peter Ochs, *The Return to Scripture in Judaism and Christianity: Essays in Postcritical Scriptural Interpretation*

Andrew E. Barnes, *The Social Dimension of Piety*